글로벌 시대를 위한

영어 천자문 에세이

글로벌 시대를 위한

영어 천자문 에세이

Essay on the Thousand-character classic
in English for the era of globalization

수필작가 호반 조광호(湖椵 曺光昊)
Essay writer, Hoban, Kwang-ho Cho

그림 김명식 | 한글 영어번역 조문희

좋은땅

i. 프롤로그 (PROLOG)

천자문은 사자소학과 함께 한자 입문서다. 고사성어 학습도 좋지만, 현실과 꽤나 거리감이 있어 동기부여가 부족하다. 따라서 자신의 주변상황에 적용하여 바라보는 천자문이라면 친근감이 있으리라 본다. 천자문은 사언고시(四言古詩 four word old poem) 250구, 팔언시어 125구, 모두 1,000자로 구성되어 있다. 자연현상과 인류, 도덕에 이르는 내용으로 한자 학습하면 떠오르는 책이다. 필자는 여기에 더해 영어와 함께, 한물갔다 하는, 지루한 꼰대적 천자문을 현실생활에 적용되도록, 생명을 불어넣은, 에세이 단상 감각으로 집필했다. 독자들도 자기의 일상생활을 사언고시에 투영하여 본인 것으로 한다면, 한결 접근하기가 쉽고, 흥미로우리라. 더구나 꿈꾸는 미래의 인생좌표를 설정하는 데 길을 찾고, 영감을 얻었으면 한다. 이런 꿈틀거리는 생생한 에세이로 독자들에게 가슴 뭉클하게 하고자 노력하였다. 지금은 별로 가치가 없는 듯하지만, 시간이 흘러 아주 먼 훗날 후손에게는 귀중한 자료가 될 수도 있으리라. 필자가 집필하게 된 동기로, 글로벌 시대, 한국과 유럽 손주들, 고전을 갈망하는 동서양 세대를 위한 에세이다.

천자문을 영어에세이로 창안한 것은 한국에서 처음이고 따라서 세계적으로도 시초가 된다. 한글을 영어로 번역하는 데 고생하여 이러한 영어천자문 에세이를 가능하게 한 딸 문희(네덜란드 시민권자)에게 한없는 고마움과 감사를 보낸다. 아울러 본 책이 발간되기까지 심혈을 기울여 노력한 좋은땅 출판사 대표님과 편집진께 감사드리며, 바쁘신 중에도 추천사를 보내 주신 교장 신병영, 서예가 조수현, 원불교 원로교무 최경도, PT SAEHO ZIPPER 회사 대표 이승구, 한의사 김도연, 회계사 조영준, IT Specialist Daniel Belter에게 마음속 깊이 감사를 보낸다. 교정과 그림으로 매번 조력해 준 아이들 엄마 김명식에게도 고마움을 보낸다.

겨울 어느 날

수필작가&시인 호반 조광호 (湖椴 曺光昊)

ⅰ. PROLOG

This is an introduction book for knowing chinese letters for children. Learning Chinese Character(The old things come from the old days, and the words used in a tolerant sense) is good, but there is a considerable distance from reality and lacks motivation. Therefore, if you apply it to your surroundings, you will have a sense of intimacy. The Thousand Character Text consists of 250 four words old poems and 125 eight words poems, all of which are 1000 characters. It is a book that comes to mind when learning Chinese characters with contents ranging from natural phenomena, human affairs and morality. In addition to this, I wrote with a life-infused essay-single sense to apply the boring, grandiose texts that went with English to real life. If readers project their daily life into their own words and say it is their own, it is easy to approach and interesting. Moreover, I want to find a way to set up a dreamy future life coordinate and get inspiration. I tried to make my readers feel heartbreaking with this wriggling essay. It may not be worth much now, but it may be valuable to future generations over time. It is an essay for the east and west generation who longs for the global era, Korean and European grandchildren, and classics.

This essay on Thousand texts is written in English for the first time in South Korea and around the world. I deeply appreciate my daughter(dutch citizen) making this essay to become true. In addition, I would like to show unbounded gratitude for the support and efforts from a publisher and editors, and I am thankful for the supports from a headmaster Sin Buyng-young, a caligrapher Cho Su-hyun, CEO from PT Saeho zipper Lee Seung-gu, an oriental doctor Kim Do-yeon, an accountant Cho Young-june, an IT Specialist Daniel Belter. Also, I can't thank a mother of my children Myungsik enough for giving her endless supports.

One winter day,

An author of an essay and poet, Hoban, Cho Kwang-ho

ii. 본문 중 표의 내용 (Contents of table in text)

天 ⟸ 한자 (Chinese character)	천 ⟸ 한자의 한글 표현(Korean expression of chinese characters)
cheon	⟸ 한자의 영어 발음 (English pronunciation of chinese characters)
하늘	⟸ 한자의 한글 뜻(의미), 한글 단어 (Korean meaning, Korean Word of chinese character)
haneul	⟸ 한자의 한글 뜻(의미) 영어 발음 (Korean language meaning english pronunciation of chinese characters)
sky	⟸ 한자의 뜻(의미) 영어 단어 (The meaning of chinese characters English words)
001. 하늘은 아득하거나 어둡고 땅(지구)은 노란색이다 ⟸ 사자성어 한글 해석(four word korean interpretation)	
The sky is faraway or dark and the ground(earth) is yellow ⟸ 사자성어 영어 번역(four word english translation)	
우천 雨天 ⟸ 상기 한자의 응용 단어 (application word of chinese character)	
rainy weather ⟸ 상기 한자의 응용 단어 영어 번역 (English translation of applied words in chinese characters)	
天천: 하느님, 임금, 운명, god, king, fate ⟸ 상기 한자의 다양한 뜻(의미)과 영어 단어 (Various meanings of chinese characters and english words)	

iii. 한자 만들어진 원리
(The principle that have been made Chinese character)

한자는 뜻글자다. 한글이나 영어 독어 불어 네덜란드어 등은 소리글자이다. 따라서 한자는 만들어진 원리를 알면 이해하기 쉽고 익히기도 즐겁다.

한자는 만들어진 원리에 따라 ① 상형(象形), ② 지사(指事), ③ 회의(會意), ④ 형성(形聲), ⑤ 전주(轉注), ⑥ 가차(假借)의 육서(六書) 분류법이 통용되고 있다.

1. 상형문자: 실제 사물의 모습을 그대로 본떠 만든 글자다.
   日(날 일: 해 모양) ⇒ ● ⇒ ⊙ 에서 유래 되어 점차 변형된 것이다.

2. 지사문자: 점과 선을 이용해 상징적인 부호로 나타낸 것이다.
   즉, 추상적인 개념을 기호로 표현한 글자라 할 수 있다.
   二(두 이) ⇒ = ⇒ 二 로 변화된 원리와 같다.

3. 회의문자: 두 개 혹은 두 개 이상의 상형문자나 지사문자를 합쳐 새로운 의미의 글자를 만드는 방법, 즉, 두 명 이상이 회의하듯 모인 글자라 할 수 있다.
   炎(불꽃 염) ⇒ '불 화火' 자를 두 개 겹쳐 '불꽃 염炎' 자가 되는 것과 같다.

4. 형성문자: 의미를 나타내는 부분과 소리를 나타내는 부분을 조합하여 새로운 글자를 만들어 내는 방법. 한자의 82%가 형성문자다. '형形'은 글자의 의미나 소속을 나타내고, '성聲'은 같거나 비슷한 발음을 표시한다.
   湖(호수 호) ⇒ (氵=水: 의미) + (호 胡: 발음)와 같은 원리이다.

5. 전주문자: 이미 만들어진 글자의 본래 뜻으로부터 유추해서 다른 글자로 호환하여 사용하는 글자의 운용 방식. 구체적인 개념을 파악하기가 쉽지 않아, 별로 사용하지 않고 있다.

예를 들면 '처음'이란 의미를 가진 '처음 시始', '처음 초初'을 서로 바꾸어 쓰는 경우이다.

6. 가차문자(빌린 글자): 기존의 글자가 담고 있는 뜻은 두고 소리를 빌어 쓰거나, 원래는 글자가 없었으나 음성에 기초하여 기존의 글자를 차용해 사용하는 글자의 운용 방식. 즉, 뜻과 무관하게 소리만 빌려 쓰는 방식이다. 외래어 표기에 많이 사용하고 있다.

네덜란드(Netherlands, Holland) ⇒ 和蘭(화란)

저머니(Germany, Deutschland) ⇒ 獨逸(독일)

위와 같이 만들어진 한자 원리가 처음 공부하려는 사람들에게 도움이 되었으면 한다.

iii. The principle of Chinese character making

Chinese characters are meaning words. Hangul, English, German, French, Dutch, etc. are sound letters. Therefore, it is easy to understand and learn when you know the principles made. According to the principles made, Chinese characters are used in the six classification of the ① Sanghyeong, ② Jisa, ③ Hoeui(meeting), ④ Hyeongseong, ⑤ Jeonju, and ⑥ Gacha.

1. Sanghyeong(hieroglyph): It is a letter that is modeled after the actual

appearance of things.

'日'(sun shape) which are derived from ● ⇒ ⊙ and is gradually transformed.

2. Jisa letter: What is represented by symbolic sign using dots and lines, In other words, abstract concepts can be said to be letters expressed in symbols.

= ⇒ 二 is like the principle changed to '二'

3. Hoeui(conference=meeting letter): How to create a new meaning of letters by combining two or more Sanghyeongs or Jisa letters, In other words, it can be said that more than two people gather as if they are meeting.

It is like being '炎' by overlapping two '火' characters.

4. Hyeongseong letter: A method of creating new letters by combining parts that represent meaning and parts that represent sound. 82% of Chinese characters are the Hyeongseong letter.

湖(ho: lake) is (氵=水 water: meaning) + (胡 ho: pronunciation) the same principle.

5. Jeonju letter: The operation method of the letter which infers from the original meaning of the already created letter and compatibles with the other letter. It is not easy to grasp specific concepts, so it is not used much.

For example, it is a case of changing 'first si 始' and 'first cho 初' which have the meaning of 'first'.

6. Gacha letter(borrow letter): The meaning of the existing letter is written by the sound, or the original letter is not used, but the existing letter is borrowed based on the voice. In other words, it is a way to borrow only sound regardless of meaning. It is used a lot for foreign language notation.

Netherlands(Holland, Dutch) ⇒ 和蘭(Hwaran)

Germany(Deutschland) ⇒ 獨逸(dokil)

I think that the above-mentioned Chinese character principle will help those who want to study for the first time.

목차 (Contents)

001. 연촌 마을의 밤과 하늘 (천지현황 우주홍황)

어렸을 적 심심산골 마을 영광 연촌의 밤하늘은 특별나게 어두웠다. 호롱불로 겨우 사람 얼굴 형태만 알아볼 수 있을 정도의 밝기로 그야말로 암흑의 밤이다. 하늘의 별들은 반짝거리며 졸고 있고, 그 별이라도 헤아려 보려는 호기심에 모든 잡념을 집어삼키고, 초승달이라도 있으면 반가울 뿐이다. 낮에는 하늘의 뭉게구름이나, 눈부셔 보기 민망한 태양빛이 얼굴을 가리니, 무심히 밝은 태양을 흘러 보낸다. 햇빛의 강렬함은 어린아이 생각까지 뭉개는 듯 뇌를 마비시켜 그냥 아무렇지도 않게 개념이 없이 나른하게 한다. 유난히 벌겋게 물들은 서산 넘어 가는 해의 매력만 가슴에 스며들 뿐이다. 저걸 화가가 되어 화폭에 담아 보고 싶은 마음이 잊혀지지 않는다. 인간은 자연 속에서 묻혀 지내고 자연과 더불어 숨 쉬는 만물 중 미물이면서 영물이 아닐까 한다. 그 미물 중 영장류라는 중생을 괴롭히는 파리 거미들을 유심히 관찰하고, 우아한 나비, 잠자리를 따라다니기도 한다. 하늘과 땅, 끝없는 우주는 넓고 아득하고 컴컴하지만 거칠지만은 않은 것 같다(천지현황 우주홍황). 어린 시절의 우주 자연은 신기할 만큼 동심을 자극하는 미묘함의 블랙홀이 아닐까 한다.

001. Night&Sky in the village of Yeonchon

When I was a child, the sky was enormously dark at night in the mountain village in Yeonggwang Yeonchon. It is an extreme darkness that can only be seen by a holong fire. Only the stars in the sky are glittering, and there is only a curiosity of counting stars without all the small ordinary thought, and there is a crescent moon in the sky that I could see, I was very happy. During the day, the sunshine is hidden by clouds in the sky, so the sun went away by time. The intensity of the sunlight anesthetizes a brain of a young child, the child feels melting with a lot of thoughts by the sun. Here members only the sun which made the mountains red. He never forgets the wish of drawing the scenery of that time on the canvas when he becomes an adult. Man is a creature of all things buried in nature and breathed with nature. Among all the creatures, only humans observe flies, spiders that bothers them, and they follow graceful butterflies and dragonflies. The sky, the earth and the endless universe seem wide, distant, dark, but not wild. Perhaps the cosmic nature to be seen by young age is a full of curiosity like a black hole.

天 천	地 지	玄 현	黃 황	宇 우	宙 주	洪 홍	荒 황
cheon	ji	hyeon	hwang	u	ju	hong	hwang
하늘	땅	검은	누를	집	집	넓을	거칠
haneul	ttang	geomeun	nureul	jip	jip	neoleul	geochil
sky	ground	dark	yellow	house	house	wide	rough
001. 하늘은 아득하거나 어둡고 땅(지구)은 노란색이다				002. 우주(세상)는 한없이 넓고 거칠게 보인다			
The sky is faraway or dark and the ground(earth) is yellow				The cosmos(universe, world) is wide and rough			
우천雨天	지구地球	현관玄關	황금黃金	우주선宇宙船		홍수洪水	황야荒野
rainy weather	earth globe	front door	gold	spaceship		flood	wilderness

천天: 하느님 임금 운명 god king fate
地지: 땅 국토 earth lands
玄현: 검다 아득하다 black faraway
黃황: 누르다 어린아이 yellow children

宇우: 집 지붕 처마 roof eaves boundary
宙주: 집 하늘 대들보 때 sky breadwinner time
洪홍: 넓다 큰물 여울 vast large water fast in water
荒황: 거칠다 어둡다 황무지 dark wilderness

21

002. 밤하늘의 달과 별들 (일월영측 진숙열장)

보름달을 보며 꿈꾸던 미지의 세계, 토끼가 절구통에 방아 찧는 영상이 그려진 달, 옛 시골은 해가 지면 암흑세계가 되니, 밝은 보름달은 신기하고 고마울 뿐이다. 재래식 화장실은 바깥 구석진 곳에 있어 여간 무서운 게 아니다. 이런 어둡고 무서운 주변을 둥근달이 밝혀 주니 얼마나 고맙겠는가. 잊혀질 만하면 한 달에 한 번씩 다시 나타나는 보름달이다(일월영측). 세월이 흐른 어느 날 달에 사람이 간다는 소문이 퍼졌다. 흑백 티브이도 별로 없던 시절, 중소도시에 몇 대 있던 시절이다. 달 착륙 모습을 티브이로 중개한다며, 구름 관중이 어느 음식점 입구까지 모여 웅성거렸다. 아폴로11호가 달에 착륙하고, 닐 암스트롱이 달 표면에 첫 발을 딛고, 이어서 에드윈 버즈올드린이 발을 디뎠다. 하늘에 떠 있는 달에 사람이 올라간 사실이 꿈속처럼 충격적인 장면이다. 동화책에 나오는 둥근 보름달 속 계수나무는 어디 가고, 방아 찧던 토끼는 어찌된 건가.

002. The moon and stars in the sky at night

I imagined unknown world by watching the full moon. And the moon included an illustration of the rabbit which pestles with a mortar. And there is no light in the countryside in the old time, the bright full moon is curious and thankful. Asquat toilet was in the corner of outside a house, thus it was so scary. However, there is a full moon to make everything so bright at night, you could imagine how grateful it was for a small child. When it seems forgotten, the full moon comes back again once a month. Longtime later than that, there was a rumor that people are going to the moon. Almost nobody even had a television at that time, a lot of people came to the main restaurant to watch the historical scene which the spacecraft landed at the moon. Apollo 11 landed on the moon, Neil Armstrong took his first step on the surface on the moon and later the historical step is followed by Edwin Buzz oldrin. It was a shocking scene like a dream. Where is the tree in the full moon in the fairy tale, and what happened to a rabbit?

日 일	月 월	盈 영	昃 측	辰 진	宿 숙	列 렬	張 장
il	wol	young	cheuk	jin	suk	ryeol	jang
날	달	찰	기울	별	잘	벌릴	베풀
nal	dal	chal	giul	byeol	jal	beolril	bepul
sun	moon	full	tilt	star	star	spread	expand
003. 해와 달은 기울거나 가득 찬다				004. 별들이 밤하늘에 고르게 펼쳐져 가득하다			
The sun and the moon is tilted or full				The stars are full of evenly spread in the night sky			
매일每日	월급月給	영월盈月	일측日昃	일진日辰	숙제宿題	일열一列	주장主張
every-day	monthly salary	full moon	sunset	day fortune	home-work	a line	argu-ment

日: 날 해 햇볕 낮의 길이 day sun
月: 달 달빛 세월 moon time
盈: 차다 넘치다 full overflowing
昃: 기울다 오후 tilt afternoon

辰: 별 때 시각 times
宿: 자다 묵다 별자리 sleep stay
列: 벌리다 줄 차례 open rows times
張: 베풀다 뽐냄 give boast posturing

003. 한여름 곤충과 고추잠자리 (한래서왕 추수동장)

고향집 앞마당 낮은 공중과 지붕 처마 아래서 비행 자랑하듯, 수많은 고추 잠자리 떼가 탱자나무 가시에 매달려 한여름을 즐기는 모습이 흥미롭다. 더위가 좋은가 보다. 아니, 가을을 재촉하는지도 모른다. 원래 가을의 빨간 고추처럼 고추잠자리는 귀뚜라미와 함께 가을 곤충의 상징이 아니던가. 이른 아침에 탱자나무에 앉아 있는 고추잠자리를 손으로 잡을 수 있을 정도로 둔하고 굼떴다. 서너 마리 잡아 잠시 관찰하면 눈은 은방울같이 보이나 눈동자의 움직임을 느낄 수 없다. 가엾고 약해 보이는 곤충이라는 생명체, 신기함보다 측은하면서 움직이는 자연의 한 조각이랄까. 인간도 비슷한 약한 존재임이 떠오른다. 그러나 사람은 끈기 있는 동물이다. 고추잠자리야, 재미있는한 세상 살다 가거라. 하면서 높이 날려 보내고, 잠시 그놈들 궤적을 멍하니 응시해 본다. 뙤약볕 여름 조금 지나면 이 한가함도 아쉬움이 되고, 바쁜 고추잠자리 대신 농부들은 가을 추수에 여념이 없으리라(한래서왕, 추수동장). 추억거리가 된 농경사회 속 농부들의 땀에 젖은 수건과 발걸음들, 고추잠자리는 아직도 그때의 흔적을 몽땅 간직하고 있다.

003. Midsummer insects and red dragonfly

As if to boast of flying under the low air and roof eaves of your home front yard, It is interesting to see many red dragonfly hanging on the thorns of the hardy-orange tree and enjoying the midsummer. I guess the heat is good. No, it may be rushing autumn. Like the red pepper in the autumn, the red dragonfly is not a symbol of autumn insects with the cricket. It was dull and slow enough to catch the red dragonfly sitting on the hardy-orange tree early in the morning. If you take three or four and observe for a while, your eyes look like silver drops, but you can not feel the movement of your eyes. A creature called a poor and weak insect, a piece of nature that moves more compassionately than wonder. It reminds me that humans are similarly weak. But a person is a persistent animal. The red dragonfly, Go to the world for a fun time. I send it high and stare at their trajectory for a while. When the summer is over, this leisure is also a miss, and farmers will not be able to keep up with autumn harvests instead of busy red dragonfly. The sweaty towels and steps of farmers in the agrarian society that became memories, The red pepper dragonflies still keep all the traces of that time.

寒 한	來 래	暑 서	往 왕	秋 추	收 수	冬 동	藏 장
han	rae	seo	wang	chu	su	dong	jang
찰	올	더울	갈	가을	거둘	겨울	감출
chal	ol	deoul	gal	gaeul	geodul	gyeoul	gamchul
cold	come	heat	go	autumn	harvest	winter	store
005. 추위가 오면 더위가 물러가고				006. 가을에는 거두어들이고, 겨울에는 저장한다			
When the cold comes, the heat backs off				It harvests in autumn, and stores in winter			
한파寒波	미래未來	피서避暑	왕복往復	추석秋夕	수입收入	동복冬服	냉장冷藏
cold wave	future	avoid heat	return	autumn holiday	imports	winter clothes	refrig-eration
寒한: 오싹하다 가난하다 천하다 creepy poor vulgar 來래: 부르다 앞으로 call future 暑서: 더위 여름 무더움 summer 往왕: 달아나다 죽다 옛날 runaway death pastdays				秋추: 결실 성숙한 나이 fruit mature age 收수: 거두다 가지런히 잡다 collect straight take 冬동: 동면 겨울 지나다 hibernation passing winter 藏장: 감추다 간직함 품다 hide keep			

004. 어머니의 윤사월 (윤여성세 률려조양)

어머니는 늦은 봄 초여름 어느 날 이렇게 지루한 윤달은 처음이라고 푸념하 듯 말하였다. 아마 윤사월인 듯하다(윤여성세 률려조양). 아침에 일어나자마 자 일과처럼 해야 하는 아침 준비, 뭉뚝한 농기구 같은 손가락은 쉴 틈이 없다. 머슴이라는 일꾼과 가족들 십여 명이고, 아이들 도시락에 단무지 무침, 어쩌다 갈치구이 한 토막 준비, 보관할 수 있는 냉장고가 없던 시절, 모든 것을 텃밭 싱싱한 야채들을 갓다 다듬어 요리해야 한다. 밑반찬은 된장 간장 콩자반 단 무지 장아찌 해초 등이 전부, 육류는 어렵고, 계란이 어쩌다 있을 정도다. 거기 다 짜다 맛없다 양이 적다 등 조잘 소곤거림 소리에 스트레스는 팔자려니 견 뎌야 한다. 남정네들 일 나가면, 참 준비, 새로운 먹거리를 만들어야 한다. 해 도 해도 쌓여 있는 농사일들, 이러한 힘든 시절을 얼른 보내려 하나, 공달이 있 어 다시 지긋지긋한 사월이 시작되니, 얼마나 지루하고 지치고 힘들었겠는가. 이럴 땐 세월이라도 게 눈 감추듯 지나갔으면 하는 마음이리라. 철들어 농경 사회 시절이던, 시경(詩經)을 풀이한 시전(詩傳)의 공자 말이 생각난다.

부모님 은혜를 갚으려 하나 하늘보다 높고 넓어 헤아릴 수조차 없더라. 문 명과 과학기술이 발전한 지금의 부모는 어떠한지. 부모에게 물려받은 무량한 은혜를 대가성이나 기대 없이 자식에게 대물림하는 것으로 갚는다 생각하면 어떨지.

004. Mother's leap april month

My mother said that one day in the late spring and early summer, Leap month was the first time She was so bored. It seems to be Leap-April. As soon as She wake up in the morning, She have no time to rest on her fingers like morning preparation and fat farm equipment. When there were a dozen workers called the farmhand and families, She's just a little pickled radish busy with her kids' lunchbox, Maybe a piece of cutlass fish, and there was no refrigerator to prepare a piece of radish, Everything should be cooked with fresh vegetables in the garden. In addition, there is no taste, there is little amount, and the stress is the destiny to be endured by the sound of whispering. When they goes to work, she has to prepare and make new food. Even if she does, She wants to spend these hard times quickly, How boring, tired and hard it must have been to start a sickly April again with a leap-month. In this case, She would like to pass by as if it had hidden crab's eyes for years. When I were agricultural society, I remember Confucius's ward, The Poem-book solved the Book of Odes. "I try to repay my parents' grace, but it is higher and wider than the sky and I can not even count it." What is the current parent of civilization and technology? What if I think of paying the irreverent grace inherited from my parents with a return to my child without consideration or expectation?

閏 윤	餘 여	成 성	歲 세	律 률	呂 려	調 조	陽 양
yun	yeo	seong	se	ryul	ryeo	jo	yang
윤달	남을	이룰	해	법	운	고를	볕
yundal	nameul	irul	hae	beop	un	goreul	byeot
leap month	remain, extra	make	year	law	female	harmonize	male
007. 윤달은 일년의 남는 일로 이루어지고				008. 음과 양은 균형과 조화를 이룬다			
A leap month is made up of the remaining days of the year				The male and female is balanced and harmonized			
윤년閏年	여유餘裕	성공成功	세월歲月	법률法律	육려六呂	조화調和	음양陰陽
leap year	margin	success	time	law	six cathode	harmony	negative positive

閏윤: 여분의 월일, month and day of the textra
餘여: 여유 여가 한가한 leisure
成성: 성숙 정성 mature sincerity
歲세: 세월 나이 일생 year age life

律률: 가락 조율 rhythm balance
呂려: 음 척추 육려 female spine six-female
調조: 조절 어울림 control matching
陽양: 양지 밝다 shining place bright

005. 계절 변화와 사색 (운등치우 로결위상)

 늦가을 초겨울 날씨에 추운 듯 옷매무새하고, 본능적으로 십 리 길 초등학교를 가던 어느 날, 다른 아이들도 여기저기서 나오는 게 보인다. 왜 학교 가는 것일까. 매일 날마다 다니다 보면 뭔가가 되겠지 라는 막연한 생각으로, 학교 가면 산수도 하고 자연도 배우고, 국어도 배운다. 그때, 이걸 어디다 써먹는지, 밥이 나오는지, 돈이 나오는지, 한석봉이 될 수 있는지, 이순신장군이 될 수 있는지, 무척 궁금했었다. 참고로, 필자는 중학교 유학시절 한참 선배의 영향으로, 섬광처럼 깨달아, 동기부여를 받고, 공부에 눈을 떴다. 주위에서 동생과 오빠와 누나와 함께, 천지가 열리는 듯, 아침 햇살의 신선함, 상쾌하고 시원하면서 쌀쌀한 바람 기운을 얼굴에 스치며 종종 걸음으로 나온다. 작은 개울과 도랑을 건너 좁은 오솔길을 따라 하염없이 가노라면, 등교하는 아이들이 서로 조잘거리면서, 하나둘씩 앞서거니 뒤서거니, 이어져 방향성 넝쿨처럼 학교행이다. 그때도 필자는 말이 별로 없었다. 궁금한 것만 하늘만큼 많을 뿐이었다. 실개천 풀 사이에 이슬인 듯 서리가, 연약한 잡초 잎을 붙들고 있다.

 하늘에서 보낸 이슬이(운등치우 로결위상) 흔적도 없이 날아가지 않고, 동심을 깨워 주며 차가운 초겨울의 생소함을 자랑하는 듯 보였다.

005. Seasonal Change and Thinking

One day I went to elementary school in the early winter weather in late autumn, in dress up as if it was cold, and instinctively. Other children are seen coming from all over the place. Why am I going to school? I think it will be something if I go every day. I go to school, I learn arithmetic, nature, and learn Korean. At that time, I wondered where I used this, whether it was rice, money, whether it could be Han Seok-bong, or whether I could be Admiral Yi Sun-shin. For reference, I was motivated, realize like flash and woke up to study because of the influence of my seniors when I was studying in junior high school. With their brother, and sister around me, the freshness of the morning sunshine, the refreshing, cool and chilly windy energy brushes my face, coming out as a quick step. If they cross a small stream and a ditch and follow a path along a narrow path, The kids schooling are chatting to each other, One by one, they goes back and forth, and I go to school like a directional vine. Even then, I didn't say much. Only as many questions as the sky. The frost, as if it were dew between the grasses of the stream, holds the fragile weed leaves. The dew from the sky didn't fly without a trace, It seemed to awaken a young child-mind and boast of the unfamiliarity of cold early winter.

雲 운	騰 등	致 치	雨 우	露 로	結 결	爲 위	霜 상
un	deung	chi	u	ro	gyeol	wi	sang
구름	오를	이를	비	이슬	맺을	할	서리
gureum	oreul	ireul	bi	iseul	maejeul	hal	seori
cloud	crime	become	rain	dew	form	change	frost
009. 구름이 위로 올라가 비가 되며				010. 이슬이 엉켜서 서리로 변한다			
Clouds rise up and rain				Dew forms and turns into frost			
운무雲霧	등락騰落	경치景致	우산雨傘	폭로暴露	결혼結婚	인위人爲	상설霜雪
cloud fog	up down	scenic	umbrella	exposure	marriage	artificiality	frost snow

雲운: 하늘 은하수 sky galaxy
騰등: 앙등 도약 jump-up jump
致치: 극치 나아가다 extreme go-on
雨우: 적시다 wet

露로: 베풀다 give
結결: 끝내다 엉키다 end tangled
爲위: 변하다 만들다 위하다 change make, do
霜상: 세월 엄하다 years strict severe

006. 금은보화보다 값진 것 (금생려수 옥출곤강)

　자식이 태어나면 힘든지도 모르게 금이야 옥이야 하면서 키운다(금생옥출). 아기를 보면 없던 힘도 생기는 게 부성이고 모성이리라. 지나고 나서 생각하면 자신이 스스로 놀랄 때가 있다. 직장 옆에 있던 교직원아파트 집안에 어린 딸이 혼자 갇혀 까무러치듯 울면서, 어쩔 줄을 몰라 하고 있다는 연락을 받고 뛰어가서, 열쇠도 없이 맨손으로 현관문을 순식간에 열은 적이 있다. 문이 어떻게 열렸는지 지금도 궁금하다. 다음에 열려고 하니, 도저히 열 수 없는 구조였다. 어떻게 열렸는지 짐작할 수 없었다. 세상 살면서 지적능력으로 이해할 수 없는 일이 발생하기도 한다. 이와 함께, 이런 모호한 심리를 이용하여 세상을 어지럽히고, 혹세무민 현상이 나타날 수도 있지 않을까하고 추측해 본다.

006. Something worth more than gold and silver treasures

　We do not know if it is hard when our child is born, and We grow him like a gold or a jade. When we see a baby, it is paternal and maternal that we have the power that we do not have. When we think about it after we have passed, we may be surprised by ourself. A young daughter was trapped in a school apartment next to my job, crying, and I got a call that she is not sure what to do, I ran to the door without a key, and I opened the front door with my bare hands in a moment. I still wonder how the door opened. It was a structure that could not be opened because it was going to open later. There's something that you can't understand in the world with your intellectual abilities. Concurrence with this, People use this vague psychology to disturb the world, I guess that there may be a phenomenon of deceiving people.

Magic

金 금	生 생	麗 려	水 수	玉 옥	出 출	崑 곤	岡 강
geum	saeng	ryeo	su	ok	chul	gon	gang
쇠	날	고울	물	구슬	날	뫼	뫼
soe	nal	goul	mul	guseul	nal	moe	moe
gold	produce	nice	water	bead	produce	mountain	
011. 금은 여수지역에서 나온다				012. 구슬은 곤강땅에서 나온다			
Gold is produced in Yeosu				The beads are produced in the Gongang			
현금現金	학생學生	여용麗容	호수湖水	주옥珠玉	출입出入	곤崑	강岡
cash	student	beautiful face	lake	jewelry	outgoing incoming	mountain	hill

金금: 황금 귀하다 gold valuable rare
生생: 살다 자라다 grow alive
麗여: 빛나다 화려함 radiant glamour
水수: 강 호수 바다 river lake sea

玉옥: 소중하다 갈다 precious grind
出출: 태어나다 뛰어나다 excel birth
崑곤: 산이름 mountain name
岡강: 언덕 산등 산봉 hill mountain ridges peaks

007. 궁금한 세상 (검호거궐 주칭야광)

미국 서부 영화를 보면 총으로 결투하거나 전쟁같이 싸우는 모습, 중국 영화를 보면 칼로 겨루는 경우가 많이 등장한다. 결투하러 갈 때 칼이 매우 중요하다며, 여러 칼 중에서 자기 목숨과 같은 날카롭고, 단단하고 빛이 나는 이름 있는 칼을 고른다. 우리나라 옛 가야국이 철강으로 유명했듯이, 메이드 인 가야국 칼이(검호거궐) 좋았으리라. 학교 앞 구멍가게에서 형광펜이나 야광 딱지를 사서, 어두운 밤에 빛이 나는 야광(주칭야광), 이불 속 어두움에서 보기도 하고, 관찰하면서 신기해한 적이 있다. 여름밤에 개똥벌레가 반짝반짝 빛내며 날아다니는 모습, 어렵게 잡아서 실제 보니, 작은 개똥 조각, 소똥 조각처럼 생긴 게 냄새도 날 것 같고, 징글맞은 벌레여서 별로였다. 날아다닐 때는 밝은 빛이 번쩍거리던 개똥벌레, 뒤꽁무니 개똥에서 뜨겁지도 따뜻하지도 않은 빛이 꺼질 듯 희미하게 나왔다. 귀신불 같지만 날아다닐 때가 역시 멋있고 구경하기 좋았다. 자연현상의 오묘함을 다시 관찰해 본다.

007. The curious world

In western American films, there are many cases where you duel with a gun, fight like a war, and compete with a knife in Chinese movies. You said that knives are very important when you go to the duel. Among the many knives, pick a sharp, hard, shining, namely knife like your life. Just as our old Gaya country was famous for steel, the Maid in Gaya country knife would have been good. I bought a fluorescent pen or a glowing scab at a hole shop in front of the school. The night lights that glow on the dark nights, I have seen it in the darkness in the blanket, and I have been surprised to observe it. The way the dog-dung-bugs flashed and flew around in the summer night, I've got it hard to catch, and I actually think it smells like a little dog shit, a piece of cow shit, It was a disgusting bug, so it was not good. The dog-dung-bug that flashed bright light when flying, The shimmering of the dog-dung poop, the light that was neither hot nor warm, came out faintly. It is like a ghost fire, but the time to fly is also cool and good to see. I observe the subtlety of natural phenomena again.

劍 검	號 호	巨 거	闕 궐	珠 주	稱 칭	夜 야	光 광
geom	ho	geo	gwol	ju	ching	ya	gwang
칼	부를	클	대궐	구슬	일컬을	밤	빛
kal	bureul	keul	daegwol	guseul	ilkeoleul	bam	bit
knife	name	big	palace	bead	call	night	luminous
013. 국보인 거궐이라는 칼이 있고				014. 밤에도 빛나는 야광구슬이 있다			
There's Geo-gwol knife called the national treasure				There are luminous beads that shine at night			
검객劍客	신호信號	거부巨富	궁궐宮闕	진주眞珠	칭송稱頌	야학夜學	영광榮光
swords-man	signal	big rich	palace	pearl	praise	night study	glorious honor

劍검: 검법 찌르다 swordsmanship stab
號호: 부르다 암호 call code
巨거: 많다 거칠다 rough many much
闕궐: 문 결원 door vacancy

珠주: 진주 보석 알 pearl jewel egg
稱칭: 칭찬 명칭 명성 praise name reputation
夜야: 어둡다 쉬다 dark rest
光광: 영광 위엄 색 glory dignity color

008. 배고픈 시절 (과진이내 채중개강)

부처님과 불경의 오묘한 진리를 언감생심 어찌 다 헤아릴 수 있을까. 구류 일체 중생 중 태생(태반에서 태어남)으로, 먹어야 살 수 있는 생명체라, 삼라 만상이 보이기 시작할 무렵, 배고픈 어린 시절 어머니가 챙겨주거나 만들어 주지 않으면, 두리번거리며 본능적으로 먹거리를 찾아 눈동자를 굴리며 번쩍 거린다. 뒷마당도 가고 장독도 가고 텃밭도 눈여겨본다. 텃밭 군데군데 서 있 는 감나무 사과나무 돌배나무 대추나무들, 생강과 옥수수들(과진이내, 채중 개강), 우리 태생 중생들은 저놈들을 여기저기 요긴한 건강식품으로 거두어 먹어야 살 수 있으니 어찌하겠는가, 저놈들은 나와 달리 배고파하지도 않고 하늘을 쳐다보고, 땅에 의지하며 우주자연으로 살고 있으니 얼마나 좋을까 하고 부러워한 적이 있다.

008. The hungry time

How can I count the subtle truths of Buddha and Buddhism? I mean, in the placenta of all the living-things, they're living things that can only be eaten, When the all creation began to appear, If your hungry childhood mother doesn't care for you or make you, I look around and instinctively find food, and I roll my eyes and flash. I go to the backyard, go to the pot of soy sauce, and watch the garden. Persimmon tree, apple tree, jujube trees, standing in the garden, ginger and corn, What can we do about our rebirths, because they have to be taken from these things with a good health food, They look up into the sky, not hungry, unlike me, I have been envious of how good it is to rely on the ground and live in space nature.

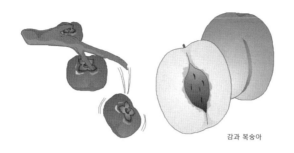

감과 복숭아

果 과	珍 진	李 이	柰 내	菜 채	重 중	芥 개	薑 강
gwa	jin	i	nae	chae	jung	gae	gang
실과	보배	오얏	능금	나물	무거울	겨자	생강
silgwa	bobae	oyas	neunggum	namul	mugeoul	gyeoja	saenggang
fruit	treasure	plum	apple	herb	important	mustard	ginger
015. 자두와 사과가 과일 중 보배다				016. 겨자와 생강이 나물 중 중요하다			
Plums and apples are the treasures of fruit				Mustard and ginger are important herbs			
과즙果汁	진미珍味	행리行李	내하柰何	야채野菜	중요重要	개자芥子	생강生薑
fruit juice	delicacy	peach plum	how?	vegetable	important	mustard seed	ginger [live]

果과: 결과 열매 resulting fruit
珍진: 귀중 맛좋다 precious delicious
李이: 자두 보따리 plum bundle
柰내: 사과 어떻게 apple how

菜채: 반찬 채취하다 side dish gather
重중: 소중 엄숙 짐 precious solemn burden
芥개: 띠끌 작다 dust small
薑강: 생강 ginger

009. 물장구치며 놀던 시절 (해함하담 린잠우상)

어렸을 적 여름에 마을 앞 금평 개울 민물에서 많이 놀았다. 물에서 한참을 놀다 보면 추워, 오들오들하면서 몸을 움츠리고, 햇볕 있는 개울가 자갈밭으로 나와, 뜨겁게 달구어진 매끈한 돌로 얼굴과 몸을 문지르며, 한기를 달래기도 했다. 귀에 들어간 물로 귀가 멍하니 소리가 잘 들리지 않아, 귓속 물 빼려고 뜨거운 돌을 귓불에 대고 흔들어 보기도 한다. 귓속 물이 빠지면서 주변 아이들, 새들, 바람소리가 맑게 들린다. 바람에 흔들리는 강아지풀, 갈대 잎, 축 늘어진 작은 버드나무 가지도 신기해 보였다. 개울 건너 산자락, 깎아지른 언덕에 큰 소나무가 매달리듯 서 있는 모습도 아슬아슬하여 눈길을 끌었다. 그때는 호기심도 궁금한 것도 많았다. 바닷물은 왜 짜고, 민물은 왜 밍밍할까 (해함하담). 물고기는 비늘이 있고 새는 날개가 있을까(린잠우상). 물고기는 숨도 안 쉬고, 미끈미끈할까. 공부하면서 서서히 그 비밀을 알게 되니, 책에 흥미를 갖게 된 듯하다.

009. The days of playing with water

When I was a child, I played a lot in the fresh water of the Geumpyeong stream in front of the village. It's cold when I am playing in the water for a while, I am shrinked trembling, I come out sunny stream-side stone field, rubs its face and body with a hot, smooth stone, and soothes the cold. I can not hear the sound of the ears because I can not hear the water in my ears, and I shake the hot stone on my ear to drain the water in my ear. As the water in my ear falls, the surrounding children, birds, and wind sound clear. The wind-shattering dog-grass, reed leaves, and the droop little willow branches looked amazing. The figure of standing, like a large pine tree hanging on a shaved hill, attracted attention with dangerous. There were many questions and curiosity. Why is seawater salty, and why is fresh water bland? Does fish have scales and birds have wings? Fish don't breathe, they're slick. As I studied, I gradually learned the secret, and it seems to have become interested in books.

海 해	鹹 함	河 하	淡 담	鱗 린	潛 잠	羽 우	翔 상
hae	ham	ha	dam	rin	jam	u	sang
바다	짤	강	맑을	비늘	잠길	깃	날
bada	jjal	gang	malgeul	bineul	jamgil	gis	nal
sea	salty	river	fresh	scale	under water	feather	wing
017. 바다는 짜고 강은 맑다				018. 물고기는 물에 있고 새는 날아다닌다			
The sea is salty and the river is fresh				Fish are in the water and birds fly			
해변海邊	鹹菜함채	銀河은하	淡水담수	은린銀鱗	잠수潛水	적우赤羽	비상飛翔
beach	pickled vegetables	galaxy	fresh water	silver scale	diving [water]	red wing	air fly
海해: 세계 넓다 world wide 鹹함: 쓰다 쓴맛 bitter taste 河하: 냇가 운하 은하 stream canal galaxy 淡담: 맑다 싱겁다 clear bland				鱗린: 물고기 이끼 fish moss 潛잠: 숨다 깊다 hide deep 羽우: 날개 새 장식 wing bird decoration 翔상: 놀다 선회하다 play turn-around			

010. 나는 이름이 여러 개다 (용사화재 조관인황)

어렸을 적에 집안 식구들이랑 동네 어른들은 필자를 만호라 불렀다. 일꾼들은 만호라는 호칭을 재미있어 하면서 그 시절 유행하던 노래 부르듯 마포리 만보하면서, 희희덕거리며 웃고 흥미 있어 했다. 초등학교 입학하여 얼마 지나자 필자를 광호라 하면서 호명하였다. 만호가 아니고 광호일까. 한동안 만호와 광호는 함께 불려졌다. 그 후로도, 필명과 예명과, 종교의 법명 등 여러 이름을 갖게 되었다. 옛적에는 전쟁과 시대의 혼란으로, 여러 이름으로 자녀들을 불렀다는 이야기가 있다. 다른 마을 아이들 부르는데 개똥아, 쇠똥아, 길똥아 라는 이름도 들은 적 있다. 사내이름을 부르면 끌려가거나 잡혀간다는 것이다. 아이들은 엉덩이에 반점이 있는데, 몽고반점이라며, 반점이 없으면 몽고사람이 아니라 하여 잡혀가므로, 어른들은 일부러 어린아이 엉덩이를 때려 푸른 반점을 만들기도 했다 하니, 침략자들의 행패를 막기 위해 나라 힘의 중요성을 절감하는 듯하다. 세상 이겨 내면서 살아가는 게 참 모질기도 한 게 아닐까. 이처럼 용사, 화재, 조관, 인황 등, 용이나 불이나 조 등은 관직이름(용사화재 조관인황)이니, 날아다니는 새가 임금이 되었다는 오해가 없길 바랄 뿐이다.

010. I have several names

When I was a child, my family and local adults called me Manho. The workers enjoyed the title of Manho, and as they sang the popular songs of those days, they were smiling and smiling, laughing and interested. After entering elementary school, Teacher called me Kwangho, not Manho. For a while, Manho and Kwangho were called together. Since then, I have had several names, including name as a writer and call-name, and religious legal name. In the past, there was a story that, due to the chaos of war and the times, they called their children in various names. I have heard the name "gaeddonga, soeddonga, and gilddonga" when I call other village children. Children have spots on their hips, they are Mongolian spots, and if they do not have spots, they are not Mongolian, Adults have deliberately hit their children on their hips to make blue spots, so it seems to reduce the importance of the country's power to prevent the invaders from being attacked. I wonder if it is really hard to live through the world. As such, The dragon, The fire, The bird, The Emperor is the name of the office. I just hope there is no misunderstanding that flying birds have become Emperor.

龍 룡	師 사	火 화	帝 제	鳥 조	官 관	人 인	皇 황
yong	sa	hwa	je	jo	gwan	in	hwang
용	스승	불	임금	새	벼슬	사람	임금
ryong	seuseung	bul	imgeum	sae	byeoseul	saram	imgeum
dragon	teacher	fire	king	bird	office	human	emperor
019. 관직 이름에 용사와 화제가 있다				020. 조류 이름을 붙인 황제가 문화를 일으켰다			
There is a dragon-teacher and a fire-king in the name of the office				The emperor, who named flying birds, created a culture			
龍宮용궁	의사醫師	화산火山	황제皇帝	백조白鳥	法官법관	인생人生	황제皇帝
dragon palace	doctor	volcano	emperor	swan	judge	one's life	emperor

龍용: 임금 호걸 king hero
師사: 어른 본받다 adult follow
火화: 타다 따르다 burn follow
帝제: 하느님 제왕 lord king of the king

鳥조: 새 bird
官관: 관청 직무 government office duties
人인: 백성 어떤 사람 People A person
皇황: 군주 가다 monarch go

011. 복장에 따른 마음자세 (시제문자 내복의상)

학창시절 제복이라 하며 학생복을 입는다. 제복에 대한 정치적 사회적 이념적 여러 견해가 존재하지만, 그걸 떠나서, 그 제복은 공부하는 걸 당연시하게 되고, 공부가 전부인 양, 의식 속에 잠재하게 된다. 제복을 입으면 학생으로서 모범되는 언행을 해야 되고 조심스러웠다. 어쩌다 체육시간이 되어 체육복을 입으면 운동하는 마음을 갖게 되고 뛰어놀게 된다. 더 나아가 나이들어 군 복무 때 군복의 신분, 관혼상제에 따른 의상변화와 조선시대의 신분차이(내복의상)에 따른 복장의 다름은 놀랍기까지 하다. 옷과 의상이 정신과 행동까지 바꾸는데, 시대를 초월하여, 어쩌면 본능적으로 옷매무새에 언제나 관심 갖고 준비하는 과정은, 나에 대한 예의 같기도 하다.

011. Attitude of dress

They wear uniforms during school days and wear student uniforms. There are many political and social ideological views on uniforms, but apart from that, the uniform takes for granted to study, and the study becomes all-in-one, and it is latent in consciousness. When I wore uniform, I had to do exemplary words and phrases as a student and was careful. When I get to physical education class and wear sportswear, I have a mind to exercise and play. Furthermore, it is surprising that the difference in costumes due to the status of military uniforms, changes in costumes according to the ceremonies of coming of age, marriage, funeral and ancestral worship, and differences in status in the Joseon Dynasty is surprising. Clothes and costumes change the spirit and behavior, and the process of preparing and preparing for the dresses, transcending the times, perhaps instinctively, is like courtesy to me.

始 시	制 제	文 문	字 자	乃 내	服 복	衣 의	裳 상
si	je	mun	ja	nae	bok	ui	sang
비로소	지을	글월	글자	이에	입을	옷	치마
biroso	jieul	geulwol	geulja	ie	ipeul	ot	chima
only then	make	text	letter	besides	clothes	clothes	skirt
021. 복희와 창힐이 처음으로 글자를 만들고				022. 황제가 윗옷과 치마를 입혀 신분구별을 하였다			
Bok-hi and Chang-hil made the first letters				Also, The emperor made a distinction by wearing a coat and skirt			
시작始作	제복制服	문학文學	흑자黑字	내지乃至	의복衣服	우의雨衣	의상衣裳
start	uniform	literature	surplus	also	clothing	raincoat	costume
始시: 처음 시작 근본 first start root 制제: 만들다 속박 making bond 文문: 책 꾸미다 book, decorate 字자: 호칭 기르다 title raise				乃내: 또한 저번 때 also last-time 服복: 입다 복종 wear obedience 衣의: 입다 덮다 wear cover 裳상: 옷 왕성하다 clothes flourish			

012. 작은 형, 인간의 선량한 본성 (추위양국 유우도당)

지금도 작은 형(조인호)은 고향 연촌에서, 농사지으며 살고 있다. 오늘날과 마찬가지로 과거에도 황소 가격은 대단히 비쌌다. 농경시대에는 소의 역할이 다양하였다. 황소는 농번기에 농부들의 힘든 농사를 도와주고, 자녀 대학교육 등록금, 결혼 등 가족의 대소사가 있을 때는 목돈의 자금줄이 되었다. 다른 가축인 개나 닭은 용돈이나 몸보신용이 되었다. 어느 날 작은 형이 시골 작은 길가 옆 도랑 풀숲에서 헝겊으로 동여맨 돈뭉치를 습득하였다. 그는 여기저기 알아보아 주인을 찾은바, 이웃 마을 사람이 5일 장날에, 소를 팔아 받은 돈임을 알고 돌려주었다 하여, 주변 온 고을에 칭송의 소문이 자자하게 퍼졌다. 황금을 돌처럼 여기고 선행한 것이, 두고두고 마을의 본보기가 되어 전해 내려오고 있다. 요순과 같은 왕조시대에 지금처럼 권력 암투 없이, 나라까지 자식이 아닌, 유능한 사람에게 넘겨주었다(추위양국, 유우도당)고 하는 아름다운 이야기가, 전설처럼 전해지고 있다.

012. A small elder brother, a good nature of man

Even now, my small elder brother lives in my hometown, Yeonchon, farming. As today, bull prices were very expensive in the past. In the agricultural age, the role of cattle varied. Bulls helped farmers to farm hard during the farming season, and when there was a family such as tuition for children's college education, marriage, etc., they became the financial support of the money. Other livestock, dogs or chickens, became pocket money or body care. One day, a small elder brother acquired a bundle of money from a ditch grass next to a small rural roadside. He found the owner here and there, and the neighboring village man returned the money, the neighboring village man had sold the cow on the fifth everyday of the market, and the rumors of praise spread to the surrounding area. The gold is regarded as a stone and the preceding is being passed down as an example of the village. In the dynasty era like Yosun, a beautiful story that says that it handed over to a competent person, not a child, without power, is said to be a legend.

推 추	位 위	讓 양	國 국	有 유	虞 우	陶 도	唐 당
chu	wi	yang	guk	yu	u	do	dang
밀	자리	사양할	나라	있을	염려할	질그릇	당나라
mil	jari	sayanghal	nara	isseul	yeomryeohal	jilgeureut	dangnara
push	state	yields	nation	be	concern	pottery	nation
023. 요의 왕은 현명한 순에게 나라를 물려주었다				024. 요와 순왕이 물려준 우, 도, 당이라는 나라가 있다			
The King of Yo yields his country to the wise Sun				There is a country called Wu, Do, and Tang that the king of Yo and Sun handed over			
추진推進	위치位置	양보讓步	국민國民	유선有線	우인虞人	도예陶藝	당면唐麵
propul-sion	location	conces-sion	people	wired	hunter	pottery	noodle
推추: 옳다 추천 right recommendation 位위: 자리 등급 seat grade 讓양: 양보할 넘겨주다 concede give-over 國국: 고향 수도 home capital				有유: 알다 소유물 know property 虞우: 편안 염려 comfort concern 陶도: 도자기 교화 ceramics edification 唐당: 갑자기 나라명 suddenly nation-name			

013. 인과응보야 궁금하다 (조민벌죄 주발은탕)

착한 사람은 상 받고, 죄 지은 사람은 죄의 값을 받아야 하는데, 받지 않고 넘어가는 경우가 상당히 많다. 초등학교 시절 연필 도난 사건 있어, 모든 학생이 책상 위에 무릎 꿇고, 손을 위로 올리며 단체 벌을 받았다. 훔친 학생이 나올 때까지 벌을 받는다고 담임선생이 말하며, 훔쳐 간 사람은 손가락이 다음 날이면 썩는다고 큰소리로 말했다. 손 썩기 싫으면 어서 나오기 바란다 하고, 몇 분 지나자 한 학생이 나왔다. 왜 훔쳤느냐 하니, 어쩌는가 보려고 그랬단다. 바늘 도둑이 소 도둑 되니, 앞으로 착하게 지내라며 용서하였다. 작은 좀도둑처럼 남의 물건 훔쳐 가는 친구, 다른 친구에게 욕하고 구타하는 친구, 그때그때 죄를 받지 않으니 짜증 날 때가 많았다. 성장하여서는 각종 범죄와 지도자라는 사람들의 악행을 보면 몸서리쳐진다. 작은 개개인의 도덕적 각성이 제도적 교육적으로 필요하지 않을까.

013. A reward in accordance with a deed, I wonder

Good people receive awards, and those who are guilty must receive the price of sin, and there are many cases where they pass without receiving it. In the case of pencil theft during elementary school, all students knelt on their desks, raised their hands and received group punishment. The teacher said that he was punished until the stolen student came out, and the person who stole it said loudly that the finger rots the next day. If you do not want to rot your hands, you want to come out soon, and after a few minutes a student came out. I was trying to see what he did, to see why he stole it. The needle thief was a cattle thief, and he forgave him to be good in the future. A friend who steals other things like a small shoplifter, a friend who swears and beats another friend, and there were irritated many times when he was not guilty. When you grow up, you are shivered by the evils of people who are various crimes and leaders. I wonder if the moral awakening of small individuals is necessary institutionally and educationally.

弔 조	民 민	伐 벌	罪 죄	周 주	發 발	殷 은	湯 탕
jo	min	beol	joe	ju	bal	eun	tang
슬퍼할	백성	칠	허물	두루	펄	성할	끓을
seulpeohal	bakseong	chil	heomul	duru	pyeol	seonghal	ggeulheul
poor	people	purnish	faulty	genera-lly	happen	eun	boil
025. 백성을 돕고, 못된 왕을 정벌하였는데				026. 주나라 발왕과 은나라 탕왕이 하였다			
He helped the poor people and punished the guilty king				He was played by King Bal of the Ju nation and King Tang of the Silver dynasty			
경조慶弔	시민市民	정벌征伐	죄벌罪伐	주변周邊	발표發表	은성殷盛	욕탕浴湯
joy sadness	citizen	punish-ment	sin punish	peripher-al	announ-cement	bustling rich	bath

弔조: 불쌍 위문 pity consolation
民민: 서민 common people
伐벌: 벌할 죽이다 punishment kill
罪죄: 죄 처벌하다 crime punish

周주: 널리 둘레 broad circumference
發발: 일어날 보내다 rise send
殷은: 은나라 번성 country prosperity
湯탕: 목욕탕 온천 bathhouse spa

014. 스님에 대한 동경 (좌조문도 수공평장)

추운 어느 겨울 대문발치에서 바랑(배낭)을 맨 스님이 목탁소리와 함께, 머리를 연신 조아리며 관세음보살 나무아미타불, 염불한다. 어린 시절에 더러 보았던 스님은 남루해 보이지만, 정성스러움에 경건함과 존경스런 마음이 들었다. 어렴풋이 속세를 떠나 깨달음을 찾는 고행자라는 인식과 고정된 그림이 있다. 언제나 머리를 짓누르고 꽉 찼던 삶의 궁금증, 처자식도 없이, 삶에서 희로애락 중, 즐거움은 어느 곳, 어떤 곳에서 찾고, 무엇으로 느낄 수 있을까. 아예 즐거움이라는 생각을 잊고 사는 것일까. 요즘엔 계절 따라, 사찰에서 수도승 체험생활을 운영하는 것으로 알고 있다. 딱딱하고 엄격하기만 할 것 같은 군대에서도 즐거운 오락생활이 있는 것처럼, 거기도 사람 사는 곳이니, 여러 오락이나 흥미로운 이벤트가 있을 것으로 짐작한다. 어쩌면 동경의 대상으로 스님이 되고 싶은 마음이 항상 자리하고 있다. 연기처럼 향기처럼 사라지는 인생은 세상을 떠날 때까지, 깨달음을 찾기 위한 삶의 끝없는 여정이 아닐런지. 하지만 깨달음은 무지개처럼 잡지 못하는, 이걸 깨달았다 생각하면 저게 궁금한 것처럼, 저 언덕 너머에서 손짓만 하는 것인 듯하다.

014. Longing for the monk

In a cold winter at the foot of the gate, the monk who has a barang(backpack) is accompanied by a wooden sound, The Merciful Goddess sound bodhisattva, Save us, merciful Buddha! and his head is kowtowed again and again, The monk who had seen some in my childhood seemed to be a poor man, but I felt reverence and respectful in his sincerity. There is a perception that it is a penitent who leaves the world vaguely and finds enlightenment and a fixed picture. Without the curiosity of life, the child who has always been crushed and filled with his head, the joy of life, where and where can pleasure be found and felt? Does he forget the idea of pleasure and live? Nowadays, according to the season, I know that I run a monk experience life in temples. As there is a pleasant entertainment life in the army that seems to be hard and strict, That's where people live, I guess there will be many entertainments and interesting events. Perhaps as the object of longing, there is always a desire to become a monk. Life disappears like a smell like smoke, and it is not the endless journey of life to find enlightenment until the world leaves. But enlightenment seems to be a gesture beyond the hill, as if I were wondering other thing when I realized this, which I could not catch like a rainbow.

坐 좌	朝 조	間 문	道 도	垂 수	拱 공	平 평	章 장
jwa	jo	mun	gil	su	gong	pyeong	jang
앉을	아침	물을	길	드리울	맞잡을	평할	밝을
anjeul	achim	muleul	gil	driul	magapeul	pyeonghal	balgeul
sit	morning	ask	way	drop	fold arms	peaceful	bright

027. 왕이 조정에 앉아 백성을 위한 도를 구하니				028. 옷을 늘어뜨리고 팔장을 껴도, 평화롭고 밝게 다스려진다			
The king sits in the court, seeks the way for the people				Even if you hang your clothes and put your arms around you, you are peaceful and bright			
좌선坐禪	조석朝夕	학문學問	도로道路	수직垂直	수공垂拱	평화平和	훈장勳章
sitdown pray	morning evening	academic	road	vertical	cross arms	peace	medal

坐좌: 앉다 자리 sit down seat
朝조: 처음 뵙다 조회 first time, see you inquiry
間문: 알아보다 보내다 know send
道도: 사리 근원 theory of things fundamental

垂수: 거의 가장자리 가까움 almost edges, close
拱공: 보옥 껴안다 jewelry hug
平평: 나누다 평평할 평정, share, calm.
章장: 조목 규정 article regulations

015. 어머니의 측은지심 (애육여수 신복융강)

환경과 가치관의 급속한 변화로 이웃사이가 사회적으로 옛날보다 정신적으로 각박해 보인다. 어머니는 언제나 손님을 귀히 여겼다. 마을 부녀자들이 오면 요깃거리 대접이 풍성하였다. 이웃이 새해 보리 고개 때 찾아오면 쌀, 보리, 곡식을 많이 베풀어 주곤 하였다. 거기에 고구마 한 보따리는 덤으로 챙겼다. 따뜻한 아랫목에 몸을 녹이도록 끌어당기고 두툼한 솜이불로 덮어 준다. 하루 종일 수다와 잡담으로 정성을 다하는 모습이 눈에 선하다. 우리는 가끔 없는 살림에 헌신적인 정신으로 자식을 사랑하고, 키운 부모의 미담을 매스컴에서 어쩌다 보곤 한다. 불효하며 패륜한 자식의 허물까지 덮어 주려는 안타까운 소식은, 평범한 사람들의 마음을 슬프게 한다. 자식 낳아서 키워봐야 부모 마음을 안다고들 한다. 일찍 철든 애어른 같은 자식들도 더러 있다. 매스 미디어가 발달한 요즘은 더욱더 서로가 깨어 있는 사랑으로 뭉쳐야 하지 않을까. 불행과 악행은 빠지기 쉽고, 사랑과 선행은 좀 번거롭고 까다롭다. 정성과 노력이 필요해서 그렇지 않을까.

015. Mother's compassion

Due to rapid changes in environment and values, it seems to be mentally more intense between neighbors and socially than before. My mother always valued her guests. When the women of the village came, there was a lot of food. When the neighbors came to the new year, early spring hungry, she would give a lot of rice, barley, and grain. I packed a bag of sweet potatoes in there. Pull your body to melt in the warm underside, and cover with thick cotton quilts. I can see she doing her best with chat and chat all day long. We sometimes love our children with a devoted spirit to the absence of living, and we often see the parents' misgivings in the media. The sad news that tries to cover up the faults of the ineffective and ruthless children makes the hearts of ordinary people sad. It is said that you know your parents' minds when you have children. Some of them are an early-aged childlike child. Nowadays, when the media has developed, should not we unite with more and more awake love? Unhappiness and evil are easy to fall out, love and good deeds are a little tricky, and they need care and effort.

愛 애	育 육	黎 려	首 수	臣 신	伏 복	戎 융	羌 강
ae	yuk	yeo	su	sin	bok	yung	gang
사랑	기를	검을	머리	신하	엎드릴	오랑캐	오랑캐
sarang	gileul	geomeul	meori	sinha	eopdeuril	orangkae	orangkae
love	raise	black	head	servant	obey	barbaian	savage
029. 임금이 백성을 사랑으로 돌보면				030. 괴롭히는 이웃 나라도 신하처럼 따른다			
If king care for your people with love				The troubled neighbors obeys like servants			
애독愛讀	교육教育	여명黎明	수석首席	공신功臣	복병伏兵	융병戎兵	강활羌活
love of reading	educa-tion	day-break	first class	contri-butor	hidden obstacle	soldier	herb name
愛애: 가엾다 편들다 be sorry take sides				臣신: 섬기다 거느리다 serve have one's own			
育육: 자라다 낳다 grow up give birth				伏복: 엎어짐 굴복하다 fall down give in			
黎려: 많다 늙다 가지런 a lot old straight				戎융: 무기 전쟁 병사 weapons wars soldiers			
首수: 첫머리 우두머리 칼자루 first head chief hilt				羌강: 고달픔 티베트족 tough Tibetans			

016. 아쉬움, 멀면서 가까운 세상 (하이일체 솔빈귀왕)

서로 지구의 반대편에 있는 유럽과 코리아, 네덜란드에는 딸 가족이 있고, 코리아에는 아들 가족이 살고 있다. 멀거나 가깝거나 모두가 하나가 되어 손자녀들을 데리고, 코리아 필자가 있는 곳으로 돌아와 모이니(하이일체, 솔빈귀왕) 이렇게 기쁠 수가 없구나. 나이 들어 보니 자손 귀한 줄을 알아가는 듯하다. 요즘은 세계가 일일생활권이 다 되어 비용이 좀 과해서 문제지, 오가는 것은 어렵지 않은 시대다. 따라서 임종 때까지 일정 재산이 유지된다면, 상속분 중 일정비율은 왕래비용 공유재산으로 유언하여, 서로 부담되지 않도록 하면 어떨까. 코로나19가 팬데믹 상태라 여간 불편한 게 아니다. 왕래한 지 꽤 되어 어린 손 자녀가 많이 성장하도록 오지 못한 실정이다. 모바일 등 정보통신이 발달하고 무료로 이용할 수 있는 아이티 기술이 제공되어, 수시로 화상통화 등으로 아쉬움을 달래고 있다.

016. Sadly, a distant and near world

Europe, Korea, and the Netherlands, on the other side of the earth, have daughters' families, and Korea has a son's family. I can not be so happy to come back to the place where I am in Korea, with my children, who are far or near, and all of them. As I grow older, I seem to know that my offspring are precious. Nowadays, the world is a daily life zone, and it is a problem because it is a little overpriced, and it is not difficult to go back and forth. Therefore, if a certain property is maintained until the end of the life, why not make a certain percentage of the inheritance as a shared property for the cost of coming and going and not being burdened with each other? Corona is not uncomfortable because it is a pandemic state. It has been a while since I have been there, and It is a situation that young children have not come to grow a lot. Information and communication such as mobile are developed, and IT technology that can be used free of charge is provided, and it is often appeases the regret due to video calls.

遐하	邇이	壹일	體체	率솔	賓빈	歸귀	王왕
ha	i	il	che	sol	bin	gwi	wang
멀	가까울	한	몸	거느릴	손	돌아갈	임금
meol	gaggaul	han	mom	geoneulil	son	dolagal	imgeum
far	near	one	body	lead	guest	return	king
031. 멀거나 이웃 나라도 하나가 되어				032. 백성을 데리고 천자에게 돌아와 굽신거린다			
Far or neighboring countries become one				He comes back to the heavens with his people			
하방遐方	원이遠邇	통일統壹	단체團體	인솔引率	귀빈貴賓	귀국歸國	왕자王子
region	far and near	unify	group	take people	VIP	return to national	prince
遐하: 가다 길다 어찌 go long how 邇이: 통속적이다 popular 壹일: 오로지 모두 같다 only all equal 體체: 모양 근본 법 shape root law				率솔: 비율 통솔 장수 ratio command general 賓빈: 물리치다 버림 defeat abandon 歸귀: 보내다 편들다 send one's side 王왕: 천자 군림함 king son overwhelm			

51

017. 새로운 나라 네덜란드 (명봉재수 백구식장)

　오래 전에 딸이 유학하면서 인연이 된 독일청년과 결혼하여, 귀여운 손녀 손자까지 갖게 되었으니 얼마나 좋고 다행인지 감동뿐이다. 그들은 네덜란드에 살고 있다. 네덜란드는 하멜이 하멜표류기로 한국을 고요한 아침의 나라로 소개하여 유명하게 되었고, 최근에는 한국에 월드컵 4강 신화를 선물한 히딩크 나라이기도 하다. 유럽에 몇 달 머물면서 어린 손 자녀와 함께 동물원에 갔다. 동물들이 우리 안에 갇혀 있는 한국 동물원과 달리, 운 좋게 울타리 없는, 넓은 들에 사람과 함께 어울리는 모습의 동물원에 가게 되어 새로웠다. 공작새는 거부감 없이 바로 앞에서 넓고 화려한 날개깃을 활짝 펼쳐 자랑스럽게 뽐내고, 새들은 지저귀며 노래하고(명봉재수), 다른 망아지나 타조 토끼들이 초원에서 풀을 뜯고(백구식장), 꽃과 나무와 어린이와 조화를 이루니 평화로움이 자연 그 자체 아닌가 싶었다.

017. A new country, the Netherlands

　I am only impressed by how good and fortunate I am to have a cute granddaughter grandson who married a German youth who had a relationship with her daughter while studying abroad a long time ago. They live in the Netherlands. The Netherlands became famous for Hamel's introduction of Korea as a calm morning country with a Hamel drifter. Recently, it is also a Hiddink country that presented Korea with a World Cup semi-finals. I stayed in Europe for a few months and went to the zoo with my young gand-children. Unlike the Korean zoo where animals are trapped in cages, it was fortunate to go to a zoo that looked like a fence-free, wide field with people. The peacock proudly shows off its wide and colorful wing feathers in front of it without any objection, The birds sing and sing, the other foals, ostriches, and rabbits graze in the grasslands, and harmonize with flowers, trees, and children. I thought peace was nature itself.

鳴 명	鳳 봉	在 재	樹 수	白 백	駒 구	食 식	場 장
myeong	bong	jae	su	baek	gu	sik	jang
울	봉황	있을	나무	흰	망아지	먹을	마당
ul	bonghwang	isseul	namu	hin	mangaji	meokeul	madang
cry	phoenix	be	tree	white	colt	meal	ground
033. 봉황이 나무에서 노래하며				034. 흰 망아지는 마당에서 풀을 뜯는다			
The phoenix sings in the trees				White puppies eat grass in the yard			
이명耳鳴	봉황鳳凰	현재現在	과수果樹	고백告白	용구龍駒	음식飲食	직장職場
tinnitus	phoenix	current	fruit tree	confes-sion	hand-some foal	food	job

鳴명: 부르다 call sing 鳳봉: 봉황의 수컷 phoenix male 在재: 찾다 살피다 look for look at 樹수: 심다 초목 plant vegetation	白백: 작위 말하다 title say 駒구: 짐승새끼 젊은이 말 cubs young men horse 食식: 음식 먹다 food eat 場장: 시험장 때, 장터 testing ground time, yard marketplaces

018. 어느 날, 가족 산책과 등산 (화피초목 뢰급만방)

보이지 않는 바람은 머리카락을 스치고, 눈에 보이는 풀과 나무 잎이 흔들려 사람 눈길을 사로잡는다. 아이들과 조그만 먹거리를 준비하여, 어느 휴일 날 구룡산 산책을 가거나 등산을 하는 경우가 더러 있다. 한가한 여느 시골처럼 김치전, 부추전, 해물파전과 막걸리를 파는 오막살이집들이 여기저기 옹기종기 있다. 산 중턱에는 각종 운동기구와, 옹달샘에 작은 물병을 줄 세워 사람들이 기다리고 있다. 사람냄새보다 풀과 나무의 풋풋한 향기가 바람에 실려 온다. 만방에 향기 퍼져라 휘날리지만 빌딩숲에 가려 하늘로 흩어져 휘발하는 듯하다. 이리 자연 속에 잠시라도 있으면 하늘의 덕이 풀과 나무에까지 미치는(화피초목) 듯하다. 그 혜택이 온 세상 만방, 보통사람들에게까지 가득 찬 듯하니(뢰급만방) 기쁘기 한이 없구나.

018. One day, family walks and hiking

The invisible wind brushes through her hair, and the visible grass and tree leaves shake to catch the eye of the person. There are some cases where children prepare small food and go for a walk or Guryong-mountain climbing on a holiday day. Like any leisurely countryside, there are many houses of kimchi-pancake, chive-pancake, seafood-pancake, and makgeolli. In the middle of the mountain, people are waiting for each species exercise equipment and a small water bottle on the Ongdalsam(small fountain) of a small fountain. The smell of grass and trees is carried in the wind rather than the smell of people. It spreads in all directions, but it seems to be volatile in the sky because it is covered by the building forest. If there is a moment in nature, the virtue of heaven seems to reach grass and trees. I am happy that the benefits are full of the whole world, the common people.

化 화	被 피	草 초	木 목	賴 뢰	及 급	萬 만	方 방
hwa	pi	cho	mok	roe	geup	man	bang
될	입을	풀	나무	힘입을	미칠	일만	모
doel	ipeul	pul	namu	himipeul	michil	ilman	mo
change	spread	grass	tree	trust	reach	ten-thousant	place
035. 조화가 풀과 나무까지 이르고				036. 신뢰(덕)는 온 세상에 도달한다			
The harmony reach grass and trees				Trust(virtue) reaches the whole world			
변화變化	피해被害	초원草原	목재木材	신뢰信賴	언급言及	만물萬物	방법方法
change	damage	grass-land	timber	trust	mention	all things	method

化화: 조화 가르치다 태어나다 harmonize teach born
被피: 이불 입다 두르다 blanket wear
草초: 잡초 비천 weeds beggar
木목: 오행(五行)의 첫째 the first of five acts

賴뢰: 힘 이득 덕 force benefit virtue
及급: 및 더불어 and together
萬만: 다수 결코 크다 majority never big
方방: 사방 방위 all directions every way

019. 철학과 종교 (개차신발 사대오상)

 거리를 걷다 보면 주택가에서 십자가 있는 교회와 절 상징의 깃발이 나부끼는 모습을 쉽게 볼 수 있다. 학창시절에 종교는 교과목에 없어 접근하기가 어려웠다. 단지 사회과목에서 토속신앙이니 토테미즘이니 하면서 지나간다. 부모와 지인들의 영향으로 어떤 종교에 관심 갖거나 속하게 되는 듯하다. 종교 이미지는 엄숙하고 희생적이고 선하고 착한 듯하다. 특별한 계기가 있으면 모를까, 쉽게 인생을 헌신하여 성직자가 되겠다는 마음과 각오는 참으로 어렵지 않을까. 자라고 나이 들면서 철학적으로 연구는 한번 해 보고 싶은 마음이 들 때가 있다. 따라서 관련 서적을 탐독하게 된다. 물론 철학과 종교는 일면 비슷한 뿌리일 수도 있지만, 전혀 별개라 본다. 철학은 논리에 따른 이론이고, 종교는 신앙에 따른 믿음을 기반으로 한다. 사주팔자, 팔괘, 육십사괘, 주역 등 어려운 사상과 마주하게 된다. 사대오상도 그 범주에 있다. 사대는 불교의 지수화풍, 또는 노자의 천지도인 또는 천지군부라고도 한다. 오상은 불교에서 성불(成佛)에 이르기까지 닦고 익히는 다섯 단계의 수행《통달보리심(通達菩提心)·수보리심(修菩提心)·성금강심(成金剛心)·증금강심(證金剛心)·불신 원만(佛身圓滿)》, 오륜의 인의예지신을 말한다. 사대 속에 오상이 함께 해야, 동물과 다른, 사람 즉 인간의 근본을 말하고 있는 듯하다.

019. Philosophy and Religion

 Walking on the streets makes it easy to see the flags of cross-border churches and temple symbols in residential areas. During school days, religion does not belong to the subject, which is making it difficult to approach. It is just a local faith and totemism in social studies. It seems to be interested in or belonging to a religion due to the influence from parents and acquaintances.

The religious image seems solemn, sacrificial, good and kind. If there is a special occasion, it will be difficult to be a priest and to be prepared to devote life easily. When I was a child, I sometimes want to do philosophical research. Therefore, I read related books. Of course, philosophy and religion may have similar roots on the one hand, but they are completely separate. Philosophy is a theory based on logic, and religion is based on faith. It faces difficult ideas such as Saju-eight-letter, Eight-gwae, Sixty-four-gwae, and Confucian scriptures. The Sadae-osang(Four-Elements and Five-Ideas) is also in that category. Four Elements are the land, water, fire, and wind of Buddhism, Or it is also called the sky, the earth, the road, the benign of Roja. Or it is also called the heaven, the earth, the king, and father. Five-Ideas refers to the benign, righteous, polite, wisdom and faith. Five stages of practice, from Buddhism to Holy Buddha, to polishing and mastering. It seems that the Five-Ideas should be together in the Four-Elements, telling the fundamentals of animals and other people, in other words humans.

蓋 개	此 차	身 신	髮 발	四 사	大 대	五 오	常 상
gae	cha	sin	bal	sa	dea	o	sang
덮을	이	몸	터럭	넉	큰	다섯	항상
deopeul	i	mom	teoreok	neok	keun	daseot	hangsang
cover	this	body	hair	four	big	five	always
037. 사람의 온몸(몸, 털)은 사대와 오상이 덮고 있고				038. 몸(사대: 흙, 물, 불, 바람)을 마음-(오상: 인의예지신)이 다스린다			
The whole body (body, hair) is covered by four big things and a five-phase				The mind (merciful, just, manner, wisdom, trust) governs the body (clay, water, fire, wind)			
화개花蓋	차후此後	신분身分	금발金髮	사방四方	대회大會	오색五色	일상日常
flower cover	after-ward	dentity	blond hair	all-sides	contest event	five colors	daily life

蓋개: 뚜껑 덮개 cover
此차: 이것 this
身신: 나 몸소 신분 I personal identity
髮발: 머리털 초목 hair vegetation

四사: 사방 all directions every direction
大대: 많다 many lots of much
五오: 다섯째 fifth
常상: 늘 all the time usually

020. 천지공사인가, 예측 어려운 시대 변화 (공유국양 기감훼상)

　학교 가는 논두렁길에 어떤 할머니가 무거운 보따리를 힘겹게 머리에 이고, 같은 방향으로 가고 있어, 도와주려 머리 위 짐을 들어 함께 가면서 중간까지 바래다주었다. 그 할머니는, 보따리는 내가 갖고 갈 테니, 학생은 공부할 때이니 어서 가서 책이나 열심히 보라 하였다. 요즘은 개성시대면서 개인시대다. 자기 몸은 자기 것이니 귀 뚫고 코 뚫고 배꼽까지 뚫어 이상한 고리 장식품(기감훼상)을 자랑하고 다닌다. 영화 속 아프리카 부족에서나 볼 수 있는 모습이다. 이것도 세계적 흐름이고 개성이리라. 모든 것이 오픈되어 글만 읽을 수 있으면 뭐든지 접근하여 알아볼 수 있는 시대다. 옳고 그름의 분별, 선과 악, 구습과 신시대 구별은 그 다음 문제가 되었다. 요즘 세상이 고상함은 조롱의 구식 문화가 되었다. 악마화는 빠지기 쉬운 길이고, 정숙함과 착함은 노력과 인내와 희생까지 해야 하니 험난한 길이다.

020. The great change of heaven and earth, The Unpredictable Changes in the Age

　On the narrow road to go to school, a grandmother was struggling to carry a heavy bundle on her head, and she was going to the same direction, and she lifted her stuff over her head, thus I would like to help het. However, the grandmother said that a student has to study and takes his own books only. These days goes for individualism. His body belongs to him, piercing his ears, his nose, his belly button, with boasting of strange ring ornaments. It is a picture that can be seen only for the African tribe in the movie. But now this is a worldwide trend and personality. This period is that you can access anything that you want to read and learn by any mean. The distinction between right and wrong, good and evil, old and new eras became the next issues. The world has neglected an old-fashioned culture these days. Bad things are easy to access and good things are difficult to reach and you need a lot of work, patience and sacrifice.

恭 공	惟 유	鞠 국	養 양	豈 기	敢 감	毀 훼	傷 상
gong	yu	guk	yang	gi	gam	hwe	sang
공손할	오직	기를	기를	어찌	감히	헐	상할
gongsonhal	ojik	gireul	gireul	eojji	gamhi	heol	sanghal
polite	only	raise	develop	how	dare	injury	hurt
039. 부모가 길러 주심을 섬기고 공경하라				040. 몸을 감히 훼손하거나 더럽히지 말아라			
Serve and honor your parents for their upbringing				Don't dare to damage or taint your body			
공손恭遜	사유思惟	국양鞠養	교양敎養	기악豈樂	용감勇敢	훼손毀損	상처傷處
civil	think	raise a child	culture-educate	enjoy music	bravery	debilita-ting	wound

恭공: 공경 섬기다 respect serve worship
惟유: 홀로 alone single
鞠국: 삼가다 refrain
養양: 양육 부양하다 bring up rear

豈기: 즐기다 enjoy like have a good time
敢감: 굳세다 strong firm stout
毀훼: 망치다 ruin destroy
傷상: 다치다 상처 injure hurt

021. 꼰대는 혐오냐, 어른스럽냐 (여모정열 남효재량)

본 책에서 자주 나오는 언급, 천자문이나 공자, 맹자 등 유익하고 쓸모 있는, 한자권 문화를 접하면 꼰대(한국의 은어=구식 사람)적 냄새가 풍기어, 젊은이들의 얼굴 표정에서 거부감이 나타나는 현실, 세월이 흘러 어느 시점에서는 르네상스로 부활할지도 모르지만, 현실은 세계화적 시대 흐름이라 어찌하겠는가. 필자라도 지켜야 하는 문화일까. 필자마저 파도타기 물결에 동참해야 할까. 소화시켜서 적응함이 일견 자연스런 현상이리라. 어릴 적 사내들은 머리가 짧고, 바지를 입고 장난스러움이 보이고, 여자애들은 그 반대 모양과 행동을 신기로워하던 시절이 있었다. 자기도 모르게 다르게 태어났으니 말이다. 단지 차별은 없애고, 구조적, 사고적 구별만은 당연 잘 분별하여 지속될 수밖에 없지 않을까.

021. Ggondae, Is it hateful against an adult?

I used a lot about useful Chinese characters, cultures such as references, confucius, and Mencius often appear in this book. Young generation thinks against about the Ggondae(Korean slang=elder-man) attitude which they might think it is an old fashion. Over the years, it may be revived as a Renaissance at some point, but what will reality do because it is a globalization era? Is it a old culture that I should keep? Should I even join the wave of the current trend? It is natural to adapt to the new thought. As a child, men had short hair, wore pants and there were times as girls who were so excited about an opposite shape and behavior. they were born differently, without knowing it. I do not think that discrimination is eliminated, and structural and thought distinctions are naturally discerning and continuing.

어른보고 놀란 어린이

女 여	慕 모	貞 정	烈 렬	男 남	效 효	才 재	良 량
yeo	mo	jeong	ryeol	nam	hyo	jae	ryang
계집	사모할	곧을	세찰	사내	본받을	재주	어질
gyejip	samohal	godeul	sechil	sanae	bonbadeul	jaeju	eojil
girl	yearn	courtesy	firmly	boy	follow	skill	good
041. 여자는 열정과 곧은 마음을 지키고				042. 남자는 재주 있고, 어진 사람을 본받아라			
She's a woman who keeps her passion and straight heart				Man is a knack, and take a model of a virtuous man			
소녀少女	사모思慕	정숙貞淑	열렬熱烈	남녀男女	약효藥效	천재天才	우량優良
girl	miss	chastity	ardent	men women	medicinal effect	genius	good-natured

女여: 여자 너 딸 girl you daughter
慕모: 그리워할 바라다 long for wish
貞정: 안정 정성 stable sincerity
烈렬: 위엄 dignity majesty

男남: 남자 젊은이 man young man
效효: 효과 보람 effect rewarding
才재: 재능 기본 기량 talent basic skill
良량: 착하다 뛰어나다 goodness excel

022. 천성과 지성 (지과필개 득능막망)

태어나면서 갖고 있는 천성은 바꾸기가 대단히 어려운 듯하다. 이러한 천성이 사주팔자(사성)일 수도 있을 것이다. 믿고 싶지 않고, 믿을 가치가 없어 보일 수 있는 천성이나 사주팔자나 운명론은, 서서히 나이 먹고 우주자연의 순환 이치를 보면서, 타고난 천성과 사주팔자가 있을 수 있겠다는 운명론으로 사고철학이 변화됨을 알게 되는 듯하다. 소위 멘토나, 존경하는 지식인의 사심 없는 충고나, 도움말은 귀담아듣고서, 인생의 좌표로 삼을 수도 있으리라. 그러한 소중한 어드바이스에 따라 모난 천성을 다듬을 수 있으리라. 멘토나 좋은 스승을 만나기 어려우므로 존경하는 분들의 자서전이나 선각자의 책을 찾아 독서하는 방법이 가장 권할 만한 대처가 아닐까. 그래서 자기의 문제점을 고치고, 터득하고, 스승을 능가하는 그릇이 될 수 있으리라. 유명한 투자가 워렌 버핏은 "독서를 이기는 것은 없다."라고까지 말하고 있다. 자기의 허물이나 잘못을 알게 되면 반성하고 고쳐야(지과필개) 하고, 젊었을 때 익힌 능력이나 지혜는 잊지 말아야(득능막망) 하지 않을까.

022. Inborn and Intelligence

The nature of being born seems to be very difficult to change. This nature may be The Four Pillars of Destiny(It is also called Four-star). The nature, the four-star, or the fatalism, which you don't want to believe, and which you don't seem worth believing, It seems to know that philosophy is changed by the theory of fate that there can be natural nature and the Four-star, slowly aging, watching the circulation of the universe nature. You can listen to the so-called mentor, who gives an advice, you meet a respected intellectual person who can be useful as the coordinates of your life. It is very difficult to meet a mentor or a good teacher, so it is the best way to find and read the autobiography of those who are respectful through a book. Through a book, you can learn how he fixed his problems in his life and you can learn them. You can get an ability to solve your own problems by this action. Renowned investor Warren Buffett goes as far as to say that nothing beats reading. If you know your fault or mistakes, you should reflect and fix it, and you should not forget the ability or wisdom you learned when you were young.

知 지	過 과	必 필	改 개	得 득	能 능	莫 막	忘 망
ji	gwa	pil	gae	deuk	neung	mak	mang
알	지날	반드시	고칠	얻을	능할	말	잊을
al	jinal	bandeusi	gochil	eodeul	neunghal	mal	ijeul
know	pass by	surely	refine	get	proficiency	not	forget
043. 자기 허물을 알게 되면 반드시 고쳐야 하고				044. 능력을 얻어 잘하게 되면, 잊지 말아야 한다			
If you know your fault, you must fix it				If you get the ability and do well, you should not forget			
지식知識	과거過去	필요必要	개선改善	소득所得	가능可能	막강莫强	망각忘却
knowledge	past	need	improvement	income	ability	strong	forget

知지: 지혜=슬기 지식 wisdom knowledge
過과: 허물 실패 잘못 fault failure
必필: 오로지 확실 only surety
改개: 새롭게 바로잡다 new correct

得득: 이익 만족, 이루다 profit satisfaction achieve
能능: 잘하다 뛰어나다 do well excel
莫막: 없다 허무 쓸쓸 futility loneliness
忘망: 건망증 끝나다 forgetfulness end

023. 어린 시절의 경영 경제 경험 (망담피단 미시기장)

어린 시절 소를 돌보고, 토끼는 키우면서 지냈다. 토끼 키우기는 호기심도 있었고, 털복숭이처럼 귀엽고, 놀란 듯 초롱한 눈, 쫑긋한 귀, 날아다니는 새처럼 사뿐사뿐 걷는 모습, 둥글둥글한 환약 같은 똥을 보면서 신기하고, 흥미가 있었다. 싱싱한 토끼풀과 쑥이나 나물종류 풀을 먹이로 주면, 붉으래한 눈을 멀뚱거리며 오물오물 잘근 잘근 귀엽게도 맛있게 빨아들이는 모습에 쏙 빠진다. 어른들은 쑥 많이 먹으면 속살 찐다고 조금만 주라고들 한다. 토끼는 몇 달 지나면 어린 토끼도 낳아, 동화책에 나오는 황금알을 낳는 거위처럼, 나의 보물이 되는 듯하였다. 귀여운 아기 토끼는 더욱 재미있게 나를 부르는 것 같다. 잠자면서까지 토끼 생각이다. 밤낮으로 몰입하여 아기토끼 돌보는 목동이 되었다. 소는 고집은 세지만 양처럼 온순하기가 그지없다. 어린 목동은 큰 소를 끌고 풀 먹이러 다니다 보면 암소 온몸에 피를 잔뜩 빨아먹은 통통한 진드기, 귀찮게 파리가 달라붙는다. 목에 달린 방울을 흔들어 대며, 파리를 쫓아내려 머리를 조아린다. 꼬리도 쉴 새 없이 좌우옆구리, 아래 종아리, 위, 등까지 흔들어 댄다. 풍물놀이 하이라이트 한국판 비보이처럼, 열두 발 상모 돌리듯 움직인다. 어린 목동은 나뭇잎이 무성한 싸리나무를 꺾어 끈질긴 쇠파리를 쫓아준다. 코를 벌렸다 오므렸다 실룩거리고, 입술을 상하좌우로 늘려 가며, 곱지 않은 누런 이빨을 드러내 보이는 소 웃음 표정이 아주 귀여워 내 마음까지 즐겁다. 코를 실룩거리며 소 웃음으로 고마움을 표시하는 듯하다.

023. Business Economy Experience in Childhood

I took care of cows as a child, and I kept rabbits. I was curious about raising rabbits, cute as a fur peaches, I was surprised and interested in watching the lantern eyes, the prickly ears, the walking like a flying bird. If you feed on fresh grass and mugwort or herb grass, I was so happy to see the red eyes from them, while they are chewing something, it seemed delicious. Old people said when you eat a lot of mugwort, you should give it a little bit since it makes them fat. The rabbits gave a birth to young rabbits after a few months, it seems like a goose that gave a birth to golden eggs in fairy tale books. A cute baby rabbit seems to give me more fun. I thought of rabbits until I slept. I became a shepherd who cared for baby rabbits during the days and nights. Cows are stubborn, but they are as gentle as sheep. When a young shepherd tries to feed a large cow, the plump ticks sucking blood all over the cow, and the flies stick annoyingly. He shakes his neck, chases the fly down and tightens his head. The tail is constantly shaking to the left and right. Pungmul-Play is like a Korean version B-boy, it moves like a twelve-length conical hat. The shepherd, breaks the leafy tree, and chases the persistent fly. The cow is very cute and enjoyable to my heart, with its nose open and close, lips stretched up and down and up and down, and when the cow smiles, while it is showing its uneven yellow teeth. He seems very satisfied.

罔 망	談 담	彼 피	短 단	靡 미	恃 시	己 기	長 장
mang	dam	pi	dan	mi	si	gi	jang
없을	말씀	저	짧을	아닐	믿을	몸	길
eopseul	malsseum	jeo	jjalbeul	anil	mideul	mom	gil
no	say	that	defect	not	rely on	body	long
045. 남의 모자란 점으로 잡담하지 말고				046. 자신의 장점을 너무 믿지 말고 겸손하라			
Don't chat about the lack of others				Don't believe in your strengths too much and be humble			
망야罔夜	속담俗談	피아彼我	단편短篇	미비靡費	시뢰恃賴	극기克己	장관長官
forget to sleep	proverb	one and the other	fragment	waste	trust	beat oneself	minister

罔망: 아니다 그물 no net
談담: 담화 농담 discourse jokes
彼피: 그것 덮다 it cover
短단: 허물 결점 blemish flaw

靡미: 쓰러지다 없다 fall no
恃시: 믿다 의지하다 faith will
己기: 자기 사욕 self private desire
長장: 장점 길다 어른 merit long adult

024. 친구와 우정 (신사가복 기욕난량)

친구를 사귀다 보면 여러 다양한 성격의 사람이 다 보인다. 가까운 사이 일수록 작은 약속이라도 지켜야, 아, 저 친구는 믿을 수 있구나 라는 믿음을 심어 주게(신사가복) 된다. 식사 약속, 술 약속 등 해 보면, 미리 오는 사람이 있는가 하면, 여러 핑계와 궁색한 변명으로 오 분 또는 십 분이라도 약속 어기는 사람이 있다. 한두 번은 그렇다 치고 세 번 이상 어기면, 그 친구와 약속은 불안해지기 시작한다. 그러면 다른 큰일도 그 친구와는 함께하기 어렵다는 고정 관념이 생기게 되어 신뢰할 수 없게 된다. 붕우유신, 즉, 친구 간에 신뢰와 믿음이 가장 중요하다는 삼강오륜까지 들먹일 필요도 없으리라. 불가측과 불신의 시대에 살고 있더라도, 우리는 스스로 신용을 무너뜨리면, 정보화 시대에 설 자리가 없어진다. 신용이 누적되어 자기에게 돌아오게 돼 있는 시대다. 시대에 관계없이 자기의 기량과 능력을 한없이 키워야(기욕난량) 하지 않을까. 그릇에 물이 차면 넘치듯, 능력이 차면, 넘쳐서 사회와 인류에 공헌할 수 있으리라. 갑자기 익숙한 사찰인 불갑사가 생각난다. 동자승은 소설의 주인공처럼, 대영웅전 앞을 발소리라도 날까 두려워하는 듯 사뿐히 이동한다. 큰 영웅이 있는 대웅전 안에는, 인자한 부처님과 함께, 인간세계 인물들은 눈을 부릅뜨고, 무서움마저 느껴지는 험악한 모습이다. 죄지은 사람을 벌하는 집행관이라 한다. 어린 시절 소풍에서 스님의 설명이다.

024. Friends and Friendship

When you make friends, you can see people of various characteristics. We have to keep a small promise as we are very close, and I have the belief that he can believe it. If you try to make an appointment for meal or a drink promise, there are people who come in advance, and there are people who break a promise before five minutes or ten minutes with various excuses and a poor explanation. If you break it more than three times, one or two times, the promise with the friends begins to get uneasy. Then there is a stereotype that other big things are difficult to be with the friend, and it becomes unreliable. There is no need to mention the three powers(Samgang-oryun: the three bonds and the five moral disciplines in human relations) of trust and faith among friends, that is, trust and faith(Bungu-yusin: Faith should reign over the relation between friends). We break our credit by ourselves, and we are out of place in the information age. It is an era when credit is accumulated and returned to oneself. I do think I should grow my skills and abilities regardless of the times. As if the bowl was full of water, if it was full of ability, it would be overflowing and contributing to society and mankind. Suddenly, I remember the familiar temple, Bulgapsa. The young monk moves smoothly like a hero of a novel, and the sound of the foot in front of the main temple. In the Great Hall, where there is a great hero, along with a generous Buddha, the human world characters are a scary figure with eyes open and fearful. It is said to be an executive who punishes the guilty. The monk's explanation in a picnic as a child.

信 신	使 사	可 가	覆 복	器 기	欲 욕	難 난	量 량
sin	sa	ga	bok	gi	yok	nan	ryang
믿을	하여금	옳을	덮을	그릇	하고자 할	어려울	헤아릴
mideul	hayeo-geum	alheul	deopeul	geureut	hagojahal	eoryeoul	hearil
trust	make	right	cover	bowl	want	hard	count
047. 내가 말한 약속은 지킬 수 있도록 하며				048. 기량은 남이 헤아릴 수 없을 정도로 크게 하라			
I'm going to make sure that you keep your promise				Do your abilities beyond what others can to the point of incalculable			
신앙信仰	사용使用	가능可能	복면覆面	악기樂器	욕심欲心	난민難民	분량分量
faith	use	possible	masked surface	musical instrument	greed	refugee	quantity
信신: 진실 성실 truth sincerity 使사: 시키다 심부름 make errands 可가: 찬성 허락 approval permission 覆복: 뒤집다 반대로 flip-over reverse				器기: 재능 도구 talent tool 欲욕: 바라다 탐내다 hope, covet 難난: 어렵다 근심 difficult, anxiety 量량: 분량 역량 quantity, competencies			

025. 동료와 소속감 (묵비사염 시찬고양)

고대중국의 철학자, 묵자는 과학자이며 사상가이며 지금으로 보면 가냘픈 시인이라 할 수 있다. 안타까운 모습을 보면 눈물을 흘렸다. 하얀 실에 까만 물들이는 걸 보면서 사람도 주변 환경에 따라, 즉, 속된 친구와 어울리면 그들과 닮고, 학구파 향기로운 친구와 어울리면 학구파 연구원이 되는 것처럼, 옆 사람도 물들여져 착하게도 되고, 악하게도 된다는 논리다. 초식동물은 대부분 온순하다. 성경에도 양이 등장하고, 사람을 해치지 않고, 양순함의 대표 동물이며, 사람에게 털의 따뜻함과 영양보고, 우유와 단백질 등 각종 이로움을 제공하는 친근한 동물이다. 처음엔 양처럼 순하다 세월이 좀 흐르면 고양이가 되더라는 속담처럼 양의 온순함을 알리고 있다, 나의 학창시절, 학교 수업 끝난 후, 염소를 끌고 다니면서 풀을 먹이다 보면, 아기염소는 무릎을 꿇고 젖을 먹는다. 사서오경 중 시경은 이것을 예의가 바르다고 찬양하였음은 가히 양 칭송가라 볼 만하다.

025. Coworkers and sense of belonging

The ancient Chinese philosopher, Mukja, is a scientist, thinker, and now a sad poet. He wept when he saw his sadness. As you watch the black paint on the white thread, people are like them according to the surrounding environment, that is, if you are with a friend, you are like them, and if you are with a fragrant friend, you become a school researcher. It is logical that the people next to you are also painted, good, and evil. Herbivores are mostly mild. It is a friendly animal that provides sheep to the Bible, does not harm people, is a representative animal of goodness, and provides people with various benefits such as the warmth of hair and milk and protein, which are nutritional storage. At first, it is as mild as a sheep. After a while, it informs the gentleness of the sheep like the proverb that it becomes a cat. When I was in school, after school, when I was taking goats and feeding grass, baby goats kneel and breastfeed. Among Confucian-bible, it is a big praise of sheep that this is such a polite attitude by Poem-bible.

墨 묵	悲 비	絲 사	染 염	詩 시	讚 찬	羔 고	羊 양
muk	bi	sa	yeom	si	chan	go	yang
먹	슬플	실	물들일	글	기릴	염소	양
meok	seulpeul	sil	muldeulil	geul	giril	yeomso	yang
ink	sad	thread	taint	writing	praise	goat	sheep
049. 묵자는 실이 염색됨을 슬퍼하고, 사람은 환경과 친구에 따라 선악에 물든다				050. 시경은 어미양과 새끼양의 예의를 노래했다			
The silk is saddened by the dyeing, and the person is stained with good and evil according to the environment and friends				The Book of Odes sang the courtesy of the mother sheep and the lamb			
묵화墨畵	자비慈悲	철사鐵絲	오염汚染	시인詩人	칭찬稱讚	고양羔羊	양모羊毛
ink painting	mercy	wire	contami- nation	poet	compli- ment	lamb	wool

墨묵: 검다 더럽다 black dirty
悲비: 자비 마음아픔 mercy heartache
絲사: 실을 잣다 take a thread
染염: 염색 더럽히다 dyeing taint

詩시: 시 악보 노래 poetry score song
讚찬: 칭찬 돕다 compliment help
羔고: 새끼양 lamb
羊양: 상서롭다 온순 auspicious gentle

026. 잡념과 성현 (경행유현 극념작성)

요즘 기타를 독학으로 배우고 있다. 유튜브가 있어 독학으로 배우기가 한결 도움이 된다. 뭐든 쉽지 않음을 몸소 체험하는 듯하다. 음악도 예술의 한 분야리라. 오선지 위 박자와 길이 고음 저음까지 몸에 익혀야 한다. 다양한 기타 코드도 순발력 있게 익혀야 한다. 노래도 대충이 아니라, 콩나물 모양 같은 박자 길이에 맞춰 정확히 불러야 한다. 유튜브 초보자 길잡이에 따라, 습관처럼 작은 시간을 만들어, 끈기 있게 진행하고 있다. 기타 연주를 조금 진행하다 보면, 기타를 치면서 주변의 필요 없는 헛생각 같은 염려를 부지불식간에 하고 있음을 깨닫는다. 기타 배우면서 가장 힘든 일이 잡념을 없애는 것이다. 무슨 일이든 방해되는 잡념을 없애면 성현이 된다 하니(극념작성) 그럴 만함을 느끼는 듯하다.

026. Every thoughts and The sages

I'm learning guitar by myself these days. Youtube helps me learning it by myself. I found through this experience that anything is not easy. Music is a field of art. You have to learn the beat and the length of the music paper to the body. You should also learn a variety of other codes with a quick start. The song is not roughly, but it should be accurately sung according to the length of the beat like a bean sprout. According to the guide of YouTube beginners, I make a small time like habit and proceed patiently. When I play a little guitar, I realize that I am unwittingly concerned about the unnecessary thoughts around me while playing the guitar. The hardest thing to learn is to get rid of the every thoughts. If you get rid of every thoughts like any obstacles, you will become The sage, so it seems to feel like it.

景 경	行 행	維 유	賢 현	克 극	念 념	作 작	聖 성
gyeong	haeng	you	hyeon	geuk	nyeom	jak	seong
볕	다닐	벼리	어질	이길	생각	지을	성인
byeot	danil	byeori	eogil	igil	saenggak	gieul	seongin
sun	go around	general plan	dick	win	thinking	build	saint
051. 큰 근본을 행하면 어진 사람이 되고				052. 잡념을 이겨 내면 성현이 된다			
If you do a great foundation, you'll become a wiseman				If you overcome your misconceptions, you will become a saint and sage			
경치景致	은행銀行	유지維持	현자賢者	극복克服	신념信念	작가作家	성현聖賢
scenic	bank	mainte-nance	wiseman sage	overcome	belief	author	saint and sage
景경: 햇볕 빛 그림자 sun light shadow 行행: 가다 줄 행위 go line action 維유: 밧줄 매다 rope string 賢현: 현명 착하다 낫다 wise good better				克극: 능히 극복 good overcome 念념: 옳다 삼가다 right refrain 作작: 짓다 만들다 원망 build make grudge 聖성: 거룩하다 슬기 holy wisdom			

027. 얼굴과 정결한 몸단장 (덕건명립 형단표정)

어린 시절 어느 여름날, 어머니는 복숭아밭 골짜기에서 고추와 오이, 가지를 따 오라 한다. 심부름과 함께, 무더움 속 코를 자극하는 고추 냄새를 맡으며, 상큼한 가지를 요깃거리 하며, 입을 정리하고 어머니에게 전달하였다. 어머니는 가지 먹고 왔구나, 음식은 소중하니 깨끗이 잘 먹어야 한다며 말한다. 가지 훔쳐 먹은 걸 어찌 알았을까 하며(형단표정), 다음부터는 정직해야겠다는 다짐을 했다. 필자는 직장 생활하면서 주위 선배, 동료교수들이 장남이냐고 물어보는 경우가 더러 있었다. 무의식중에 집안과 부모 걱정하며 말하는 모습을 보았던 것 같다. 그러면서 필자는 셋째라니, 발 뻗고 신경 쓸 것 없다고 조언해 주는 경우까지 있었다. 모든 삶이 그리 호락호락 할까만은 어찌 그래도 된다는 마인드일까. 성품과 행실이 단정하면 얼굴에도 그 모습이 나타나 보이는 것 같다(형단표정).

027. A clean body and face

One summer in childhood, my mother asks me to pick up peppers, cucumbers and eggplants from a field valley. Along with the errand, I smelled the red pepper that stimulated my nose and I made a refreshing nose by eggplants, arranged my mouth and delivered them to my mother. My mother says that she has eaten an eggplant, and that food is precious and should be eaten cleanly. How did she know that I had stolen an eggplant, and I vowed to be honest next time. I often asked my seniors and fellow professors if they were the eldest sons. I seem to have seen the unconsciousness of talking about my family and parents. In the meantime, I had a third case, even when I advised that I had nothing to worry about. Is it a mind that all life is so good that it can be done? If the character and the behavior are clear, it seems to appear on the face.

德 덕	健 건	名 명	立 립	形 형	端 단	表 표	正 정
deok	geon	myeong	rip	hyeong	dan	pyo	jeong
덕	세울	이름	설	모양	바를	겉	바를
deok	seul	ireum	seol	moyang	bareul	geot	bareul
virtue	build	name	stand	shape	right	appearance	right
053. 덕을 쌓으면 이름을 알리는 것이며				054. 몸매가 단정하면 겉에 나타나는 모습도 바르게 된다			
If you build a virtue, you'll tell them your name				When you are in shape, you will be right on the outside			
미덕美德	건강健康	명예名譽	자립自立	인형人形	남단南端	표정表情	진정眞正
virtue	health	honor	self-reliance	doll	southern tip	facial expres-sion	calming

德덕: 어진 인품 sage character
健건: 굳세다 마련 firm preparation
名명: 평판 유명 reputation
立립: 세우다 자리 make seat

形형: 형상 용모 몸 shape appearance body
端단: 끝 실마리 end clue
表표: 나타남 뛰어나다 appearance excel
正정: 품위 정당하다 dignity justify

73

028. 어려운 공감정서 (공곡전성 허당습청)

장애인 단체에서 봉사 활동한 적이 있다. 장애인은 눈으로 보이는 장애인 도 있지만, 눈으로 보이지 않은 장애인이 여러 가지 많았다. 장애인 정의는 신체적 정신적으로 오랫동안 일상생활이나 사회생활에 일정한 장애를 받는 자라 한다. 그토록 고통과 어려움을 몸소 경험하였을 장애인이나 장애인 가 족들이, 장애인의 어려움을 가슴으로 진정 느끼는지, 의심스러울 때가 여러 번 있었다. 그들은 서로들 알게 모르게 놀리며 즐거워하고 있어, 의아함마저 들었다. 그들은 여러 명의 장애인과 그 가족이 모인 장소에서, 난청으로 소리 를 제대로 듣지 못하는 옆 아주머니를 놀리고 있었다. 말을 제대로 듣지 못하 니 서로가 답답하긴 마찬가지일 것이다. 장애의 상태가 서로 다를 뿐이다. 저 것 하면서 욕하면 그건 알아듣고 버럭 화낸다면서 가짜 귀머거리라고 놀리고 있었다. 국가의 난청 장애인 등록은 대화 중 삼십에서 사십 프로 알아듣지 못 할 때로 돼 있다. 익숙한 말은 그런대로 들리고, 생소한 말은 어렵게 듣는 형 태, 아나운서나 가족 간의 대화는 그런대로 들을 수 있는 난청, 즉, 난청 단어 뜻대로 듣는 데 어려움이 있는(습청) 사람이다. 보통의 중생들은 어떤 문제 든 서로의 아픔을 헤아리기가 참 어려운 현실이 아닐까 생각해 본다.

028. Difficulty empathy

I have been working as a volunteer for a group of people with disabilities. There are many people with disabilities who are visible, but many people with disabilities who are not visible as well. Definition of the disabled grows physically and mentally with a certain disability in a daily life or a social life for a long time. It is often that a disabled or a family member who has disabled people in a family have experienced such pain and difficulties.

But many people were laughing and making a joke with each other without knowing them. They were teasing a lady who was unable to hear properly. It must be frustrating for them not to hear it properly. Everybody has a different problem. Normal people think that it is a difficult reality to count for other peoples shoes.

空 공	谷 곡	傳 전	聲 성	虛 허	堂 당	習 습	聽 청
gong	gok	jeon	seong	heo	dang	seup	cheong
빌	골	전할	소리	빌	집	익힐	들을
bil	gol	jeonhal	sori	bil	jip	ikhil	deuleul
empty	valley	deliver	sound	empty	house	learn	listen
055. 빈 골짜기에서도 소리가 퍼지듯, 옳은 말은 멀리 전해지고				056. 빈 방에서 하는 말도 누군가 듣는다			
As the sound spreads in the empty valley, the right words are conveyed far away				Someone hears what you say in an empty room			
공항空港	계곡溪谷	전설傳說	음성音聲	허공虛空	식당食堂	연습練習	시청視聽
airport	valley	legend	voice	airspace	restaurant	practice	watch

空공: 구멍 곤궁 공허 hole poverty emptiness
谷곡: 골짜기 계곡 valley
傳전: 전기 전달 autobiography deliver
聲성: 음악 명예 소문 music honor rumor

虛허: 허무 빈틈 하늘 futility empty-gap sky
堂당: 마루 궁전 floor palace
習습: 숙달 습관 mastery habit
聽청: 허락 순종 permission obedience

75

029. 인내의 고통, 지은 대로 받을까 (화인악적 복연선경)

자동차 고치러 카센터에 간 적이 있다. 사무실에 복연선경이라는 큼지막한 액자가 보였다. 물어보니 필자와 같은 나이다. 그 사장은 고객 차 세차하는 세차보이라며 싱글벙글 즐거워하였다. 미륵 부처님 세상이 오길 바라는 것은 무지개를 잡으러 쫓아가는 어린아이가 아닐까. 공사나 사무를 하다 보면 작은 일에 심리가 움직인다. 사람 됨됨이와 천부적 품성은 있으리라. 성선설과 성악설처럼 수많은 동화책과 이솝우화에도 선과 악이 교차하고 있다. 우리들은 안이함을 벗어나, 순간적이고 동물적인 감각으로 상황에 대비하고 본능적으로 준비성이 있어야, 좋은 결실을 맺을 수 있으리라.

029. The pain of patience, will it be what it is?

I went to the car center to fix the car. I saw a large frame of the Bokyeon-Seongyeong(Blessing is good and happy to build up) in my office. I asked him, and he was the same age as me. The president was a car washr and was happy. I wonder if it is a child who chases the rainbow to catch the world of Mireuk Buddha. When you work or business, you are psychologically moved by small things. There will be human beings and natural personality. Like the theory that man's inborn nature is good and the theory that human nature is fundamentally evil, many fairy tales and Aesop fables are also crossed by good and evil. We must prepare instinctively with a spotanious and senses to make good results.

천사와 악마

禍 화	因 인	惡 악	積 적	福 복	然 연	善 선	慶 경
hwa	in	ak	jeok	bok	yeon	seon	gyeong
재앙	인할	악할	쌓을	복	인연	착할	경사
jaeang	inhal	akhal	ssaheul	bok	inyeon	chakhal	gyeongsa
catast-rophic	cause	bad	build up	fortune	cause	good	happy

057. 악한 일을 거듭하면 불행이 오게 되고	058. 착하고 기쁜 일을 쌓으면 복이 온다
If you do evil things again, you will be unhappy	Blessing is good and happy to build up

화복禍福	인연因緣	악마惡魔	면적面積	행복幸福	우연偶然	선심善心	경축慶祝
disaster happy	affilia -tion	devil	area	happiness	accidental	good heart	celebration

禍화: 황폐 죄 devastation crime
因인: 의지 유래 원인 will derived causation
惡악: 미움 더럽다 불길 hate dirty unhappy
積적: 저축 포개다 save fold

福복: 행운 간직하다 luck keeping
然연: 따르다 인연 follow affiliation
善선: 좋다 good
慶경: 축하 기쁨 칭찬 congratulations joy praise

030. 시간과 절제된 인격 (척벽비보 촌음시경)

구술치기, 팽이치기, 딱지치기 놀이를 많이 하면서 어린 시절을 보냈다. 대부분 몸을 움직이면서 하는 놀이다. 시대가 변하여 어린이 노는 모습도 많이 달라졌다. 몸 운동보다는 머리 운동으로 하는 놀이다. 미래에는, 몸에 비해 머리가 큰 외계인 ET 같은 세상이 될는지 모르겠다. 어른도 잘 모르거나, 까다로워하는 컴퓨터 다루는 모습이 능수능란하다. 옛날에 할아버지나 할머니가 들려주던 재미있는 전설 이야기 같은 역할을 노트북이나 아이패드가 해주고 있다. 어린 손 자녀 노는 모습을 물끄러미 쳐다보고 있을 뿐이다. 놀 거리가 다양하여, 작은 시간도 놓치지 않고(촌음시경), 자동차 놀이며, 블록 놀이며, 인형 놀이며, 집중과 끈기가 필요한 그림 맞추기 놀이를 쉼 없이 하고 있다. 필자도 새롭고 다양한 취미거리를 찾아야 할 듯하다.

030. Time and Understated personality

I spent my childhood playing a lot of bead, top, and scabs. Most of them are playing with body movements. The times have changed so much that children play. It is a game of head exercise rather than body exercise. I do not know if it will be a world like alien ET with bigger head than body in the future. Adults are not familiar with it, or they are skilled at dealing with difficult computers. A laptop or iPad plays a role like a funny legend story that my grandfather or grandmother once told me. I am just staring at the young children playing. There are various things to play, so I do not miss a small time, I play a car, play a block, play a doll, and play a picture matching game that requires concentration and persistence. I think that I try to find new and diverse hobbies.

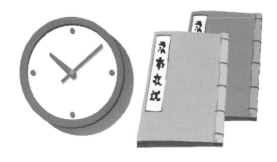

尺 척	璧 벽	非 비	寶 보	寸 촌	陰 음	是 시	競 경
cheok	byeok	bi	bo	chon	eum	si	gyeong
자	구슬	아닐	보배	마디	그늘	이	다툴
ja	guseul	anil	bobae	madi	geuneul	i	datul
scale	bead	not	treasure	spacing	shade	this	compete
059. 훌륭한 사람 되려면, 길이가 한 자 되는 큰 보배보다				060. 짧은 시간을 더 소중히 여긴다			
To be a good person, you're gonna be more than a big treasure				cherish a short time more			
지척咫尺	완벽完璧	비난非難	보물寶物	삼촌三寸	음양陰陽	시비是非	경쟁競爭
close contact	perfect	reproach	treasure	uncle	negative positive	right -wrong	competi -tion

尺척: 법 가깝다 길이 law close length
璧벽: 옥 아름다움 jade beauty
非비: 비방 거짓 slanderous lie
寶보: 돈 귀하다 money precious

寸촌: 조금 마음 헤아리다 little mind count
陰음: 음지 어둡다 shade dark
是시: 옳다 진실 곧다 right truth straight
競경: 쫓다 다투다 follow fight

031. 부모님 은혜는 하늘 같구나 (자부사군 왈엄여경)

장성하고 자식 키워 보니 부모의 헌신이 가히 짐작하기도 어려운 것 같다. 옛날에는 자녀가 보통 다섯에서 열 명 정도니, 나이 들어 보면, 자식 키우는 그 고생이 짐작하고도 남는다. 그래서 요즘 젊은이들은 아예 고생하기 싫어서 결혼을 기피하던가, 아이를 갖지 않는 젊은이가 조금씩 늘어간다. 구식 같다는 옛날 성경, 시경은 거의가 민중, 즉, 국민, 서민들, 필부들의 생로병사 애환을 담은 노래를 시어로 이루어져 있다. 시경(詩經)을 풀이한 시전(詩傳,공자가 만든 책)은, "부모님 은혜를 갚으려 하니 하늘보다 넓어 끝이 없구나." 필자가 나이 들어, 보고 싶은 부모의 흔적을 찾고자 하나, 아무것도 없으니 안타깝기만 하구나. 과거 언젠가 집에 가니 아버지가 일일 달력에 일기장처럼 깨알 같은 메모가 정신 유품이었는데, 하늘로 연기처럼 사라졌으니 어찌하랴. 그 달력이라도 보존하였으면 그때의 모습이 생생할 텐데 하는 아쉬움을 감출 길이 없구나. 이제나마 필자의 집필로 그때의 애처로움을 달래노라. 우리는 부모님 은혜를 깊이 간직하면서 보은하는 마음가짐이 좋으리라. 하지만 지난 일에 너무 얽매여 있지 말고, 현재에 충실하고 미래를 준비하여 입신양명하면, 부모님 은혜에 조금이나마 보답되리라.

031. Parents' grace is like heaven

It seems that the devotion of the parents is difficult to guess when they grow up and raise their children. In the old days, there are usually five to ten children, so when you get older, you can guess the hardship of raising your child. So nowadays, young people do not want to suffer at all, so they avoid marriage, and there are a little more young people who do not have children. The old Bible, which is like an old style, is almost composed of poets who sing songs about the people, that is, the ordinary people, the common people, and the working class. A Sijeon(Poetry book: A Book by Confucius) with a Description of the Book of Odes, I am trying to repay my parents' grace, so it is wider than heaven. I am getting old and I want to find traces of parents that I want to see, but it is pity that there is nothing to find. When I went hometown someday, my father had a diary which described on a daily lives, and it was a memorial reminder, but it unfortunately disappeared like a smoke in the sky. If I had preserved that diary, I would be much happier now without lot of regrets. Now, through my writing, my memory is coming slowly with that time. We have a good mindset to keep a grace of our parents deeply. We should not be too restrained by our past. If we are faithful to our present and prepare for the future, we will give a little reward back for our parents' grace.

資 자	父 부	事 사	君 군	日 왈	嚴 엄	與 여	敬 경
ja	bu	sa	gun	wal	eom	yeo	gyeong
재물	아비	섬길	임금	가로	엄할	더불	공경
jaemul	abi	seomgil	imgeum	garo	eomhal	deobul	gonggyeong
wealth	father	serve	king	say	strict	together	respect
061. 아버지 공경하는 자세로 임금을 섬기라				062. 섬기는 자세란 엄숙하고 공손하고 공경이다			
Serve the King, as in the respect of your father				Serving posture is solemn, polite and respectful			
자본資本	부모父母	기사記事	군주君主	소왈所日	위엄威嚴	참여參與	존경尊敬
capital	parent	article	monarch	speak in the world	dignity	participa -tion	respect

資자: 재화 방종 goods unruly
父부: 아버지 father
事사: 일하다 부리다 work provide
君군: 그대 자네 you my lord

日왈: 말하다 say
嚴엄: 삼가다 경계 caution wary
與여: 주다 참여 give participation
敬경: 정중 예의 admiration etiquette

032. 한결같은 마음 (효당갈역 충즉진명)

어린 시절 시골 작은 마을 옹기종기 모여 살았다. 해가 서산에 걸리는 저녁 쯤에는 집집마다 굴뚝에서 나무 연기가 작은 뭉게구름처럼 몽실몽실 거리며 오르다 사라진다. 울타리를 지나가다 보면 군침 넘어가는 고소한 음식 냄새가 코를 스친다. 그 시절이기도 하지만, 마루 한 쪽에 볏짚 돗자리 위에 조그마한 상을 놓고, 물과 밥 한 공기와 맑은국을 차려 놓고, 조상에 정성을 다하는 모습이 천사처럼 보였다(효당갈역). 어쩌면 저렇게 지극 정성 효성스러울까 하는 마음에 절로 존경의 마음이 감동스러워 그때 그 모습이 아직도 가슴에 남아 있다. 지금은 산업화 사회와 민주화 사회 정보화 사회를 거치면서 그 자손들이 인연 따라 전국 각처와 세계로 흩어져 옛날을 추억하고들 있겠지. 그려 어쩔 거냐, 밥 주는 곳이 고향이라 하더라.

032. A consistent mind

As a child, we lived in small rural villages, and by the evening when the sun was on the western mountains, a smoke from chimneys at each house was rising and disappearing like a small cloud. As you pass through the fence, the smell of savory food that goes over the nose is crossed. It was those days, but it seemed like an angel to put a small table on the rice straw mat on one side of the floor, to set up a cup of water, a bowl of rice, and a bowl of soup, in order to devote himself to his ancestors. Maybe it is so sincere, and respectful mind is impressed, and the figure still remains in my heart. Now, through the industrialization society and the democratization society information society their descendants will be scattered all over the country and remember the old days. What are you going to do? I feel that a place where I feed is my hometown.

孝 효	當 당	竭 갈	力 력	忠 충	則 즉	盡 진	命 명
hyo	dang	gal	ryeok	chung	jeuk	jin	myeong
효도	마땅	다할	힘	충성	곧	다할	목숨
hyodo	mattang	dahal	him	chungseong	got	dahal	moksum
filial piety	natural	do one's best	power	loyalty	soon	devote	life
063. 효도는 당연히 있는 힘을 다하고				064. 임금에 대한 충성은 목숨이 다할 때까지 한다			
serve one's parents does all his strength				Loyalty to king is until your life is over			
효자孝子	당장當場	갈력竭力	노력努力	충고忠告	원칙原則	진력盡力	생명生命
filial piety	now	craving power	effort	advice	principle	best	life
孝효: 부모 섬기다 serve one's parents 當당: 당연 주관 natural subjectivity 竭갈: 다하다 가뭄 do one's best drought 力력: 힘쓰다 애쓰다 power try				忠충: 정성 곧다 sincerity straight 則즉: 법 규칙 law rule 盡진: 힘을 다하다 do one's best 命명: 운수 명령 luck command			

033. 내리 사랑의 본성 (임신리박 숙흥온청)

어머니는 마음이 여리어 언제나 노심초사 자식 걱정에 여념이 없다. 밖이 엄동설한처럼 추운지, 푹푹 찌듯 무더운지(숙흥온청), 물가에 가면 깊은 물이 마음에 걸리고(임신리박), 산에 가면 낭떠러지가 눈에 가시다. 자식들은 호박처럼 주렁주렁 많이 매달렸으니, 열 손가락 물으면, 모두 아프더라. 장성한 자식에게도 차 조심 물 조심하라 하니, 그런 지극 정성이 난초 향처럼 은은하고 소나무처럼 사계절 무성하다. 세월을 보내고 나니, 눈감을 때까지 자식 걱정하다 한평생 보내는 게 부모 마음 아닐까 한다.

033. The nature of love flowing down

My mother has always been worried about her child, burning inside with a struggle in mind. If you go to the water, you will feel the deep water, and if you go to the mountain, you will see the cliff. The children hung like pumpkins a lot, so if you bite ten fingers, they're all sick. I'm telling my eldest son to watch out for the car. Parents' mind is the same as the orchid scent and like a pine tree after years, it is parents' mind to spend a life time worrying about their children.

臨 림	深 심	履 리	薄 박	夙 숙	興 흥	溫 온	淸 청
rim	sim	ri	bak	suk	heung	on	cheong
임할	깊을	밟을	엷을	일찍	일어날	따뜻할	서늘할
imhal	gipeul	balbeul	yeolbeul	iljjik	ileonal	ttatteuthal	seoneulhal
come down	deep	step on	thin	early	get up	warm	cool

065. 깊은 물가에 있는 듯 조심하고, 살얼음을 밟듯이 조심하라				066. 일찍 일어나, 따뜻한지 추운지 살펴, 부모 몸을 보살핀다			
Be careful as if you were on the deep water, stepping on thin ice				Wake up early, watch for warmth or cold, and take care of your parents' bodies			
왕림枉臨	심야深夜	목리木履	박봉薄俸	숙세夙世	흥미興味	온풍溫風	청소淸掃
come	late night	wooden shoes	small salary	past era	interest	hot wind	cleaning

臨림: 곡하다 뵙다 sad-cry meet
深심: 심하다 무성하다 prosper lush
履리: 걷다 신발 신다 walk shoes wear
薄박: 가볍다 천하다 light vulgar

夙숙: 이른 빠르다 지난 early fast past
興흥: 흥거움 이루다 excitement achieve
溫온: 온화 원만 mild amicable
淸청: 맑다 춥다 차다 clear cold

034. 향기는 언제나 (사란사형 여송지성)

　필자는 수필집으로『어머니 향기』를 집필했다. 고향집은 탱자나무 울타리로 빙 둘러져 있고, 전원주택처럼 마당에는 과실나무와 화초가 전후좌우로 심어져 있다. 석류가 익어 껍질이 터져 갈라지며 내미는 꽉 찬 알이 탐스럽지만, 분홍빛 살구꽃은 그야말로 눈을 유혹하듯 화사하며 향이 좋았다. 탱자나무 울타리 넘어 앞산의 활엽수와 언제나 변함없이 사시사철 무성하고 푸른 소나무는 지칠 줄 모르는 모성애와 같았다. 가깝지도 멀지도 않은 도로에 가끔씩 지나가는 삽자루 든 농부와 머리에 수건 두른 아낙네가 있어 사람 사는 시골의 정취를 느끼게 한다. 이러한 한 폭의 그림 같은 동양화는 계절 따라 세월 따라 사람의 얼굴과 함께 조금씩 변한다.

034. The scent always

　I wrote 『Mother's Scent』 as an essay book. The home is surrounded by a hardy-orange tree fence, and fruit trees and flower plants are planted in the yard like a garden-house. The pomegranate is riped, the shells are cracked, the pink apricot flowers are bright and fragrant as if they are really luring eyes. The broad-leaved trees of the mountain and the ever-changing green pine trees over the hardy-orange tree fence were like tireless motherhood. There is a farmer with a shovel that passes occasionally on a road that is not close or far away, and a woman with a towel on his head, making him feel the mood of the countryside. This one-width, picturesque oriental painting changes slightly with the face of a person by season, by the years.

似 사	蘭 란	斯 사	馨 형	如 여	松 송	之 지	盛 성
sa	ran	sa	hyeong	yeo	song	ji	seong
비슷할	난초	이	향기	같을	소나무	갈	성할
biseuthal	nancho	i	hyanggi	gateul	sonamu	gil	seonghal
alike	orchid	this	scent	like	pine	go	flourish

067. 현자의 향기는 난초향기처럼 멀리 퍼지고				068. 소나무처럼 사철 내내 번성하다			
The sage's scent spreads as far away as the orchid scent				The flourish like a pine tree in all seasons			

유사類似	옥란玉蘭	사수斯須	형향馨香	여옥如玉	해송海松	형제지간兄弟之間	성업盛業
alike	jade orchid	short moment	flower smell	like a jade	sea pine	Brother-hood	work well

似사: 같다 닮다 흉내 like look-alike mimic	如여: 따르다 말잇다 follow follow one's words
蘭란: 목련 모란꽃 magnolia peony-flower	松송: 솔 pine
斯사: 쪼개다 떠나다 split-off leave	之지: 가다 변하다 go change
馨형: 꽃다울 명성 flowery reputation	盛성: 담다 번성 put prosperous

035. 말없이 가르친다 (천류불식 연징취영)

그 시절 내 고향 금평 시냇물은 아주 맑았다. 물속에 있는 작은 조약돌이나 작은 물고기, 송사리며 이끼까지 돋보기로 보듯 선명하게 보였다. 시냇물이 너무 맑고 깨끗하여 내 마음까지 비추는 듯하다(연징취영). 쉬지 않고 흐르는 시냇물(천류불식)은 거울처럼 맑아 온몸이 물에 비춰, 잔잔한 너울 물결 춤에 얼굴이 움직인다. 어린이의 동심이 맑은 물에 흐느적거리며 아리랑 노래하는 듯하다. 시원하고 조용하고 맑은 시냇물은 여름 한 철 온 동네 아우성치는 어린이를 흥분시키는 시원한 놀이터가 된다. 개울은 졸졸 흐르며, 뭔가를 말하는 듯하다. 어린 필자에게 시냇물은 말이 없어도 많은 것을 가르쳐 주었다. 말없이 깨닫게 해 주는 것이 있음을 많은 세월이 흐른 후에 알았다, 자연은 말없이 사계절을 순환시키고, 땅은 말없이 만물을 낳으며, 사람은 말이 없어도 모범을 보여 인재를 기른다. 어느 더운 여름날 논두렁 구불구불 따라가서, 물장구치며 관찰하던 어린 시절 모습이 말없이 떠오른다.

035. Teaching in silence

At that time, my hometown Geumpyeong Stream was very clear. The small pebbles in the water, the small fish, the small-fry, and the moss seemed clear as if they were magnifying glass. The stream is so clear and clean that it seems to shine to my heart. The stream that flows without rest is clear as a mirror, and the whole body is reflected in the water, and the face moves in the calm wave dance. The child's concentricity seems to be singing Arirang in the clear water. The cool, quiet and clear stream becomes a cool playground that excites children who are clamoring all over the summer. The stream is a stream, and it seems to be saying something. For the young writer, the stream taught me a lot without words. I knew after many years that there was something that made me realize without saying anything, Nature circulates the four seasons in silence, the land produces everything in silence, and people set an example even if they do not speak. One hot summer day, I went along the river, and I remember such a silent moment about the childhood which I was watching in the water.

川 천	流 류	不 불	息 식	淵 연	澄 징	取 취	映 영
cheon	ryu	beul	sik	yeon	jing	chui	yeong
내	흐를	아니	쉴	못	맑을	취할	비칠
nae	heureul	ani	suil	mot	malgeul	chuihal	bichil
stream	flow	not	rest	pond	clean	have	show

069. 냇물이 쉬지 않고 흐르듯, 꾸준히 공부하고 독서하면				070. 맑은 연못에 그림자가 비치듯, 세상의 온갖 일들이 보인다			
As the stream flows without rest, it studies steadily and reads				As shadows shine in clear ponds, all sorts of things in the world are visible			

산천山川	교류交流	부동산 不動産	자식子息	연어淵魚	징수澄水	섭취攝取	영화映畵
mountain stream	interact	real estate	born child	salmon	clear water	uptake	movie

川천: 하천 시냇물 river stream
流류: 갈래 학파 계파 branch school sect
不불: 크다 없다 large no
息식: 숨쉬다 호흡 휴식 breathe resting

淵연: 깊다 연못 조용 deep pond quiet
澄징: 맑다 맑은 물 clear clear water
取취: 가지다 받아들이다 have accept
映영: 비추다 덮다 햇살, light cover sunlight

036. 성직자의 모습 [용지약사 언사안정]

여기 저기 등산이나 여행 다니다 보면, 전국 어느 곳이나 사찰 하나 쯤은 있다. 우리나라에 들어온 지 오래되지 않은, 교회는 대부분 도심이나 사람 세계와 함께 있으나, 오랜 역사를 자랑하는 사찰은 산속에 있다. 조선시대 유교에 밀려나, 불교 탄압 정책으로 산속으로 피신한 것이 그 이유다. 그 시대 흐름과 참다운 불교 교리와 다르게 불교인들이 민폐 끼쳐, 대대적인 정화운동이 있었다. 지금은 본래의 불교 모습으로 가고 있는 듯하다. 어느 종교든 눈살 찌푸리는 일부 부도덕한 종교 종사자들이 있기 마련이다. 종교로 인하여 전쟁도 일어나는 경우가 있으니 말이다. 하늘과 나무와 새소리 들으며, 낙엽 쌓인 오솔길을 지나고, 실바람에도 풍경소리가 울리는 고요하고, 한적한 사찰을 지나가게 된다. 운수 좋으면 정신수양을 하여 지식이 머리에 꽉 찬 것 같은 선비 모습의 흰 고무신 스님을 보게 된다. 옷매무새가 흐트러짐이 없고, 절제된 참선생활의 결정체인 수정처럼 밝은 얼굴이, 깨달은 사람의 풍미를 절로 느끼게 한다. 짧은 말에도 맑은 목소리, 정리되고 안정됨(언사안정)이 중생의 몸으로 다가온다.

036. The image of a priest

Here and there, if you go hiking or traveling, there is one temple anywhere in the country. Most of the churches, which have not been in Korea for a long time, are with the city center or the people's world, but temples that boast a long history are in the mountains. This is why Confucianism in the Joseon Dynasty was pushed out and fled into the mountains due to the policy of Buddhist suppression. Unlike the trend of the times and true Buddhist doctrines, Buddhists were in trouble and there was a massive cleanup movement. It seems to be going to the original Buddhist figure now. There are some immoral religious workers who are frowned upon by any religion, as there are times when wars arise due to religion. Hearing the sky, trees and birds, passing through the a narrow path of fallen leaves, passing through the quiet, quiet temple where the tinkling of a wind-bell even in the small wind. If you are lucky, you will be able to see a white rubber-shoes monk who seems to have full knowledge in his head in a self-discipline. The attire is undisrupted, and the crystal-light face, the crystal of the understated life of the meditation in Zen Buddhism, makes the flavor of the enlightened person feel like a temple. Even in short words, clear voices, cleanliness and stability come to the body of the common people.

容용	止지	若약	思사	言언	辭사	安안	定정
yong	ji	yak	sa	eon	sa	an	jeong
얼굴	그칠	같을	생각	말씀	말씀	편안	정할
eolgul	geuchil	gateul	saenggak	malsseom	malsseom	pyeonan	jeonghal
face	behave	equal	think	word	word	comfor-table	stable

071. 모든 행동은 사물을 생각하듯이 신중히 하고	072. 말은 편안하고 안정되게 하거라
All actions are as careful as thinking about things	Make the word comfortable and stable.

용모容貌	정지停止	약간若干	사상思想	언론言論	사전辭典	안정安定	선정選定
appea-rance	stop	a little	thought	press	diction-ary	stability	selec-tion

容용: 꾸미다 몸가짐 decorate body-attitude
止지: 끝나다 억제하다 end suppress
若약: 같다 건초 만약 like dry-grass if
思사: 원하다 사모하다 want adore

言언: 말 화평 논의 speech peace discussion
辭사: 하소연 말하다 plead say
安안: 즐기다 아닐 enjoy complacent
定정: 바로잡다 반드시 correct surely

037. 제주도 하늘 [독초성미 신종의령]

학창시절 어느 여름날, 제주도 한라산 등반을 친구와 셋이 갔다. 등산코스 출발점을 성판악으로 하여, 돈 없이 가는 무전여행 식으로 계획하여 기차타고 배타고, 제주항구 선착장에 도착하였다. 처음 보는 외국 같은 낯선 우리 땅, 걸어 걸어 여러 해수욕장과 폭포를 구경하며, 온힘을 다하여 첫발을 참으로 설레며, 아름답게 시작(독초성미) 하였다. 열대나라 같은 야자나무 그늘에서 쉬기도 하고, 늘어지기도 하였다. 준비해 온 미숫가루로 허기증을 달래기도 하였다. 불볕더위에 걸으며 걸으며 몸과 마음 지칠 대로 지쳤다. 우리들은 서로 얼굴만 쳐다보며 웃기도 하였다. 무얼 찾고자 하는지 젊음이 궁금하기만 하였다. 하늘과 땅 더위 지침 속에서 번개처럼 깨달음이 올까. 이것보다 책에서 인생을 찾아보는 게 좋을 거야. 멀리 보고 살자. 오늘의 작은 낙담에 너무 실망말자. 과거에 크게 몇 번 웃었던 것도 별것 아닌 과정이다. 유종의 미를 거두는 사람이 가장 크게 웃을 수 있지 않을까(신종의령). 한라산 백록담에 오르듯~.

037. The sky of Jeju-Island

One summer day during school days, three friends went to the climbing of Halla Mountain in Jeju Island. The starting point of the mountain climbing course was set as Seongpanak, and it was planned to go without money, and it was taken by train and by ship, and arrived at the marina of Jeju Port. The foreign-like unfamiliarity that I have never seen before is to walk on our land, to see various beaches and waterfalls, I started my first step with all my strength and started beautifully. It rested and stretched in the shade of palm trees like tropical countries. We also appease hunger with the powder we have prepared. I was tired of my body and mind as I walked in the heat of the sunshine-heat. We looked at each other and laughed. What we were looking for were a youthful man. Will we come to enlightenment like lightning in the sky and the heat of the earth? You better find life in a book than this. Let's live far away. Let's not be too disappointed with today's little fail. It is a little process such as when you have laughed a few times in the past. I feel that a person who finishes completely can laugh the most like climbing the mountain Halla to see Baekrokdam.

篤 독	初 초	誠 성	美 미	愼 신	終 종	宜 의	令 령
dok	cho	seong	mi	sin	jong	eui	ryeong
도타울	처음	정성	아름다울	삼갈	마칠	마땅	하여금
dotaul	cheo	jeongseong	areumdaul	samgal	machil	mattang	hayeogeum
kind heart	begin -ning	sincerity	beautiful	careful	finish	right	order
073. 어려서 부모 따르듯, 자라면서도 그 마음을 잊지 말고				074. 장성하여 마칠 때까지 하면, 훌륭하게 될 것이다			
As you are young and follow your parents, do not forget your heart while growing up				By the time you're done with your long life, you'll be great			
독지가 篤志家	최초最初	성금誠金	미술美術	신중愼重	시종始終	편의시설 便宜施設	호령號令
bene -factor	first	donation	art	prudence	start end	conve- nient facility	command

篤독: 돈독 인정 성실 strong gentle sincere
初초: 먼저 시작 first start
誠성: 삼가다 참으로 refrain reluctance
美미: 예쁘다 경사스럽다 pretty festival

愼신: 신중 조심 prudence careful
終종: 끝나다 마침 be over end
宜의: 당연 화목 naturally peaceful
令령: 명령 부리다 command try

038. 잡지 못하는 무지개 같은 세상 (영업소기 적심무경)

세상에 끝이 없는 게 있을까. 즉, 무경, 필자의 지식으로는, 뭐라 단정하기 어렵다. 세상의 종말론도 있으니까. 그러나 종말 다음 세상도 있다. 중생과 만물은 있음도 없고 없음도 없다고 부처가 알려준 바 있다. 그래도 선배 철학자, 소크라테스, 괴테, 셰익스피어 등이나 성현들, 부처, 예수, 공자 등, 집념의 과학자들, 아인슈타인, 에디슨, 장영실 등의 명성은 끝이 없을 것 같다. 그들은 연구하는 게 취미고 생활이고 코미디고 운동이고 오락거리가 아닐까. 요즘은 과학적으로 빛도 파동 즉, 물질임을 밝혀 주고 있다. 그러니 빛도 휘어지고, 구부러진다는 것이다. 그릇에 담을 수 없는 소리(음파), 파도(호수의 물결 파)와 같은 물질, 그러면 빛보다 빠른 게 뭘까, 물질이 아닌, 보이지 않는 영(靈), 즉, 영혼이나 신령이 아닐까 하고 생각해 본다. 참, 어느 영화에서 영혼도 실물처럼 액션으로 표현한 걸 본 적이 있다.

038. The world that you can't catch like a rainbow

Is there something that has no end in the world? In other words, never-ending, in my knowledge, it is difficult to say. But there is a world after the end. There is also the apocalypse of the world. There is no creature and everything, and there is no none, Buddha has informed me. Still, the reputation of senior philosophers, Socrates, Goethe, Shakespeare, and other saints, Buddha, Jesus, Confucius, and the scientists of commitment, Einstein, Edison and Jang Youngsil seem to have no end. They think that studying is a hobby, a life, a comedy, a movement, and entertainment. These days, the scientific light is also a wave, a substance, so that the light is curve and bent. Materials like sound (sound waves), waves (waves of

water), which cannot be put in a bowl, and then what is faster than light?
I wonder if it is an invisible spirit, not a substance, that is, a soul or a spirit.
I have seen in a movie that the soul could be expressed in action like real
life.

榮 영	業 업	所 소	基 기	籍 적	甚 심	無 무	竟 경
yeong	eop	so	gi	jeok	sim	mu	gyeong
영화	업	바	터	온화할	심할	없을	마침
yeonghwa	eop	ba	teo	onhwahal	simhal	eobseul	machim
excel-lent	work	this	basic	gentle	well	non without	end
075. 공적 쌓는 일은, 고위 관직의 기초가 되고				076. 훌륭해짐은, 끝이 없을 정도로 좋으리라			
Public building is the foundation of a high-ranking office				To be honorable, it will be endlessly good			
영광榮光	업무業務	장소場所	기본基本	국적國籍	심풍甚風	무료無料	경야竟夜
honor	work	place	basic	nationality	heavy wind	free	all night
榮영: 꽃 번성하다 flowers flourish 業업: 생계 일 직업 living work job 所소: 곳 도리 관청 this office moral-reason 基기: 사업 근본 business fundamental				籍적: 문서 책 이름 document book name 甚심: 무엇 지나침 what overpassing 無무: 허무 대체로 nihility broadly 竟경: 끝나다 마침내 be-over at-last			

039. 친구처럼, 고행을 벗 삼아 (학우등사 섭직종정)

요즘은 도시 대부분 5일마다 열리는 시장이 필요 없다. 일상적으로 매일 시장이 열린다. 재래시장에 가다 보면 노인이 조그마한 좌판을 늘어놓고 푸성귀와 몇 가지 과일을 팔고 있다. 용돈과 손주 사탕이라도 사줄 요량으로 한단다. 자력으로 호구지책하고 베풀며 살아가려는 대단한 어른이다. 옛날 옛적 농경시대에는, 많이 배워 사회 진출하여 보람 있는 일을 하면서 의식주를 해결할 수 있는 자리가 관직(학우등사)을 제외하고는 별로 없었다. 부모들은 자식 가르쳐 벼슬, 즉, 고위관료 되길 바랐으리라. 요즘은 각고의 노력을 하면 의식주를 해결하면서, 다방면으로 인류에 공헌하고, 나라와 가문의 별이 될 수 있는 분야가 무궁무진하다. 릴랙스한 여유로운 휴식도, 집안 수리나 청소 등 육체적이든 정신적이든 힘든 일 다음 시간에 커피향기 같은 달콤함을 자주 느끼는 듯하다.

039. Like a friend, with a penance

Nowadays, most cities don't need a market every five days. Every day, there are markets. When you go to the traditional market, the elderly are selling a small seat and selling some herbs and fruits. They're a great man who wants to buy pocket money and grandchild candy, and to live on his own and give. In the old agricultural age, there were not many choices except for the office working in order to support own life with the clothes, food and shelter. Parents would have wanted to teach their children, that is, to be a high-positioned official workers. Nowadays, there are many fields that can contribute to society in various ways and become a famous person of the country and family. It seemed that I felt the more sweetness like coffee smell often in the break time after I did hard working physically or mentally, such as house repair or cleaning the house.

學 학	優 우	登 등	仕 사	攝 섭	職 직	從 종	政 정
hak	u	deung	sa	seob	jik	jong	jeong
배울	넉넉할	오를	벼슬	잡을	벼슬	좇을	정사
baeul	neokneokhal	oreul	byeoseul	jibeul	byeoseol	jocheul	jeongsa
learn	generous	climb	office	hold	office	follow	politics
077. 배운 것이 많으면, 벼슬에 오를 수 있고				078. 벼슬에 오른 후 정사에 참여할 수 있다			
If you have learned a lot, you can go to office				You can participate in politics after you get into office			
학생學生	배우俳優	등산登山	봉사奉仕	섭취攝取	직업職業	주종主從	정치政治
student	actor	climb a mountain	serve	ingest	vocation	main follow	politics
學학: 학문 학파 academic academic-faction				攝섭: 당기다 다스리다 take control			
優우: 뛰어나다 부드럽다 excellent soft				職직: 직책 일 position work			
登등: 얻다 밟다 높다 get step high				從종: 시중들다 나아가다 serve go-on			
仕사: 관직 배우다 office learn				政정: 구실=핑계 바로잡다 pretext correct			

97

040. 조상들의 지혜 (존이감당 거이익영)

먹을 것이 부족한, 배고픔의 한국 표현인, 보리 고개 즈음, 앞마당에 달콤한 앵두, 비교적 늦은 봄에 열리는 앵두, 먹어야 생명을 유지하는 사람들 모두는 달콤한 열매의 유혹에서 벗어나기 어려우리라. 복용하는 방법에 따라 효과, 즉, 약효가 다름을 알고 가공 발효하여 그 이로움에 따라 섭취하였다. 그들은 기본적으로 소주발효, 설탕발효, 엿물발효, 조청발효, 꿀 발효 등 여러 비법이 있고, 발효 기간도 짧게는 몇 주, 길게는 몇 년씩 숙성시키기도 한다, 서양의 양주나 포도주 발효와 비슷한 숙성기간을 두어 거친 맛을 순하고 부드러우면서 이로운 효과를 극대화시키는 방법이리라. 사실, 어머니께서 위암으로 고생할 때, 뱀 소주를 담아 텃밭 탱자나무 울타리 아래 웅덩이를 파고 묻어 숙성시키는 걸 보고서 관심을 갖게 되었다. 민간 치료법을 전수한 선조들은 영영 갔어도 그 음덕과 가치에 시를 짓고 비법을 칭송하고 대대로 노래(거이익영)하리라.

040. The wisdom of ancestors

By the time of the barley hill, a Korean expression of hunger, which lacks food, sweet cherry in the front yard, a relatively late spring cherry, and those who maintain life to eat are all attracted to sweet fruit. The effect, that is, the effect of the drug was different according to the method of taking, and it was processed and fermented and consumed according to the benefits. They basically have various secrets such as soju fermentation, sugar fermentation, malt fermentation, grain syrup fermentation, honey fermentation, etc., and the fermentation period is short for several weeks and years for a long time, It is a way to maximize the smooth, soft and beneficial effect of rough taste by having a ripening period similar to Western brewing and wine fermentation. In fact, when my mother suffered from a stomach cancer, I was interested in seeing the snake fermented wine and ripening a puddle under the garden tangle fence. The ancestors who passed on the private treatment would write poems and praise the secrets of the wisdom and sing for generations.

存 존	以 이	甘 감	棠 당	去 거	而 이	益 익	詠 영
jon	i	gam	dang	geo	i	ik	yeong
있을	써	달	아가위	갈	말이을	더할	읊을
isseul	sseo	dal	agawi	gil	malieul	deohal	eulpeul
be	with	sweet	hawthorn	go	but	more	recite
079. 호라는 선비가 아가위나무 아래 머물며, 백성에게 헌신하니				080. 그가 떠난 뒤, 백성은 시를 읊어 추모했다			
Ho is a scholar who stays under the tree of the hawthorn and devotes himself to the people				After he left, the people recited and remembranced the poem			
존재存在	이후以後	감언甘言	감당甘棠	과거過去	이립而立	이익利益	영음詠吟
existence	after-ward	flattery	adzuki bean	past	self-reliance	profit	read aloud

存존: 보존 살피다 conservation look
以이: 닮다 함께 resemblance together
甘감: 익다 맛있다 ripeness delicious
棠당: 해당화 correspondingization

去거: 덜다 떠나다 lessen leave
而이: 그러나 곧 but soon
益익: 넘치다 보태다 overflow add
詠영: 시를 짓다 노래하다 make a poem sing

99

041. 새로운 질서 (악수귀천 예별존비)

유럽 딸집에 갈 일이 있어, 비행기 좌석으로 퍼스트, 비즈니스, 이코노믹을 구분하여, 예약한다. 새로운 신분사회의 보편화이다. 과거에 많은 사람들은 대중가요라 하여 라디오에서 흘러나오는 노래 소리 들으며, 힘든 농사일에도 흥겨워하였다. 지금은 옛이야기가 되었지만, 왕조시대에, 모내기 하면서 부르던, 어얼러 상사 뒤야 올해도 대 풍년이야. 시대를 초월하여 만담과 풍류가 있었다. 지난 것은 추억으로 아름답다. 옛것은 소중한 것이여 하는 복고주의도 있고, 서양의 르네상스도 옛것의 부흥을 노래한 것이리라. 놀이 문화도 신분에 따라 다름이(악수귀천) 있었다. 현대는 대중문화 시대라 다양화되고 오픈되어 함께 즐기게 된 것이다. 야구 농구 등 스포츠놀이와 각종 콘서트 등 음악회, 미술, 서예 등 박람회가 대중의 품 안으로 들어왔다. 그 속에서도 특등석, 보통석 등 귀함과 천함, 높고 낮음이 새로운 방식으로 변천하여 이어지고 있는 듯하다. 자본주의적 사고방식, 사실, 이러한 새로운 패러다임의 신분 상승을 위하여(예별존비), 알게 모르게 사람들은 스스로 노력하고 있다.

041. The new order

I have to go to my daughter's house in Europe, and I make reservations for the seat among the choices of first, business, and economics as airplane seats. It is the universalization of a new social status. In the past, many people heard songs from the radio, saying that they were popular songs, and were excited about hard farming. It was an old story now, but in the dynasty, They has been calling rice-planting, "Eo eolreo sangsa dwiya" This year is a good year. There was a lot of talk and entertainment beyond the times. The past is beautiful with memories. The old is precious, and the

Western Renaissance sang also the revival of the old. The play culture was different according to the status. Modern times were diversified and opened as popular culture era, and they enjoyed together. Sports such as baseball basketball, concerts, art, calligraphy, etc., such as sports games and various concerts, came into the public's arms. Such as special class and ordinary class, it seems to be changing in a new way. For capitalistic thinking, in fact, to raise the status of this new paradigm, people are unconsciously trying themselves.

樂 락	殊 수	貴 귀	賤 천	禮 례	別 별	尊 존	卑 비
rak	su	gwi	cheon	rye	byeol	jon	bi
즐거울	다를	귀할	천할	예도	다를	높을	낮을
jeulgeoul	dareul	gwihal	cheonhal	yedo	dareul	nopeul	najeul
fun	different	noble	low	aptitude	different	high	low
081. 풍류도 신분의 높고 낮음에 따라 다르고				082. 예의는 윗사람과 아랫사람을 구별하여 지켰다			
The song and play is different depending on the high and low status				The courtesy was kept by distinguishing the superior from the lower			
음악音樂	특수特殊	부귀富貴	귀천貴賤	혼례婚禮	개별個別	존중尊重	비속卑俗
music	special	wealthy& noble	valuable vulgar	wedding ceremony	individual	respect	vulgar
樂락: 놀이 좋아하다 노래 play enjoy song 殊수: 죽이다 결심하다 kill determine 貴귀: 자랑 고위급 proud-boast high-status 賤천: 낮은 신분 low-identity				禮예: 예절 예물 manners etiquette gift 別별: 나누다 구별 divide distinguish 尊존: 중히 여기다 높다 seriously upper 卑비: 천하다 낮은 사람 ignoble low-person			

042. 더 어울려 살 수 있는 희망 (상화하목 부창부수)

어린 시절, 가뭄이 심하던 어느 여름 농사철, 논에 물이 부족하여 벼가 마르거나 자라지 못하던 한 여름, 농부는 하늘만 쳐다보는 논(천수답)에 조금이라도 물을 자기 논에 보내기 위해 동분서주한다. 여기 저기 흩어져 논이 있으니 항상 지킬 수도 없고, 오밤중에 어떤 사람이 나와 삽으로 물줄기를 바꿔 버리니 어찌하겠는가. 서로 자기 논에 물을 보내기 위해서는 화목한 이웃되기(상화하목)가 쉽지 않았다. 얌전한 이웃집 아저씨도 화내며 소리 지른다. 아주머니도 함께 목소리가 높아진다. 지아비 따라 소리 높일(부창부수) 수밖에 없으리라. 앞집 뒷집 등 화목한 집안도 있으나, 시끄러운 집도 더러 있다. 대대로 많은 세월을 살면서 의견 충돌은 인간사에서 불가피한 경우가 많다. 알콩달콩 하면서 사는 사바(현실)세계 중생들이다.

042. Hope to live more together

In childhood, during a summer farming season when the drought was severe, a summer when rice was dry or could not grow due to lack of water in rice paddies. The farmer is busy sending water to his rice paddies at least in the rice field (Cheonsu-paddy field: a land that gazes at the sky) that only look at the sky. There are fields scattered here and there, so you can not keep them all the time, and what would you do if someone changed the water stream with a shovel in the night? It was not easy to be a harmonious neighbor to send water to each other's rice paddies. The nice neighbor is angry and screaming. His wife also raises her voice. She would have to sound up after her husband. There are harmonious houses such as the back house of the front house, but there are some noisy houses. Many years of conflict of opinion are inevitable in human history. They are Sabah-world people who live in lovey-dovey.

上 상	和 화	下 하	睦 목	夫 부	唱 창	婦 부	隨 수
sang	hwa	ha	mok	bu	chang	bu	su
위	화할	아래	화목할	지아비	부를	지어미	따를
wi	hwahal	arae	hwamokhal	jiabi	bureul	jieomi	ttareul
top	peaceful	bottom	peaceful	husband	song-call	wife	follow
083. 남편이 따뜻하게 대하면 아내도 화목하고				084. 남편이 이끌면 아내가 따른다			
If he was warm, she would be in harmony				When the husband leads, the wife follows			
세상世上	평화平和	지하地下	친목親睦	농부農夫	합창合唱	신부新婦	수필隨筆
world	peace	under-ground	friend-ship	farmer	chorus	newlywed-wife	essay

上상: 오르다 표면 ascending surface
和화: 고르다 harmony
下하: 내리다 하위 lower below
睦목: 공손하다 온순 polite gentle

夫부: 남편 일꾼 husband worker
唱창: 노래 song
婦부: 아내 며느리 wife daughter-in-law
隨수: 동반하다 accompany

043. 어머니의 솔선수범 (외수부훈 입봉모의)

아주 어렸을 때 어머니 꽁무니 따라 다니는 걸, 당연 좋아했다. 어린 나는 어머니가 행주치마 입고 밥그릇, 국그릇, 젓가락 등을, 설거지하는 모습을 유심히 쳐다본다. 고춧가루, 소금, 참기름, 볶음깨, 간장을 요리 저리 하면서 반찬 하는 걸, 새롭고 신기한 것을 좋아하는 마음으로 관찰한다. 호미, 쇠스랑, 곡괭이, 낫으로 밭에서 흙을 갈고, 가꾸는 걸 호기심 갖고 배운다. 어머니는 낮에 힘든 일하고, 밤에는 안방에서 바느질하고, 대대로 전해 내려왔을 것 같은 전설의 고향 비슷한 옛날이야기들도 한다. 그 시절엔 동화책이라든가, 당연 텔레비전, 컴퓨터 등 정보통신 시설도 없었다. 모든 것이 구전 문화였다. 그렇다고 말을 많이 하던 시절도 아니었다. 그나마 여자들 수다가 좀 있었고, 남자들은 말수가 적고 점잖아야 한다는 문화였다. 남아일언은 중천금이라며, 말조심하고 신중하라는 무언의 압력문화였다. 이러한 것이 모두 어린 시절의 머리에 기억으로 남아 사회생활의 바탕이 되는 듯하다. 부모형제자매와 생활하면서 알게 모르게 배우게 되고, 세월이 흐르고 시대가 바뀌어도 어머니의 자식에 대한 사랑은 변함이 없는 것 같다. 자식에 대한 헌신적이고 어질고 착한 모성본능이리라.

043. Mother's lead by example

When I was very young, I liked to follow my mother. I look at my mother wearing a dish skirt, washing rice bowls, soup bowls, chopsticks, and dishes. I look into the side dish while cooking red pepper powder, salt, sesame oil, stir-fried sesame, soy sauce with curiosity. I learn curiously to grind and cultivate soil in the field with small-hoe, forked-rake, hoe, and sickle. My mother works hard during the day, sews in her room at night, and tells old stories about the legendary hometown that seems to have been passed down for generations. In those days, there were no fairy tale books, no TV, no computer, no information and communication facilities. Everything was a word-of-mouth culture. It was not a time when I talked a lot, but there were some women talking, and men were less talkative and It was a culture that should be a demure. A man's word was a silent pressure culture, like heavy gold, to be prudent and careful. All of these seem to be memories of childhood and become the basis of social life. I learn without knowing it while living with my parents and sisters, and even if the years pass and the times change, mother's love for her child seems to remain unchanged. She would be devoted, merciful, and good motherly instinct to her children.

外 외	受 수	傅 부	訓 훈	入 입	奉 봉	母 모	儀 의
oe	su	bu	hun	ip	bong	mo	eui
바깥	받을	스승	가르칠	들	받들	어미	거동
baggatt	badeul	seuseung	gareuchil	deul	baddeul	eomi	geodong
outside	receive	teacher	lesson	come	respect	mother	behavior
085. 밖에 나가서는 스승의 가르침을 받고				086. 집에 들어와서는 맹자처럼 어머니의 모범을 보고 배운다			
I went out and I was taught by my teacher				When I come home, I learn from my mother's example, like Mencius			
외국外國	수상受賞	사부師傅	교훈敎訓	입시入試	봉사奉仕	부모父母	의식儀式
foreign	award	mentor	message	entrance examination	service	mom and dad	cere-mony

外외: 외가=처가 멀리 mother's side far
受수: 얻다 응하다 get response accept
傅부: 펴다 베풀다 spread give
訓훈: 길 인도하다 road lead

入입: 수입 income earnings
奉봉: 기르다 돕다 따르다 raise help follow
母모: 어머니 땅 근원 mother land root
儀의: 모형 본뜨다 pattern imitate

044. 백부의 멸사봉공 (제고백숙 유자비아)

아버지는 사 남매로 백부와 작은 고모 둘 있었다. 필자가 어렸을 때 백부 (조희석)는 바로 옆에 살며 아버지와 함께 농사를 지었다. 초등학교 들어갈 쯤 도시로 이사 갔다. 소소한 여러 가지 기억이 잠재의식에 남아 있다. 그런 기억은 문득 문득 기회가 될 때마다 떠오른다. 백부는 종중과 집안의 장손이 다. 보시감과 책임감이 남다르다는 인상이 있다. 도시로 이사 가서, 조카 되 는 필자뿐 아니라, 다른 고모네 조카도 챙겨 배움의 길로 인도(제고백숙 유자 비아)하였다. 더구나 보리고개 넘기 힘든 빈농으로 소득이 변변치 않은 농사 일 외에 먹거리가 없던 고향마을 아이들도 수시로 챙기고 인도하여 호구지책 하도록 일자리를 마련해 주어 정착하도록 도왔다. 이에는 거기에 뒷받침되는 헌신이 있어야 가능하다. 백모는 백부의 뜻이라면, 어렵고 쪼들리는 생활에 도 불평 없이 즐겁게, 모두 받아 드리고 헌신적 희생정신으로 뒷바라지 임무 를 다했다. 백부모는 모두를 자식으로 여겼을 정도로 지극정성으로 습관처럼 하였다. 원불교 교리 사요(四要) 중 타 자녀 교육을 몸소 실천하고, 헌신하는 부처님 같은 큰 어른이며, 본보기라 할 수 있다. 그 은혜를 입은 사람들은 감 사하고, 고마움을 마음 깊이 헤아릴 수 있을는지.

044. The elder father, abandon one's own desire and work for the public good

My father had a brother and two sisters. When I was a child, the elder father(Cho Hui-Seok) lived next to me and farmed with my father. I moved to the city by the time I entered elementary school. There are many small memories in the subconscious. They come to mind every time they get a chance. The elder father is the eldest son of the clan and family. The elder father has an impression that he has a give mind and responsibility. He moved to the city and led not only my nephew but also other aunt's nephew to the way of learning. In addition, he provided jobs for the children of the hometown village, which had no food other than farming, to take care of and guide them from time to time. It is possible only with the sacrifice supported. If elder mother is the will of elder father, he has done his duty with a spirit of sacrifice, delightful and devoted to all of his needy and difficult life without complaining. The elder parents were so habitual as to regard everyone as a child. The elder parents are big adults such as Buddha who practice and devote themselves to the education of other children among Won Buddhism doctrines. The people who have been blessed are grateful, and they can deeply count their gratitude.

諸 제	姑 고	伯 백	叔 숙	猶 유	子 자	比 비	兒 아
je	go	baek	suk	yu	ja	bi	a
모두	시어미	맏	아저씨	같을	아들	견줄	아이
modu	sieomi	mad	ajeossi	gateul	adeul	gyeonjul	ai
all	mother-in-law	elder	younger	like	son	match	child
087. 고모와 백숙부는 아버지와 한 뿌리므로				088. 조카를 자기 아이처럼 다정하게 대해야 한다			
My aunt and my uncle are rooted in my father				You have to treat your nephew as sweet as your own child			
제반諸般	고부姑婦	백부伯父	숙부叔父	유예猶豫	자녀子女	비교比較	아동兒童
various	mother&daughter-in-law	elder uncle	father's brother	morato-rium	sons&daughters	compare	kid

諸제: 모으다 간수하다 gather keep
姑고: 고모 시누이 aunt sister-in-law
伯백: 형 어른 elder adult
叔숙: 어리다 young

猶유: 같다 오히려 닮다 as resemble similar
子자: 자녀 열매 child fruit
比비: 돕다 이웃 help neighborhood
兒아: 연약 아들 tender son

045. 형제들 우애 (공회형제 동기연지)

옛 적에는 보통 오남매 칠남매가 보통이다. 아들 딸 남매만 있는 집은 마을에서 불쌍히 여길 정도였다. 유명 가수인 윤항기 윤복희 남매는 뛰어난 가창력으로 대중의 인기도 받았지만, 남매라는 것이 매스컴으로 알려져, 불쌍하다는 동정심까지 더하여, 인기가 전국을 떠들썩하게 한 것으로 짐작된다. 그들 외에 형제들이 많은 만큼 즐겁고 다정할 때도 있지만, 다투고 시끄러울 때도 가끔 있는 듯하다. 궁굽하고 어렵고 철없고 어린 시절이니 어쩌겠는가. 놀다 보면 여러 경우가 있으리라. 그 이후 인구 팽창을 막기 위해 국가적 산아제한 정책으로 전환되고, "많이 낳아 고생 말고 적게 낳아 잘 키우자.", "덮어놓고, 아이를 낳다 보면 거지꼴을 못 벗어난다.", "서구 유럽 선진국 본받아 아들 딸 구별 말고 둘만 낳아 잘 기르자."라는 표어까지 나왔을까. 이런 후 요즘은 신생아 출생이 너무 낮아, 국가 소멸론까지 들먹이며 출산 장려정책으로 전환되고 있다. 장성하고 보니 그리운 건 형제들이요 남매들이더라(공회형제). 같은 뿌리와 가지인 남매들(동기연지)이니, 우리는 철없을 때의 작은 흠들은 잊은 듯 눈감아 주거나, 강물에 흘려보내고 정다웠던 기억만 살리면 원만하지 않을까. 욕심내지 말고, 주지 못해서 안타까웠던 추억이 있으리라.

045. The brotherhood fraternity

In the past, seven or five siblings were usually common. The house with only the son and daughter was pitying in the village. Yoon Hang-ki, a famous singer, Yoon Bok-hee, was popular with the public with his excellent singing ability, but his brother and sister are known as media, and he is pitying that he is sorry, It is presumed that popularity has made the whole country buzz. There are times when the brothers are as pleasant and friendly as many other than them, but sometimes they seem to be arguing and loud. What if it was a poverty, difficult, immature, and childhood? There would be many cases when they were playing. Since then, it has been converted into a national birth control policy to prevent population expansion, and "Let's raise a lot of births and raise less than hardships.", "If you put it on and give birth to a child, you can not take off the beggar." and "Let's raise it well, not just the distinction between the daughters of the sons and daughters of the Western European advanced countries." Nowadays, newborn births are too low, and the theory of national extinction is being turned into a policy to encourage childbirth. I missed the brothers and sisters when I saw them. We are brothers and sisters with the same roots and branches, so if we can make small flaws when we are able to fly, shed, and save memories that were neat, it would be good. We do not want to be greedy, we will have memories that were sad that we could not give.

孔 공	懷 회	兄 형	弟 제	同 동	氣 기	連 련	枝 지
gong	hoe	hyeong	je	dong	gi	ryeon	ji
구멍	품을	맏	아우	한가지	기운	이을	가지
gumeong	pumeul	mad	au	hangaji	giun	ieul	gaji
hole	hold	elder	brother	same	spirit	stem	branch
089. 몹시 그리워 잊지 못하는 것이 형제 사이다				090. 부모로부터 같은 기운을 받아 이어진 가지와 같다			
It is between brothers that I miss so much				It is like a branch that has been given the same energy from parents			
공작孔雀	감회感懷	형부兄夫	제자弟子	동생同生	용기勇氣	일련一連	분지分枝
peacock	feelings	elder sister's husband	student, disciple	younger brother or sister	courage	sequence chain	share branch
孔공: 매우 크다 very large 懷회: 마음 생각 포용 mind think embrace 兄형: 형 어른 older-brother adult 弟제: 동생 순서 little-brother order				同동: 한가지 함께 same-stem with 氣기: 숨 날씨 공기 breath weather air 連련: 잇다 연속 series continuum 枝지: 나뭇가지 나누다 branch divide			

046. 새로운 시대, 친구 찾기 (교우투분 절마잠규)

어린 유년 시절부터 친구들이, 어느 겨울 밤 눈처럼 누적된다. 어린 눈으로 보고, 덜 익었지만 작은 머리로 판단하고, 부모의 속삭임을 참고하면, 친구의 기준이 어느 정도 감이 잡히게(교우투분)된다. 마음에 내키지 않는 친구는 경외의 관계를 유지하도록 한다. 갈수록 험한 세상이라 도리를 절실히 하면서도 항상 경계를 늦추지 않아야 하리라. 선지자가 오죽했으면 염화시중의 미소나, 관포지교처럼 진정한 친구하나만 있어도 행복하고 성공한 사람이라 했을까. 유구한 역사를 통해서도 그만큼 배반의 시대에 살고 있는지도 모른다. 성장하면서 각자가 너무 많은 경우의 수 들을 경험하고 살기 때문일까. 한때는 믿는 도끼에 찍히더라도 믿어야 한다는 생각까지 한 바 있다. 어느 스님이 이야기했다. 도둑은 대부분 믿었던 사람, 절친, 공신력 있는 신분, 고향 친구, 동료 등이 포함된다고, 믿음은 철저한 의심과 검증에서 나와야 하리라. 그래야 상대방도 살리고 본인도 살리는 일이다. 어리숙한 선의는 상대의 탐욕에 당할 수밖에 없지 않을까. 어리숙함은 견물생심의 희생자가 되고, 욕심을 조장하게 된다. 그러니 불신의 시대로 인하여, 혼술 혼밥 비혼 등이 대세로 자리 잡는 시대로 변할 조짐이 보이는 게 아닐까. 물론 다른 이유와 사연도 있으리라.

046. New Age, Finding Friends

Since childhood, friends accumulate like snow in one winter night. If we look at it with our young eyes, judge it with a less cooked but small head, and refer to our parents' whispers, our friend's standards will be somewhat felt. Friends who are unwilling to be in awe, and we will be in a more and more difficult world, so we must be desperate and always alert.

If it was a bad thing, would the prophet be happy and successful even if he had a true friend like a smile on the Yeomhwa-sijung(The Buddha gave flowers, and only the Gaseop smiled) or a Gwanpo-jigyo(Damon and Pythias friendship)? Through the long history, it may be living in the age of betrayal. Is it because each person experiences too many cases of growth and lives? Once, I even thought that I should believe even if I was stamped on an ax I believed in. Most thieves include those who believed, best friends, credible identities, home friends, and colleagues, and faith must come from thorough doubt and verification. That way, you can save the other person and save yourself. I wonder if the foolish good will be greedy. Foolishness becomes a victim of the life of the beast, and encourages greed. So, due to the era of distrust, there is a sign that drinking alone, eating alone, not marrying will become a trend. Of course, there are other reasons and stories.

交 교	友 우	投 투	分 분	切 절	磨 마	箴 잠	規 규
gyo	u	tu	bun	jeol	ma	jam	gyu
사귈	벗	던질	나눌	끊을	갈	경계	법
sagwil	beot	deonjil	nanul	ggeunheul	gil	kyeonggye	beob
socialize	friend	throw	share	cut	grind	carefull	law
091. 신분에 맞는 친구를 사귀고				092. 친구와 학문과 덕을 닦아 경계하며, 인격 수양을 이룰 수 있다			
I'm gonna make friends that fit one's identity				You can be wary of your friends, your studies and virtues, and you can achieve personality training			
외교外交	우정友情	투자投資	신분身分	친절親切	안마按摩	잠언箴言	규칙規則
diplo-matic	friend-ship	invest-ment	status	friendly	massage	apho-rism	rule

交교: 바꾸다 왕래 change come&go
友우: 우애 친구 fraternity friend
投투: 머무르다 주다 stay give
分분: 가르다 신분 separate identity

切절: 모두 친절 절실 all kind earnest severe
磨마: 문지르다 연마 쓰다듬다 rub practice touch
箴잠: 감시 바늘 꽂다 watch needle stick
規규: 모범 도리 exemplar justice

047. 측은함과 배려 (인자은측 조차불리)

어머니는 필자와 다닐 때, 머리에 수건 질끈 동여매고 저 멀리서 밭일하는, 춘흥마을 아주머니를 보고 불쌍히 여기고 슬퍼하며, 항상 안타까워(인자은측)하였다. 그녀는 멀리서 시집와서, 딸만 다섯 낳고 아들도 없이 고생 고생한단다. 그들 중에 지금은 어디서 살고 있는지도 모르는 초등학교 동기 동창도 있었다. 딸만 둔 아저씨는 주눅 들어 힘이 없는 듯한, 표정을 하고 다녔다. 필자는 그들로부터 부러운 눈빛을 받고 살았다. 어머니 옷자락 따라 뒷마을 지나 이리저리 돌아다니며, 친구와 소꿉장난하며 놀던 윗마을 뒷산 비탈 깊이 들어간 또 다른 마지막에 집이 있다. 필자보다 나이가 몇 살 많은 거복이, 거복이는 한때 초등학교를 함께 다닌 적이 있는데, 그는 중간에 가정 사정인지, 학업을 포기한 것 같다. 그는 쓰러져 가는 허름한 토담집, 그는 때가 꼬질꼬질한 누더기 옷을 입고 살고 있었다. 이름도 잊혀진 영광댁 노부부 가족들, 우리 집 탱자나무 울타리 뒷길로 땔감을 아주머니는 머리에 이고, 아저씨는 지게에 지고, 땅거미가 내리는 저녁쯤에 지나갔었다. 아마, 사기정굴 계곡 깊숙한 끝머리에 논과 밭에서 일하며, 방 아궁이에 불을 지필 나무를 마련한 듯하다. 거칠게 자랐던 거복이 가족의 영상이 아스름한 눈빛 뭉게구름처럼, 측은스럽게 어린 가슴에 아로 새겨져(조차불리) 있다.

047. The pity and consideration

When my mother was with me, she was pitied and saddened by seeing a woman in Chunheung village who was working in the field from a distance with a towel on her head. She is married from afar, has five daughters and suffers without a son. Among them was an elementary school classmate who did not even know where he lived now. The uncle, who had only a daughter, looked helpless and weak. I lived with envy from them. There is another house at the end of the hillside of the village where I walked around the back village along the back of my mother's clothes and played with my friend. A friend Geobok who is a few years older than me, He once went to elementary school with me, and He seems to have given up on his studies, whether it is family affairs in the middle. He was living in a collapsing, shabby house, he wore a ragged rag suit, The name of the old couple of the Yeonggwang house, the old couple's family, my house, the back road of the tangle fence, the firewood was on her head, the uncle was on the A-frame, and they had passed the evening of the dusk. Perhaps, they worked in rice fields and fields at the end of the Sagi-jeonggul valley, and they had prepared a tree to fire the room. The image of the family, which grew rough, is carved into the young breast like a cloud of gray eyes.

仁 인	慈 자	隱 은	惻 측	造 조	次 차	弗 불	離 리
in	ja	eun	cheuk	jo	cha	bul	ri
어질	사랑	숨을	슬플	지을	버금	아닐	떠날
eojil	sarang	sumeul	seulpeul	jieul	beogeum	anil	tteonal
virtue	love	hide	sad	build	next	not	leave
093. 현자는 어질고 사랑하고 슬퍼하고 불쌍히 여기는 마음				094. 이러한 마음이 잠시라도 떠나면 안 된다			
The wise man is a heart that merciful, loves, grieves and pityes				This mind should not leave for a moment			
인효仁孝	자선慈善	은어隱語	측심惻心	구조構造	차례次例	불소弗素	거리距離
merciful &filial	charity	slang	pitying heart	structure	proce-dure	fluorine	distance

仁인: 인자 자애 benign-man affection
慈자: 인정 자비 kindly-feelings mercy
隱은: 가여움 의지함 compassion depend
惻측: 측은 간절 pitiful desperately

造조: 만들다 이르다 세우다 make reach set-up
次차: 차례 다음 order next
弗불: 달러 어기다 dollar break disobey
離리: 이별 헤어짐 parting separation

113

048. 칠전팔기의 정신 (절의염퇴 전패비휴)

 그 시절에는 대부분, 필자 등 모두가 초등학교까지 십 리 길을 걸어 다녔다. 먼지 일어나는 비포장 도로, 산마루 고갯길, 시냇물 흐르는 바위와 돌멩이 나뒹굴던 갓길을 걸어서, 방학과 휴일을 빼고, 눈과 비가 오는 날에도 매일 다녔다. 그 시절 시골버스는 있었으나 어린이는 태워 주지 않았다. 우리는 넘어지거나, 쓰러져 다치고, 피가 나도 울 수도 없었다. 지금은 폐교된 시골 묘량 초등학교는 일 학년에서 오 학년까지 한 반에 오십여 명 정도의 두 개 반이었던 것 같다. 육 학년은 빈곤한 가정 사정으로 학생 수가 육십여 명으로 많이 줄어, 합반하여 한 반으로 수업하였다. 그 시절 시골에서, 전체 학생 수가 칠백 명 정도로 제법 큰 학교였다. 어린 친구들과 작은 개울에 두 손을 담그고 작은 물고기 잡던 시절, 은빛 모래 만지던 시절, 맑은 물 반짝이는 물결 속 고동 줍던 시절, 지나고 보니 주변 사람과 친구 이름은 잊혀지지만, 어려서의 기억과 추억이 한 폭의 그림처럼 가장 오래 남고, 길게 가는 듯하다.

048. The indomitable spirit(seventh falls, but spirit of stands up again for the eighth time)

 In those days, most of them, including myself, walked to elementary school. We walked on dirt roads, mountain ridges, streams of rocks and stones, and walked on the shoulder of the rocks, except for vacation and holidays, and every day on snowy and rainy days. There was a country bus then, but the child did not give a ride. We couldn't fall, collapse, get hurt, get blood or cry. Now, the closed rural Myoryang elementary school seems to have been two or more classes in the first and fifth grades. Sixth graders were taught in one class by combining the number of students with the number of poor families decreased to about sixty. In the countryside at that time, the total number of students was about seven hundred, which was a fairly large school. When I was soaking my hands in small streams with my young friends, catching small fish, touching silver sand, picking up the marsh-snail in a clear water sparkling wave, As I pass by, the names of the people and friends around me are forgotten, but remembrances and memories of my childhood seem to remain for a long time as a picture.

節 절	義 의	廉 렴	退 퇴	顚 전	沛 패	匪 비	虧 휴
jeol	ui	ryeom	toe	jeon	pae	bi	hyu
마디	옳을	청렴	물러날	엎어질	자빠질	아닐	이지러질
madi	olheul	cheongryeom	mulreonal	eopeojil	jabbajil	anil	ijireojil
joint	right	integrity	retreat	fall over	tumble	not	wane

095. 신하는 절개와 의리와 청렴과 물러남의 도리를 지키고	096. 넘어지고 쓰러져도 약해져서는 안 된다
The servant keep reasonable of the incision, the righteousness, the integrity, and the withdrawal	You should not be thrown away even if you fall and tumbledown

계절季節	강의講義	청렴淸廉	퇴근退勤	전복顚覆	전패顚沛	토비土匪	휴월虧月
season	lecture	clean	off work	overthrow	tumble down	gang of robbers	littered moon

節절: 절개 예절 fidelity etiquette, manner
義의: 정의 의리 justice righteousness
廉렴: 검소 살피다 frugality look at
退퇴: 사양하다 떠나다 decline leave

顚전: 기울어지다 뒤집다 collapse capsize
沛패: 넘어지다 늪 fall swamp
匪비: 도둑 악한 thief=steal evil
虧휴: 약해지다 줄다 weaken reduce

049. 몸과 마음의 휴식 (성정정일 심동신피)

초등학교 시절 여섯 해 동안, 가깝지 않은 불갑사로 소풍 갔다. 웅장해 보이는 기둥과 기초 석으로 만들어진 위대한 영웅의 건물은 어린이 시선을 압도하기에 충분했다. 그 안에 있는 부처님은 묵직하게 어린이를 내려다보고만 있다. 뭘 말하려는지 언제나 궁금했다. 아무도 알려주는 사람이 없다. 사실 몇 마디로 그 누가 말로 표현할 수 있겠는가. 그저 염불이나 듣고, 호기심 자극하는 것으로 어린이를 안내하는 것이리라. 나는 그냥 물끄러미 바라보고 있노라면, 마음이 고요하고 잔잔해진다. 흔히들, 관심 있는 종교 실내에 들어가면 마음이 편안해진다고들 한다. 많은 중생이, 많은 세월 동안 의지하고, 위안 삼고, 깨닫고, 포교하고 사라졌으리라. 갖가지 고통을 참고 견뎌야 하는 사바세계 중생들 중 하나인, 시끄럽고 술주정하며 어머니에게 화풀이하는 아버지 얼굴이 떠오른다. 아버지의 모습이 일제 강점기의 트라우마일지도 모른다. 여러 모순과 실책도 있었겠지만, 한 가정의 생계를 책임지고, 기둥 노릇한 것도 사실이다. 이것 또한 나의 마음을 움직여 정신을 피곤하게 만드는 잡념(성정정일, 심동신피)일까.

049. A rest of body and mind

During the six years of elementary school, the picnic went to the Bulgab-temple, which was not close. The building of great heroes made of magnificent-looking pillars and foundation stones were enough to overwhelm the children's gaze. The Buddha in it is looking down heavily at the child. I always wondered what he was going to say. No one tells me. In fact, in a few words, who can put it in words? It will just guide the child by listening to the pray to Amitabha and stimulating curiosity. If

I am just looking at it, my heart becomes quiet and calm. It is often said that when you enter a religious room of interest, your mind becomes comfortable. Many people, many years, will depend, comfort, realize, preach, and disappear. One of the real world people who have to endure various sufferings, the face of a father who is loud, drunk and angry with my mother comes to mind. The appearance of his father may be a trauma during the Japanese colonial rule. He may have had many contradictions and mistakes, but it is also true that he is responsible for the livelihood of a family. Is this also a miscellaneous idea that makes my mind tired by moving my mind?

性 성	靜 정	情 정	逸 일	心 심	動 동	神 신	疲 피
seong	jeong	jeong	il	sim	dong	sin	pi
성품	고요할	뜻	편안할	마음	움직일	귀신	피로할
seongpum	goyohal	tteut	pyeonanhal	maeum	umjikil	gwisin	pirohal
nature	quiet	meaning	comfortable	mind	move	ghost	fatigue
097. 태어날 때부터 지닌 성품을 고요하게 가라앉히면, 마음이 편안하고				098. 마음이 흔들리면, 정신이 고달프다			
When you calm down your personality from birth, you feel comfortable				When you feel shaken, you are in a state of distress			
성격性格	안정安靜	표정表情	안일安逸	진심眞心	운동運動	신화神話	피곤疲困
character	stability	expression	indolence	sincere	exercise	myth	tiredness

性성: 모습 개성 image personality
靜정: 침착 고요함 composure calm
情정: 감정 진심 feeling emotion sincere
逸일: 만족 숨다 satisfy hide

心심: 느낌 의지 가슴 feeling will heart
動동: 변하다 행동 motion shake action
神신: 정신 신령 마음 spirits deity mind
疲피: 지치다 고달픔 exhaustion wearing

050. 큰 꿈으로 잠을 설치자 (수진지만 축물의이)

강변도로를 출퇴근 겸, 드라이브하면서 듣던 라디오 프로에서, 한 상담자가 사업에 실패한 후 돈을 벌기 위해 물불 안 가리고 몇 년을 허둥댔지만 항상 그 자리였다고 한다. 한동안 책과 함께 휴식과 명상을 하며 마음의 여유를 찾은 후, 물질을 쫓기보다 작은 현실에 적응하며 즐겁게 일하니, 자연스럽게 돈은 따라 오더라 한다. 돈을 쫓기보다 뒤에서 다가오도록 해야 함을 배웠다 (수진지만, 축물의이) 한다. 자본주의 사회에서 개인도 국가도 부의 축적이 모든 것의 기본이 되고 있다. 사리사욕에서 벗어나, 사회에 공헌하고, 헌신하고자 하는 원대한 목표를 세우고, 업무에 접근한다면 좋지 않을까.

050. Let's set up a big dream at night

In a radio that I was listening to while driving by the riverside road, a counselor talked about the story of somebody that he had been in the same spot for years, although he tried to make money after failing his business. After a while, he rested and meditated with books, found his mind, and then he adjusted to the small reality rather than chasing the material, and he worked happily. Naturally, money comes along. In capitalist society, the accumulation of wealth is the basis of everything, both individuals and countries. It would be nice to get out of self-interest, contribute to society, set a grand goal to devote, and approach work.

守 수	眞 진	志 지	滿 만	逐 축	物 물	意 의	移 이
su	jin	ji	man	chuk	mul	ui	i
지킬	참	뜻	찰	쫓을	물건	뜻	옮길
jikil	cham	tteut	chil	jjocheul	mulgeon	tteut	omgil
keep	true	will	fill	pursue	thing	meaning	change

099. 신념을 지키면, 의지로 가득 차게 되고				100. 욕망을 쫓아가면, 신념도 흔들린다			
If you keep your faith, you're filled with will				If you follow desire, your beliefs are shaken			

수비守備	사진寫眞	의지意志	만족滿足	각축角逐	동물動物	합의合意	이민移民
defense	photo	will	satisfy	rivalry	animal	consen-sual	immigra-tion

守수: 임무 보살피다 duty care
眞진: 순수 천성 pure nature
志지: 감정 절개 will intention integrity
滿만: 풍족 가득 rich full

逐축: 빠르다 돼지 구하다 fast pig, rescue
物물: 만물 재물 all-things property
意의: 감탄사 추측 exclamation guess
移이: 떠나다 이민가다 leave emigration

051. 나의 작은 노력이 인류에 공헌 (견지아조 호작자미)

어린 철부지같이 앞뒤 안 가리고 놀던 시절, 공부만 해야 하는 지루한 중고 등학교 시절, 어쩌다 주변 동산이라도 오르면 다른 세상이 보이고, 공부하고는 좀 거리가 있는 것 같은 오솔길, 언덕길 잡초들, 소나무들 밤이든 낮이든 제자리 지키고 있다. 잡념들로 갈등하고, 고민했던 작지 않은 세월들, 성취를 위해 날밤을 세워야 했던 시절들, 그러한 것들이 지나고 보면, 언제나 다시 그리워지는 좋은 시절의 조각들이 아닌가 싶어진다. 왕조시대 옛 선비의 덕목으로, 쇠와 돌 같은 깊은 마음을 지키고, 소나무와 대나무 같은 깨끗한 지조를 다듬었다. 그러면 자연히 좋은 관직이 스스로 온다(견지아조, 호작자미). 다른 말로 하면, 목숨까지 받쳐 충성하라 하니, 요즘과 다른 세상인 듯하다. 요즘은 개인의 발전이 국가와 민족과 인류발전에 공헌하는, 국가가 각 개인의 인권을 포함하여 지식까지, 보호해 주는 보호주의로, 아름다운 시대가 되고 있다. 공공과 개인이 서로 상호작용하는 사회로의 변화되는 시대라 함 직하다.

051. My little effort contributed to humanity

When I was playing like a young man, I was in a boring middle and high school where I had to study, and when I climbed the surrounding garden, I saw another world through the trails, hill weeds, pine trees, which seem to be a little distance from studying, are kept in place at night or day.

The small years of conflict and trouble with the misconceptions, The days when I had to set up a night for achievement, when those things pass, I wonder if they are the pieces of good times that I always miss again. It was the virtue of the old learned-man of the dynasty, keeping a deep heart like iron and stone, and refining clean branches like pine and bamboo. Then, naturally, a good office comes to itself. In other words, it seems to be a different world than these days because it is loyal to life. Nowadays, the current state is a beautiful era with protectionism that protects the knowledge including the human rights of each individual, where the development of individuals contributes to the development of the nation and humanity. It is a changing era in which the public and the individual interact with each other.

堅 견	持 지	雅 아	操 조	好 호	爵 작	自 자	麋 미
gyeon	ji	a	cho	ho	jak	ja	mi
굳을	가질	바를	잡을	좋을	벼슬	스스로	얽어 맬
gudeul	gajil	bareul	jibeul	joheul	byeoseul	seuseuro	eolgeomael
firmly	have	right	hold	likable	office	naturally	bind
101. 바르게 수신하여 의지를 지키고 있으면				102. 좋은 벼슬 기회가 스스로 오게 된다			
If you keep your body and mind right, and keep your will				A good chance of a court will come for oneself			
중견中堅	긍지矜持	아량雅量	체조體操	호감好感	공작公爵	자연自然	계미繫麋
back-bone	pride	toler-ance	gymnas-tics	attractive	top office	nature	hold and tie

堅견: 강하다 단단 strong hard
持지: 보전 지키다 preserve keep
雅아: 우아하다 맑다 elegant clear
操조: 지조 절개 principle unchange

好호: 아름답다 친하다 beautiful friendly
爵작: 술잔 참새 glass sparrow
自자: 저절로 itsel automatically
麋미: 꼬삐 일이 생기다 rein happen

052. 견문을 실생활에 적용 (도읍화하 동서이경)

고등학교 시절 서울이라는 대도시를 입시 때문에 처음 왔다. 시골 도시에서 올라온 촌놈은 거의 상상을 초월하는 문화적 충격이었다. 서울은 빌딩이며, 도로며, 사람들이며 전혀 다른 세상이었다. 필자는 우물 안 개구리마냥, 살던 지방 도시가 대단히 큰 것처럼 생각하고 살았던 것이다. 그만큼 교통도 불편했고, 경우에 따라서는, 경제적 이유로 다른 곳을 잘 다니거나 여행을 하지 않던 구석기 같은 시절이다. 책에서만 보았던 역사적 창경궁, 비원, 남대문, 거리 표지판에 여러 나라 대사관들, 말로만 듣던 한강철교와 한강다리, 애국가에 나오는 남산, 경복궁, 청와대, 사람은 이러한 곳에서 살아야 하는 것 아닐까 하는 마음이 들었다. 그 후 많은 세월이 흐른 뒤 논문 지도교수가, 유학을 위해 도착한 미국 뉴욕 거리를 보고서, 그는 입이 쩍 벌어져 다물어지지를 않을 정도로 놀라고, 넘어질 뻔했다는 그의 말이, 필자와 비슷한 문화적 충격이 아니었을까(도읍, 이경) 하고, 짐작해 본다. 그 후로 필자는 길에서 길을 찾고, 더욱더 큰 꿈을 그려 보고자 여행을 즐겨 하기도 했다.

052. Minds to apply knowledge to real life

It was the first for me to come to Seoul in my high school time because of my big exam for entering university. As a village man from the countryside, city was a cultural shock that was almost beyond imagination. Seoul was surrounded by a building, a road, a people, that was a completely different world, and I lived like a frog in a well, thinking that the local city I lived in was very big. Traffic was so uncomfortable that it was in some cases, such as the Paleolithic period, where people did not visit each other or travel for economic reasons. The historical Changgyeong Palace, Biwon,

Namdaemun, the various embassies on the street sign, the Han River iron-Bridge and the Han River Bridge in the words, Namsan, Gyeongbok Palace, Cheong-Wa-Dae of The Blue House, and people in the national anthem were wondering if they should live in these places. After many years, the paper advisor, after seeing the streets of New York, where he arrived to study, He is surprised that his mouth is open and not closed, and he guesses that his words that he almost fell, were cultural shocks similar to my own. Since then, I've been looking for new directions on the road, and have enjoyed traveling to draw a bigger dream.

都 도	邑 읍	華 화	夏 하	東 동	西 서	二 이	京 경
do	eub	hwa	ha	dong	seo	i	gyeong
도읍	고을	빛날	여름	동녘	서녘	두	서울
doeub	goeul	bichnal	yeoreum	dongnyeok	seonyeok	du	seoul
town	county	bright	summer	east	west	two	capital
103. 화하는 빛나고, 큰 나라 중국을 말한다				104. 동경과 서경 두 개의 수도가 있다			
Hwa-Ha refers to China, a bright and big country				There are two capital cities, East and West			
도시都市	읍내邑內	호화豪華	하계夏季	동양東洋	서양西洋	이중二重	귀경歸京
city	city town	luxury	summer season	oriental	Western countries	duplex double	return to capital
都도: 도시 성 city urban castle 邑읍: 마을 도읍 downtown town 華화: 꽃 화려하다 flower magnificent 夏하: 중국 하나라 china Ha-nation				東동: 동쪽 봄 주인 east spring, owner master 西서: 서쪽 서양 west western 二이: 다음 같다 following as same 京경: 수도 크다 capital big great			

053. 산천은 영원하리 (배망면락 부위거경)

　필자의 선산은 시골 마을 연촌 뒷산이다. 선조들 묘는 경치 좋은 산자락 여러 곳에 각자 흩어져 고인의 직계 자손 나름 명당자리라 여겨 오던 곳에 있었다. 집성촌 문화와 농경사회를 벗어난 산업화와 정보화시대에 이르러, 자손들이 전국 각지, 세계 도처에 거주하게 되었다. 자손들은 한식 즈음의 시제나, 추석 명절에 많은 묘지를 찾아가 성묘하거나, 벌초하기도 쉽지 않았고, 백 여분에 가까운 선조를 납골당이 아닌, 납골묘 형식(화장하여 유골함에 유분과 기념문 넣음)으로 하나의 묘지에 합묘하여 한 군데로 모시게 되었다. 선산은 나지막한 산이지만 배산임수(배망면락, 부위거경)로 시골치곤, 교통이 좋아 찾아보기도 편리한 곳이다. 선산에는 북카페(도서관 카페 제실 용도), 주차장, 조형물, 꽃동산, 포장된 임도, 작은 휴식공간과 전망대인 연휴정이라는 정자까지 있다. 우리는 선산을 창조공원이라 부른다. 제사 지내는 건물(제각)은, 옛날 명칭에서 벗어나, 북카페 등 여러 명칭 중 협의하여 선택 후 정하고, 후손들이 즐거워하는 기념관이 되고, 더불어 자손들 모두의 고향이 되길 바란다.

053. The mountain-stream and nature will last forever

　My ancestral graveyard is a back of mountains of rural village Yeonchon. The ancestors' tombs were scattered in various scenic mountains and were in the honor-place where they were regarded as the direct descendants of the deceased. In the era of industrialization and information, which is out of the culture and agricultural society of the village, the descendants have lived all over the country and all over the world. The descendants visited many cemeteries during the Korean ceremony and Chuseok holidays, and it was not easy to visiting their ancestor's grave(Seongmyo) or to cutting the weeds around a grave(Beolcho), The ancestors close to a hundred minutes were gathered in a cemetery in the form of a crypt-grave(Put bone-powder and memorials in the ashes-bowl by cremation), not a crypt-room, and were brought to one place. Seon mountain is not that high, but there is a lake in front of this mountain, which looks very rural but because of the good road infrastructure it is easy to go there. There are sufficient parking facilities, sculptures, flower gardens, paved forest-road, small resting spaces and even a pavilion nearby. A observation platform where you can take a rest, it is called Yeonhyujeong. Another name for Seonsa is Chang-Cho park. The building, referred as Jegak, is a memorial hall. In addition, I hope that this place would be like a home for all the descendants.

背 배	邙 망	面 면	洛 락	浮 부	渭 위	據 거	涇 경
bae	mang	myeon	rak	bu	wi	geo	gyeong
등	퇴	낮	낙수	뜰	물이름	의지할	물이름
deung	toe	nat	naksu	tteul	mulireum	uijihal	mulireum
back	mountain	front	water	float	water	will	water
105. 동경은 뒤로 북망산, 앞에 낙수가 있고				106. 서경은 위수와 경수 두 갈래 물줄기가 합하는 근거지에 있다			
East capital is back in Bukmangsan mountain, front in Naksu stream				West capital is located on the base where Wisu, Gyeongsu, and two-way water stream are combined			
배경背景	북망北邙	화면畵面	낙양洛陽	부상浮上	경위涇渭	근거根據	경수涇水
back-ground	bukmang mountain	screen	city name	catch the public eye	whole story of an affair	basis	river name

背배: 배반 배경 betrayal backdrop
邙망: 북망산 bukmang mountain
面면: 앞 겉 front external
洛락: 낙수 fall-water

浮부: 가볍게 덧없다 light fleeting
渭위: 위수 wisu of water name
據거: 근거 증거 ground evidence proof
涇경: 통하다 흐르다 through run

054. 가끔은 해변 구경도 (궁전반울 루관비경)

산악인은 산이 있어 산에 오른다고 한다. 한국의 유명 등산가 고상돈도 이와 다르지 않았다. 운동을 위해, 건강을 위해, 높은 곳에서 전망을 보기 위해 등등, 그럴싸한 명분이 아니었다. 그냥 산이 좋은 것이리라. 남녀가 한눈에 반하듯이 그 사람이 그냥 좋은 것이리라. 눈에 보이는 것은 언제나 가까운 땅이나 방바닥, 벽, 책이다. 다람쥐 쳇바퀴 돌듯이 말이다. 이러한 감옥 같은 생활을 하다 보면 스트레스가 누적될 수 있다. 어쩌다 한 번쯤은 확 트인 곳을 보고 싶을 때가 있다. 높은 산 위에 올라가서, 거기서도 더 위, 안전한 바위 꼭대기, 또는 해변의 모래사장에서 저 멀리 수평선을 보고 싶으리라. 보통 사람이고 평범한 일상이니 어찌 하겠는가. 전국 삼천리강과 산 방방 곳곳 유랑인 김삿갓은 아니라도, 다리 힘 있을 때, 하고 싶을 때 시간 내서 둘러보는 것(루관비경)도 좋으리라.

054. Sometimes the beach view

Mountain climbers are said to climb mountains because of mountains. Korea's famous mountain climber, Gosangdon, was no different. For exercise, for health, for a view from a high place, etc., it was not a good cause. It would be a good mountain. He would be just as good as men and women would be at a glance. What is visible is always the land, the floor, the wall, the book. Like a squirrel wheel. This prison life can lead to a cumulative stress. Sometimes you want to see a place that is open. You'd like to climb a high mountain, and see the horizon further up there, on a safe rocky top, or on a beach sandy beach. What can I do because it is ordinary people and ordinary everyday life? It is not a Kim Sat-gat, who walked all over the country, but it would be good to look around when you still have strength.

宮 궁	殿 전	盤 반	鬱 울	樓 루	觀 관	飛 비	驚 경
gung	jeon	ban	ul	ru	gwan	bi	gyeong
집	전각	소반	우거질	다락	볼	날	놀랄
jip	jeongak	soban	ugeojil	darak	bol	nal	nolral
house	palace	tray	many	upstair	see, look	fly	surprise
107. 진시황 때, 궁전 건물들이 울창한 숲처럼 빽빽하게 있고				108. 루각와 관대는 새가 날고 말이 놀라 솟구치는 듯 화려했다			
At Chin-si emperor, the palace buildings were dense as dense forests				The castle stand and sightseeing deck were gorgeous, with birds flying and horses rising in surprise			
왕궁王宮	신전神殿	기반基盤	우울憂鬱	종루鐘樓	관객觀客	비약飛躍	경이驚異
royal palace	temple	base	melan-choly	bell tower	audience	leap jump	miracle marvel
宮궁: 담 궁궐 wall palace 殿전: 대궐 great-palace palatial-residence 盤반: 대야 쟁반 basin tray 鬱울: 답답할 무성하다 stuffy overgrown				樓루: 망루 겹치다 누각 watchtower attic palace 觀관: 경치 view landscape scenery 飛비: 오르다 높다 climb high 驚경: 빠르다 fast quick rapid			

055. 화가와 사진작가 (도사금수 화채선령)

　해변가에서의 석양 갈무리, 설악산의 경이로운 단풍, 한라산 백록담의 신비로움들, 여행 자유화 바람타고, 중국을 경유하여, 우리의 영산이라는 백두산 천지의 웅장함, 아름답고 놓치고 싶지 않는 경치를 보면 화가가 되고(도사금수) 싶을 때가 많았다. 쉽게 볼 수 없는 백두산 천지는 애국가 첫머리서부터 수없이 노래 불렀던 구절이라, 언제나 궁금했던 신비로움의 산이다. 그런 산을 본 것만으로도 내 인생의 영광이고 행운이라 여겼다. 해 보고 싶은 것은 태산처럼 많으나 인생은 짧으니, 아쉬울 뿐이다. 요즘 직장인이라면, 예전보다 휴가도 많고 공휴일도 많아 여행도 많이 다닐 수 있다. 거기다 아이티 기술도 발달하여 일순간을 포착하여 간직할 수(도사금수, 화채선령)도 있다. 인간성도 함께 성숙한다면 지상 낙원처럼 좋은 세상이 아닐까.

055. Painter and Photographer

　There were many times that I wanted to become a painter when I saw the magnificentness of Baekdu Mountain, which is our Mountain of soul, via China, when I saw the liberalization of travel, and the beautiful and unforgettable scenery, the wonderful autumn leaves of Mt. Seorak, with the sunset on the beach, and the scenery that we do not want to miss. Baekdusan Mountain, which can not be easily seen, is a verse that has been rekindled countless times since the beginning of the national anthem, and it is a mountain of mystery that I always wondered. I thought it was the glory and luck of my life just to see such a mountain. I want to try it like Taesan, but life is short, so it is only a pity. If you are an employee these days, you can travel a lot because you have more vacations and holidays than before.

In addition, IT technology has developed and can be captured and kept for a moment. If humanity matures together, it will be a good world like paradise on earth.

圖 도	寫 사	禽 금	獸 수	畫 화	彩 채	仙 선	靈 령
do	sa	geum	su	hwa	chae	seon	ryeong
그림	그릴	새	짐승	그림	채색	신선	신령
geurim	geuril	sae	jimseung	geurim	chaesaek	sinseon	sinryeong
painting	draw	bird	animal	painting	coloring	hermit	spirit
109. 봉황 등 상상 속 동물과, 십장생 짐승들을 그렸고				110. 이러한 궁전의 벽에, 신선과 신령스럽게 색칠하여 그렸다			
He painted Imaginary animals such as phoenix, and the ten-year-old beasts				On the walls of these palaces, they were painted with freshness and divine coloring			
시도試圖	사진寫眞	금수禽獸	맹수猛獸	만화漫畫	광채光彩	선녀仙女	성령聖靈
try attempt	photo	birds& animals	wild beasts	comic	rilliance luster	angel nymph	holy spirit

圖도: 그리다 지도 drawing picture map
寫사: 베끼다 모방 copy imitate
禽금: 짐승 날짐승 beast teflying-animal
獸수: 야생동물 wild-animals

畫화: 그리다 채색 drawing coloring
彩채: 무늬 모양 pattern shape figure
仙선: 도교 Taoism
靈령: 영혼 정성 soul sincerity

129

056. 그리운 군대 생활 (병사방계 갑장대영)

어디서나 마찬가지겠지만, 의무 복무인 일반 사병은 진급에 대한 부담이 없어, 군대 내 임무에만 충실하면 되니, 군 생활이 행복했었던 기억이다. 세상은 마음대로 되지 않지만, 예기치 않은 행운은 일어나는 것 같다. 역시 예측 못한 역경도 있으리라. 앞 군번 동료가 고위급 장성 자녀로, 줄 잘 서서 수도권 후방 편하고 좋은 부대에 귀속되었다. 부대에 배치되어 가 보니, 친구가 장교로 있고, 장교가 친구라는 이유로, 나는 졸병이고 계급이 낮다고, 선임병들이 쉽게 건들지 못하는 것 같은 분위기였다. 그러한 분위기를 군 생활 내내 감지할 수밖에 없는 행운이 있지 않았나 싶었다. 가끔 장교들과 회식도 하고 했으니, 선임병과 동료 사병 주변에서 익히 알았으리라. 하지만 특수 조직인 군대이고, 행운은 언제나 곁에 있는 게 아니므로, 조심하고 본분을 다해야 하는 것은 당연하리라. 유구한 역사 속에 군 조직이란 불가피한 조직이고, 현 시대도 마찬가지다. 영화에서처럼, 깃발과 함께 죽 늘어선 병사들, 고대 로마 시대 창과 방패로 싸우는 병사들(병사방계, 갑장대영), 단한번의 인생에서 추풍낙엽처럼 사라져 가는 병사들을 볼 때마다 안타까운 생각이 든다. 상하 엄격한 복종 관계로 자유로운 영혼을 옭아매야 하는 건, 길지 않은 짧은 삶에서 너무 비참하고 안타까운 게 아닐까. 인생은 새처럼 자유롭게 날면서 꿈을 찾아가는 것이 행복이 아닐는지.

056. The longing army time

As everywhere, the general soldier, who must follow a mandatory service, has no burden on promotion. I remember my military life being happy. So I had to be faithful to my duties in the army. The world is not at its disposal, but unexpected luck seems to happen. The former military colleague was a high-level general, standing in line and belonging to a comfortable and good unit in the rear of the metropolitan area. When I was deployed to the unit, because my friend was an officer, and because the officer was a friend, I was a soldier and low class, and the seniors seemed to be unable to touch easily. I wanted to have the luck to sense such an atmosphere throughout my military life. I had a dinner with the officers sometimes, so I would have known it around the senior and fellow soldiers. But it is a special organization, an army, and luck is not always around, so it is natural to be careful and do my duty. Military organizations are inevitable organizations in a long history, and the same is true in the present age. As in the movie, it is a pity to see soldiers lined up with flags, soldiers fighting with ancient Roman spears and shields, and soldiers disappearing like autumn wind leaves in a single life. It is too miserable and sad to have to entrap a free soul in a strict obedience relationship in a short life that is not long. Life would be a happy thing when you can fly freely like a bird and find a dream.

丙 병	舍 사	傍 방	啓 계	甲 갑	帳 장	對 대	楹 영
byeong	sa	bang	gye	gap	jang	dae	yeong
남녘	집	곁	열	갑옷	장막	대할	기둥
namnyeok	jip	gyeot	yeol	gapot	jangmak	daehal	gidung
south	house	side	open	armor	curtain	reply	pillar
111. 황제를 중심으로, 신하들 머무는 집은, 양옆으로 나란히 열려 있고				112. 눈부신 휘장들은 양 기둥 사이에 세워져 있다			
The house where the servants stay, centered on the emperor, is open side by side				The dazzling insignia is erected between the two pillars			
병월丙月	청사廳舍	방청傍聽	계몽啓蒙	갑판甲板	통장通帳	대화對話	영내楹內
byeong-moon between sky	government building	hear audience	enlight-enment	deck	bankbook	convert-sation	inside of home
丙병: 불 셋째 fire third				甲갑: 껍질 병사 첫째, shell soldier first			
舍사: 두다 풀다 put solve free				帳장: 휘장 천막 insignia tent			
傍방: 기대다 옆 lean next				對대: 마주 대답 put-opposite answer			
啓계: 깨닫다 인도하다 realize lead				楹영: 기둥 막사 post barracks			

057. 기타 퉁기는 음악가가 되고 싶다 (사연설석 고슬취생)

여름휴가를 선호도에 따라 계곡이나, 드넓은 바닷가 해수욕장으로 간다. 바닷물 파도가 닿지 않아야 하고, 전망 좋고 자리가 평평하고, 고른 곳에 자리를 잡고 텐트를 친다(사연설석). 해수욕도 좋지만, 여정으로 시장기가 있으니 먹거리부터 찾아 요기를 해야 한다. 항상 머물던 곳을 떠나, 여행하며 먹는 재미가 사실 너무 좋은 것이다. 어디서 들려오는지 모르게, 잔잔한 노래 소리가 메아리친다. 젊음을 발산하는 노래 「해변의 여인」이다. 이어서 「밀짚모자 목장아가씨」, 「모닥불」 노래로 이어진다. 저 멀리서 누군가 기타 연주하고 옆에서 노래도 부르고(고슬취생) 있다. 어린 아이들이 모래 놀이를 한다. 모래 속 조개껍질들이 신기한 모양이다. 찌는 듯한 더위, 짭쪼롬하고 비릿한 바다 바람, 푸른 바다, 각지에서 모여든 여행객, 각양각색의 텐트들, 어릴 때는 모든 게 신기했다. 지나갈 것 같지 않던 한여름도, 흩어져 멀어져 가는 기타 소리처럼 사라지리라.

057. I want to be a musician with a guitar

Depending on your preference for summer vacation, you chose to go to a valley, a wide beach, and a bathing resort. The sea waves should not reach, the view is good, the place is flat, and the tent is settled in the even place. The sea bathing is good, but there is a hungry feeling on the journey, so you have to find food and eat. It is actually too good to leave the place where I always stayed, to travel and eat. Without knowing where it comes from, the sound of a calm song echoes. It is a song that emits youth, "The Woman on the Beach." It leads to "The Straw Hat Ranch Girl" and "The Campfire". From afar someone is playing guitar and singing next to him.

Young children play sand. The shells in the sand seem strange. It was all strange when I was a child, with the hot heat, the salty and fishy-smell sea breeze, the blue sea, the travelers from all over the place, the various tents. The summer, which did not seem to pass, will be scattered and will disappear like a guitar sound that is moving away.

肆 사	筵 연	設 설	席 석	鼓 고	瑟 슬	吹 취	笙 생
sa	yeon	seol	seok	go	seul	chwi	saeng
베플	자리	베플	자리	북	비파	불	생황
baepeul	jari	baepeul	jari	buk	bipa	bul	saenghwang
place	seat	give	seat	drum	harp	blow-play	flute
113. 돗자리를 펼쳐 잔치 자리를 마련하고				114. 하프 같은 현악기를 연주하고, 플루트 같은 관악기를 분다			
We'll spread the mat, make a feast				Play a harp-like string instrument, and play a flute-like wind instrument			
책사冊肆	강연講筵	설치設置	수석首席	고무鼓舞	금슬琴瑟	고취鼓吹	요생瑤笙
book-store	preach place	install	first-chief	inspire stimulate	conjugal harmony	inspire	jade-flute

肆사: 시장 늘어놓다 marketplace spread
筵연: 좌석 돗자리 seat mat
設설: 만들 연회 make banquet party
席석: 깔다 앉음 lay cover sit-down

鼓고: 맥박 연주 두드리다 pulse play tap knock
瑟슬: 거문고 Korean-harp
吹취: 바람 숨쉬다 wind, breathe respire
笙생: 작다 대나무악기 small bamboo-instrument

058. 고궁 관람도 즐거워 (승계납폐 변전의성)

어느 봄날 아이들과 일요일에 덕수궁 나들이를 갔다. 덕수궁은 조선말 순
종왕이 덕이 많은 아버지의 장수를 바라면서 지은 이름이란다. 거대한 대한
문 입구 지나 오른쪽 연못이 있다. 연못 입구 커피숍의 진한 커피 향 유혹을
뿌리치고, 연못 속 작은 섬에 핀 화려한 철쭉꽃으로 눈길이 간다. 작은 오리
가 헤엄치며, 이리저리 어미오리 찾는 듯 바쁘게 물을 가른다. 역사가 숨 쉬
는 함녕전, 덕홍전, 대한제국 역사관인 석조전, 국립현대미술관인 덕수궁 관
들이 우리의 역사를 느껴 보려는 관람객을 말없이 기다리고 있는 듯하다. 석
어당 옆, 바람결에 떨어진 듯, 덜 익은 살구를 몇 개 집어 본다. 운수 좋게, 깃
발과 문을 지키는 병사, 군졸 격식에 맞는, 예식 갓을 쓰고, 다양한 색상의 전
통 의상을 입은, 병사 교대식도 함께 구경하는 행운이 있었다(승계납폐 변전
의성).

058. The enjoy of watching the old palace

One spring day, I went out to Deoksugung Palace on Sunday with my
children. Deoksugung Palace is the name built by King Sunjong at the end
of the Joseon Dynasty, hoping for the longevity of his father. There is a
pond on the right side of the entrance to the huge Korea-gate. The entrance
to the pond The coffee shop is attracted to the dark coffee flavor, and the
eyes are turned to the colorful royal-azalea on the small island in the pond.
A small duck swims around, busy cutting water like looking for a mother
duck. It seems that the museums of Hamnyeongjeon, Deokheungjeon,
the Korean Empire Historical Museum, and the Deoksugung Palace, the
National Museum of Modern and Contemporary Art, are waiting for mutely

visitors to feel our history. Next to the Seokeo hall, I pick up a few less ripe apricots, as if they were falling in the wind. Fortunately, there was a good chance to watch the soldiers' shifts, wearing flags and doors, ceremony hats for military graduation, and traditional costumes of various colors.

陞 승	階 계	納 납	陛 폐	弁 변	轉 전	疑 의	星 성
seung	gye	nap	pye	byeon	jeon	ui	seong
오를	섬돌	들일	섬돌	고깔	구를	의심할	별
oreul	seomdol	deulil	seomdol	goggil	gureul	uisimhal	byeol
go up	stair	enter	stone-step	hat	wave	doubt	star
115. 신하들이 계단을 올라 궁전에 들어가서 구경하니				116. 잔치에 고깔모자 움직임이, 반짝이는 별인 듯 어리둥절하다			
The servants climbed the stairs, entered the palace, and seeing				The movement of the cone hat at the feast is puzzled as if it were a glittering star			
승천陞遷	계급階級	납득納得	폐하陛下	무변武弁	운전運轉	의문疑問	위성衛星
advance -ment	class grade	unders- tand	majesty	sword office	driving	question	satellite

陞승: 나가다 승진 proceed promotion
階계: 사다리 계단 ladder staircase
納납: 바치다 받다 dedicate accept
陛폐: 오르다 서열 rise rank

弁변: 즐거움 joy pleasure
轉전: 돌리다 움직임 turn roll move
疑의: 의혹 wonder suspicion
星성: 세월 many years

059. 인생은 선택의 운명과 함께 (우통광내 좌달승명)

누구나 갈림길에서는 선택을 강요받는다. 필자가 강의를 들었던 철학자이며 계몽가인 안병욱 교수는 인생살이는 수많은 선택의 순간이라 하였다. 심지어 옷을 입을 때라든가, 아침밥을 먹을 때도 밥상에서 여러 반찬 중 선택해야 한단다. 소금과 간장밖에 없는 어려운 시기도 있어 안타깝지만, 선택의 연속이다. 좌로 가야 할지 우로 가야 할지 중간 길로 가야 할지(우통, 좌달), 인생의 갈림길에서 지혜는 목표에 집중이다. 요즘은 네비게이션이 있어 올바른 목적지에 도착하도록 잘 안내하고 있다. 앞으로는 인공 지능에 의해서 인생의 네비게이션이 등장할 수도 있지 않을까 싶다. 그래도 목표는 꿈과 희망에 따라 각자 본인이 정해야 한다. 인생의 네비게이션은 선각자들의 많은 책(광내=도서관 명칭, 승명=도서관 옆 기숙사)일 것이다.

059. Life is the fate of choice

Everyone is forced to choose at the crossroads. Professor Ahn Byung-wook, a philosopher and enlightenmentist who I listened to the lecture, said that life is a moment of many choices. Even when you wear clothes, or when you eat breakfast, you have to choose from various side dishes at the table. It is a shame that there are difficult times with only salt and soy sauce, but it is a series of choices. Whether to go left or right or middle, wisdom at the crossroads of life is focused on goals. Nowadays, there is navigation, so we are well guided to get to the right destination. In the future, I think that the navigation of life may appear by artificial intelligence. Still, the goal should be set by humans according to their own dreams and hopes. The navigation of life may be many of the prophets' books (The Gwangnae is the name of the library, The SeungMyeong is the dormitory next to the library).

右 우	通 통	廣 광	內 내	左 좌	達 달	承 승	明 명
u	tong	gwang	nae	jwa	dal	seung	myeong
오른	통할	넓을	안	왼	통달할	이을	밝을
oreun	tonghal	neolbeul	an	oen	tongdalhal	ieul	balgeul
right	pass	wide	inner	left	pass	join	bright

117. 오른쪽으로 가면, 광내라는 도서관이 있고				118. 왼쪽으로 가면, 학자들이 책을 보며 머무는 승명이라는 곳이 있다			
To the right, there's a library called Gwangnae				On the left, there is a place called the seungmyeong where scholars stay in the book			

우측右側	교통交通	광고廣告	시내市內	좌측左側	달성達成	승계承繼	설명說明
right side	traffic	advertise -ment	down- town	left side	achieve	succeed	explana -tion

右우: 서쪽 돕다 west help assist	左좌: 왼쪽 멀리하다 left-side stay away
通통: 오가다 사귀다 come and go date	達달: 엇갈리다 보내다 conflicting send
廣광: 퍼지다 광범위한 spread broad	承승: 받들다 건지다 respect pick-up
內내: 들이다 아내 let in wife	明명: 나타나다 깨끗하다 appear clean

060. 사색의 즐거움, 독서 삼매경 (기집분전 역취군영)

책 읽는 즐거움. 독서 삼매경처럼 사고의 즐거움은 거의 중독의 마력이다. 필자도 한때 독서하지 않고 성공할 수 있을까 라고 고민한 적이 있다. 노력하여 찾아보니, 독서하지 않고, 유명해지거나, 성공한 사람을 찾을 수 없었다. 공자는 주역을 백 번 이상 읽고도 아쉬워했다 한다. 나폴레옹이나 이순신장군, 고려 말 최영장군, 위런버핏, 빌게이츠 등 수많은 영웅들(역취군영)은 영민하고 학식을 쌓고 밤샘하며 독서하는 학구파들(기집분전=책이 가득한 도서관)이다. 그런데 세상은 어지럽다. 많은 시간이 흐른 지금도 왜 이리 인간은 잔인하고 가혹하고 불지옥을 만드는지 궁금할 따름이다. 세계적 갈등을 중재하기 위한 유엔이라는 평화조직 등 여러 기구도 있지만 말이다. 동서양과 남북을 불문하고, 권모술수와 배반이 춤추고 있다. 유구한 역사 속에 누적된, 서로의 원한이 근본이겠지만, 명분은 국민을 위하고 평화라 한다. 사바세계에서의 천국이란, 무지개 같은 유토피아로 백과사전에나 나오는 단어일 뿐이다.

060. The Pleasure of Thinking, a state of abandoning the mind and concentrating on reading

The pleasure of reading books, like concentrating on reading, the pleasure of thinking is almost the magic of addiction. I have also wondered if I could succeed without reading books. I tried and found that I could not find anyone who did not read, became famous, or succeeded. Confucius said he was sorry to read The Book of Changes in the Bible more than a hundred times. Many heroes, such as Napoleon, Admiral Yi-sunsin, General Choi-yeong of korea term, Wiren Buffett and Bill Gates, are the school districts(The Gijip-Bunjeon is the book-filled library) who are brilliant, learned, and read at night. But the world is dizzy, and even after a lot of time, I wonder why humans are cruel, harsh, and fire hell. There are several organizations, including the United Nations peace organization, to mediate global conflicts. Regardless of the East and the West and the North and the South, there are dancing trickery and betrayal. The resentment of each other accumulated in the long history is the basis, but the justification is for the people and peace. Heaven in the real world is a rainbow-like utopia, only word that comes out in encyclopedias.

旣 기	集 집	墳 분	典 전	亦 역	聚 취	群 군	英 영
gi	jip	bun	jeon	yeok	chwi	gun	yeong
이미	모을	무덤	법	또	모을	무리	꽃부리
imi	moeul	mudeom	beop	tto	moeul	muri	ggotburi
ahead	collect	grave	law	also	gather	group	flower
119. 삼황기록 등 모든 고전을 모아 준비하였고				120. 많은 인재들이 모여들었다			
All the classics, including the Three Emperors, were collected and prepared				Many talented people gathered			
기존旣存	시집詩集	고분古墳	고전古典	역시亦是	취합聚合	군중群衆	영웅英雄
existing	poetry book	old tomb	classic	also	collect	crowd masses	hero

旣기: 쌀 미리 rice beforehand already
集집: 이르다 가지런하다 reach arrange
墳분: 언덕 둑 크다 hill bank big large
典전: 책 본보기 book model

亦역: 모두 그래도 all total but still
聚취: 누적 저축 cumulate save store
群군: 많은 군중 친족 many herd relative
英영: 인재 장식 talent decoration

061. 두문불출의 추억 (두고종례 칠서벽경)

노무현 대통령이 암자에서 고시 공부했다 하듯, 두문불출에 대한 우리 조상들의 거룩한 태생만큼이나 남다른 추억(두고종례)이 있다. 인생의 전환기적인 나이에 교과서를 외워야 했다. 머릿속에는 나름 나 자신과 가문과 나라가 보이기도 하고, 가끔 사색거리가 되기도 하였다. 이러한 그림이 필자를 지탱 했으리라. 돌부처처럼, 조금의 흐트러짐, 작은 빈틈으로 잘못하면 무너질 수 있으니, 심지를 굳게 해야 했다. 늦겨울부터 초겨울까지, 계절 변화의 냄새와 작은 창으로 보이는 별과 달이 가끔 대화하는 친구였다. 인생은 장거리 경주라 했다. 달리기 초등학교 대표로 출전한 바 있다. 장거리는 나와의 싸움이다. 매일매일 새롭게 자신과, 괴롭지만 즐기면서 싸워야 한다. 석가모니의 보리수나무 아래 좌선과 비할 바는 아니지만, 정신적 육체적으로 온갖 방해꾼들이 수시로 기웃거린다. 이걸 이겨 내는 필자의 비법은 책 속으로 들어가는 것이다. 그리고 구름과 별과 달과 시골향기가 매력적이고, 좋은 친구였다.

061. The memories a stay-at-home life

Just as Ex-president Roh Moo-hyun studied at the hermitage, there are extraordinary memories for me as our ancestors' holy births on the stay-at-home life. I had to memorize textbooks at a turning point in my life. In my head, I can see myself, my family and my country, and sometimes it became a contemplation. These paintings would have supported me. Like a stone Buddha, a little distraction, a small gap, could collapse, so I had to solidify my mind. From late winter to early winter, the smell of seasonal change and the stars and moon seen as small windows were occasional conversational friends. Life was called a long-distance race. I was a representative of running elementary school. Long distance is a fight with me. Every day you have to fight with myself, with pain, but with pleasure. It is not comparable to the sit still for Zen-editation under the barley tree of The Sakyamuni-Buddha, but mental and physical all kinds of interrupters are snooping from time to time. My secret to overcoming this is to enter into books. And clouds, stars, moons and country scents could be my attractive, good friends.

杜 두	藁 고	鍾 종	隷 례	漆 칠	書 서	壁 벽	經 경
du	go	jong	rye	chil	seo	byeok	gyeong
막을	짚	쇠북	글씨	옻	글	벽	경서
makeul	jip	soebuk	geulssi	ot	geul	byeok	gyeongseo
protect	straw	drum	text	lacquer	book	wall	bible
121. 글씨는 두백도 초서, 종요의 예서가 있고				122. 대나무에 옻칠하여 쓴, 벽 틈 사이에서 찾은 경전이 있다			
The writing is a brief and rapid of Dubaekdo handwriting, wave-shaped of Jongyo and writing				There is a scripture found between the walls, written in bamboo with lacquer			
두절杜絶	맥고麥藁	종유석 鍾乳石	하례下隷	칠판漆板	서류書類	벽화壁畵	경제經濟
interrup-tion	straw of barley	stalactite	servant	black-board	document	wall painting	economy
杜두: 팥배나무 감당 adzuki-bean persimmon 藁고: 마르다 원고, dry manuscript 鍾종: 술병 bottle of wine 隷례: 노예 부하 slave subordinate				漆칠: 삼가다 검다 refrain avoid abstain black 書서: 쓰다 장부 글씨 write book letter 壁벽: 담 울타리 절벽 wall fence cliff 經경: 법 이치 law reason			

062. 행운, 결코 바라지 말자 (부라장상 로협괴경)

필자에게 운이 좋았던 때가 여러 번 있었고, 죽을 고비를 넘긴 경우도 몇 번 있었다. 그러다 죽으면 인생은 종료된다. 종교적이 아닌 현실적으로, 다시 부활할 수 없는 것이 사람이기 때문이다. 행운은 최선을 다한 다음에, 스스로 오는 것이지, 바란다고 오지 않는다. 자기의 일에 전력을 다하라, 그리고 하늘의 명령을 기다리라는, 진인사 대천명과 같다. 어려서 고향 금평 개울에서 여름에 친구들과 물놀이 하며 놀다, 개울 중간 커다란 바위 아래 작은 구멍이 있었고, 그 물속 바위 구멍으로 아이들이 드나들며 노는데, 필자도 구멍을 통과하려다, 머리는 나오고, 몸이 끼어, 나오질 못했던 순간에, 상처 나는 몸부림으로 겨우 빠져나와 죽음 직전을 경험했던 운 좋은 사건이 있었다. 중년의 나이에 졸음운전 후 죽음의 문턱에서 깨어났던 운 좋은 사건, 그 후 운전 중에는 졸음 쫓는 방법으로 껌 씹는 것을 철칙으로 여기며 실천하고 있다. 지금 생각해도 아찔하기만 하다. 지금 삶은 행운스런 덤이라 본다. 사람에게 행운은 자주 오지 않는 법이다. 운을 바라지 말고 한 순간이라도 조심해야 하리라. 비운의 홍길동, 임거정, 홍경래, 전봉준 등 참 안타까운 인재들(장상)이며 슬픈 역사의 희생자들이 문득 떠오른다. 지금 세상은 자기의 노력에 따라 성취할 수 있는 시대라 본다. 글로벌 기회의 시대, 젊은 날의 유혹들을 잠시 붙들어 매 놓고, 학문에 매진하면 목표에 맞는 성취의 기회는 반드시 오리라.

062. Dont expect a good luck

There were many times I was lucky, and there were several times I passed the death penalty. Then, when you die, your life ends because you are a human who can not be revived, not religious, but realistically. Luck comes after doing its best, coming on its own, not wishing. Do your best in your work, and wait for the command of heaven, like the Jininsa-Daecheonmyeong. As a child, I played with my friends in the summer in my hometown Geumpyeong stream, and there was a small hole under a large rock in the middle of the stream, The kids are playing in and out of the rock hole in the water, I was trying to get through the hole, but my head came out, my body was stuck, and at the moment I could not get out, there was a lucky event that I barely escaped with a wounded struggle and experienced the death before. I'm lucky event to have woken up at the threshold of death after drowsy driving at a middle age, After that, during driving, chewing gum is considered a rule of law and practice. I think it's a bit of a dizzying thing. I think life is a lucky thing. Luck does not often come to a person. Do not wish luck, but be careful for a every moment. It is a sad talent such as Hong Gil-dong, Lim Geo-jeong, Hong Gyeong-rae, and Jeon Bong-jun of emptiness, and the victims of sad history suddenly come to mind. The world now is an era that can be achieved according to its own efforts. In the era of global opportunities, the temptations of young age period must be held for a while, and if you are committed to learning, the opportunity to achieve your goals will come to you straight.

府 부	羅 라	將 장	相 상	路 로	挾 협	槐 괴	卿 경
bu	ra	jang	sang	ro	hyeop	goe	gyeong
관청	벌일	장수	서로	길	겹	회화나무	벼슬
gwancheong	beolil	jangsu	seoro	gil	gyeop	hoehwanamu	byeoseul
office	stand	general	together	road	overlap	sophora	office
123. 관청에는 장수와 정승들이 모여 있고				124. 길 양쪽에는 관리들의 집들이 줄지어 았다			
The government office has a group of longevity and high-ranking officials				There are rows of officials' houses on both sides of the road			
행정行政	염라閻羅	대장大將	상대相對	도로道路	협공挾攻	괴화槐花	추기경樞機卿
administration	yama	admiral/captain	partner/mate	roadway	pincer attack	sophora-flower	cardinal

府부: 마을 창고 village storage
羅라: 그물 돌다 순찰 net web turn patrol
將장: 인솔자 장래 leader guide future
相상: 보다 돕다 see look help assist

路로: 방법 연줄 고달프다 way connection tire
挾협: 끼우다 같이 insert together
槐괴: 삼공 three-officer
卿경: 귀족 noble aristocratic

063. 호구지책의 시대 변화 (호봉팔현 가급천병)

가족과 함께 대형 서점도 가고, 탑골공원 같은 역사 유적지도 볼 겸 시내 나들이를 가곤 한다. 광화문 거리 분수대, 청계천 개울가, 사람 눈을 끌고, 유혹하는 매력이 있다. 예쁜 꽃을 무심코 바라보듯이, 물보라가 어린 시절처럼 멋있다. 광화문광장에 이순신장군 동상이 보인다. 왕조 시절에는 영화나 삼국지에 나오듯이, 중생을 왕이나 귀족의 사치품이나 장식품으로 여기는 때가 있었다. 왕은 공적이 크고 유능한 관료 선비에게 고을과 병사와 노예를 쌀 배급하듯, 나눠 주었다(호봉팔현, 가급천병). 지금은 월급을 매개로 대기업 종업원이나 공무원 등을 공개 채용하고 있으니, 비슷한 듯, 뭔가 좀 달라지지 않았나 싶다.

063. The changes of the times in a means of livelihood

I go to a large bookstore with my family, and I go to a historical site such as Topgol Park and go out to the citycentre. There has a charm that attracts people's eyes and seduction by famous places such as Gwanghwamun Street Fountain, Cheonggyecheon Stream . Just as I look at flowers casually, the spray is as cool as my childhood. A statue of Admiral I Sun-sin is seen at Gwanghwamun Square. During the dynasty, there were times when the regeneration was regarded as a luxury or ornament of the king or noble, as in movies and the Three Kingdoms. The king gave out the high-ranking, capable bureaucrats, as if he were distributing rice, soldiers and slaves. Now people are hiring employees of large corporations and civil servants from government offices through salary, I think something has changed.

戶 호	封 봉	八 팔	縣 현	家 가	給 급	千 천	兵 병
ho	bong	pal	hyeon	ga	geup	cheon	byeong
지게	봉할	여덟	고을	집	줄	일천	군사
jige	bonghal	yeodeolp	goeul	jip	jul	ilcheon	gunsa
A-frame	seal /shut	eight	county	house	give	thousand	soldier

125. 황제는 친척이나 공신들에게 많은 마을을 주고				126. 그 가문에 많은 병사를 주었다			
The emperor gave many villages to relatives and meritorious people				He gave the family many soldiers			
문호門戶	봉지封紙	팔순八旬	군현郡縣	가족家族	월급月給	천금千金	파병派兵
open the door	bag /pack	eighty years	state -county	family	pay /salary	a lot of money	dispatch

戶호: 집 문 주민 house door resident	家가: 마나님 가문 elderly-lady family
封봉: 주다 봉투 give envelope	給급: 넉넉하다 더하다 enough add
八팔: 나누다 share divide	千천: 많다 반드시 lots of much surely
縣현: 매달다 hang suspend	兵병: 병사 전쟁 soldier war battle

064. 구경거리와 낭만 (고관배련 구곡진영)

　필자가 기타를 늦깎이로 배우면서 부르는 「밀짚모자 목장 아가씨」 노래다. 시원한 밀짚모자 포푸라 그늘에 양(소) 떼를 몰고 가는 목장의 아가씨, 실버들 바람에 머리카락 휘날리며, 연분홍 빛 스카프, 입술에는 살며시 웃음 머금고, 널따란 푸른 들판, 하늘엔 조각구름 지나가네. 기타 치면서 소몰이 하던 어린 시절을 생각하며 가사를 조금 개작해 보았다. 옛날 지위 높은 관리가 갓을 쓰고, 말이 끄는 수레를 타고, 울퉁불퉁한 비포장도로를 달리며 갓 모자 반짝이는 장식의 휘날리는 모습(고관배련, 구곡진영)이 멋있고, 아름다웠으리라.

064. The romance

　It is a song 「Miss Straw Hat Ranch」 that I call while learning guitar late. lady of the ranch who drives sheep (cattle) time in the poplar-tree shade of a cool straw hat, she was flying my hair in the wind of the wicker, a pink scarf, with a little smile on her lips, a vast blue field, passing by a piece of cloud in the sky. While playing guitar, I changed the lyrics a little bit, thinking about the childhood of the cow. There is an old-fashioned man, wearing a hat, and riding a horse-drawn cart. It would have been nice and attractive to see the man with the glittering decorations of the hats on unpaved roads.

高 고	冠 관	陪 배	輦 련	駒 구	轂 곡	振 진	纓 영
go	gwan	bae	ryeon	gu	gok	jin	yeong
높을	갓	모실	수레	몰	바퀴통	떨칠	갓끈
nopeul	gat	mosil	sure	mol	bakwitong	tteolchil	gatggeun
high	hat	serve	wagon	drive	wheel	shake	hat-string
127. 고위급관리들이 모자를 쓰고, 황제의 수레를 몰고 가고				128. 말을 몰아 수레바퀴가 구를 때 마다 모자가 흔들린다			
High-ranking officials wear colorful hats and drive the emperor's cart				The hat shakes every time the wheel rolls on the horse			
최고最高	왕관王冠	배석陪席	여련輿輦	용구龍駒	추곡推轂	진동振動	주영珠纓
best/ highest	crown	it with	king- wagon	handsome -horse	support	vibration /shake	string of jewels

高고: 비싸다 훌륭하다 expensive excellent
冠관: 관례 성년 customary adulthood
陪배: 더하다 쌓다 add build stack
輦련: 가마 cart palan-quin

駒구: 돌다 망아지 달리다 turn foal run
轂곡: 수레 밀다 wagon push
振진: 열다 흔들리다 open wave swing
纓영: 장식 끈 decorative-string

065. 입신양명과 건강이 효도 (세록치부 거가비경)

결혼하여 자식을 갖게 되니, 세상살이가 자연의 섭리대로 흐르는 듯하다. 결혼 전에는 부모의 마음을 절감하지 못했다. 차츰 아버지 역할이 지대함을 알아가게 되어, 매사가 나만의 일이 아닌 가족 공동체 의식의 책임성을 깨닫게 되는 듯하다. 이와 함께 부모는 자식 키우는 재미와 보람, 고통과 시련 속에서 살아가는 듯하다. 어머니는 더욱 그렇다. 아버지 날 낳으시고 어머니 날 기르시니, 라는 시가 있듯이 말이다. 낳기보다 기르기가 훨씬 어렵다. 갓난아기 때부터 성인이 되기까지, 성인이 되고, 함께 늙어 가면서도 어머니는 자식을 길러야 하는 본능이 있다. 그러니 기르는 어머니가 아버지보다 평생을 두고 고생한다. 자식은 힘없고 가엾은 어머니를 잘 모셔야 하리라. 한평생 찌들려 살고, 어렵게 사는 것에 대한 보상으로, 자식이 잘되어, 가문을 일으키길 바라는 마음이 누구든 다 있기 마련이다. 어머니의 혼신 기도를 느껴, 주변의 달콤한 유혹을 물리치고, 주경야독 노력해야 하지 않을까.

065. Success, Fame and Health is dutiful to one's parents

When I got married and have a child, the world seems to flow according to the providence of nature. Before marriage, parents' minds were did not feel keenly. Gradually, father's role seems to be getting to know the greatness, and everything seems to realize the responsibility of the family community consciousness, not my own work. In addition, parents seem to live in the fun, reward, pain and trials of raising their children. Mother is more so, as there is a poem called "Father gives birth to me and my mother raises me." It is much harder to raise than to give birth. From birth to adulthood, to adulthood, and to grow old together, the mother has an instinct to raise her child. So the mother who raises suffers for a lifetime more than her father. The sons and daughters must be good at the helpless and poor mother. As a reward for living worn a lifetime and living hard, there is a desire for all the children to be good and to raise the family. I must feel my mother's heart, thus I should defeat from sweet temptations around me, and try to do my best for my life.

世 세	祿 록	侈 치	富 부	車 거	駕 가	肥 비	輕 경
se	rok	chi	bu	geo	ga	bi	gyeong
인간	녹봉	사치할	부자	수레	멍에	살찔	가벼울
ingan	nokbong	sachihal	buja	sure	meonge	saljjil	gabyeoul
human	pay	luxury	wealth	wagon	yoke	fat	light
129. 고위급관리는 많은 봉급을 받아 대대로 부유하고 잘 살아				130. 그들은 좋은 수레와 살찐 말을 타고 다닌다			
High-level officials are rich and well-off, paid a lot of salaries for generations				They ride a good cart and a fat horse			
세계世界	관록貫祿	사치奢侈	부귀富貴	기차汽車	능가凌駕	비만肥滿	경중輕重
world	dignity/ stipend	extrava- gant /indulge	wealthy& noble	train	superb /exceed	obesity /over- weight	light weight
世세: 대를 잇다 generation connect 祿록: 복 기록하다 fortune record 侈치: 거만하다 proud haughty 富부: 풍성 재산 enrich property				車거: 도르래 바퀴 pulley wheel 駕가: 탈것 임금수레 vehicle king-wagon 肥비: 거름=비료 manure 輕경: 조급 경솔 impatient hasty indiscretion			

066. 임무에 대한 충실 (책공무실 늑비각명)

임무에 충실하다 보면 별이 보인다. 호랑이는 죽어 가죽을 남기고, 사람은 죽어 이름을 남긴다고 한다. 인생의 의미를 누구나 고민해 봤을 것으로 생각한다. 어찌 보면 이름을 남긴들 무엇 하겠는가 라고 단순히 여길지 모르나, 안 남기고 자연 속으로 사라지면 또 무엇 하겠는가. 인생에 대한 시간을 허비하지 말고 최선을 다 하면서 살라는 의미리라(책공무실). 태어나서 단 한 가지라도 후세 또는 인류 발전에 공헌함이 인간으로서 동물과 다름이 아닐까. 끝없는 노력에도 공헌함이 없다면, 후손을 남긴 업적만으로 미완성 마무리 지을 수밖에 없으리라. 사실 인격이 잘 갖춰진 후손 양육이 위대한 업적일 수 있다. 공공을 위하여 멸사봉공하면 후세가 그 이름을 새겨 역사로 기억하고 기념하리라(늑비각명). 작게는 가족과 자손이 기억하고, 문중이 기억하고, 크게는 고을이 기억하고, 나라가 기억하고, 온 세상이 기억하리라. 지식을 갖춘 사람(지자본위)으로 큰 공헌에 목표를 두면 작고 사사로운 욕심이나 갈등은 큰 뜻에 소멸되고 괴로움은 감소하게 되리라.

066. Fidelity to duty

When tigers die, leave its own leather, and when people die and leave their own names. I think everyone has thought about the meaning of life. In some ways, what do you do if you leave your name, but what if you disappear into nature without leaving it? It means not to waste time on life but to live while doing your best. Perhaps the contribution to the development of the future or human being is different from that of animals as a human being. If you do not contribute to endless efforts, you will have to finish the unfinished work with the accomplishments that left your descendants. In fact, nurturing a well-equipped descendant can be a great achievement. If you serve humanity, you will remember and engrave the name in the monument and celebrate it with history. Smallly, family and descendants remember, the their kinsfolk remembers, and the big town remembers, the country remembers, and the whole world remembers. If you aim at a great contribution to the world with a great found of knowledge, small and private greed or conflict will disappear and the suffering of life will decrease.

策 책	功 공	茂 무	實 실	勒 륵	碑 비	刻 각	銘 명
chaek	gong	mu	sil	reuk	bi	gak	myeong
꾀	공	무성할	열매	새길	비석	새길	새길
ggoe	gong	museonghal	yeolmae	saegil	biseok	saegil	saegil
wit	merit	increase	fruit	engrave	tombstone	engrave	engrave
131. 공로 실적이 많고, 노력하여 충실히 쌓으면				132. 꽃다운 이름을 새기고, 글을 지어 기념 돌에 새겨, 후세에 알린다			
If you have a lot of achievements and you try hard and build up faithfully				Inscribed with a flowery name, written in a stone, and informed in the future			
산책散策	성공成功	무림茂林	실험實驗	미륵彌勒	비석碑石	시각時刻	감명感銘
walk	success	lush-forest	experi-ment	Maitreya	grave-stone	time	impress

策책: 채찍 기록 계획 whip record plan
功공: 업적 보람 achievement reward
茂무: 우거지다 왕성 풍족 overgrown full rich
實실: 결실 실적 fruitful result

勒륵: 묶다 굴레 tie bind bridle
碑비: 돌기둥 비문 stone-column inscription
刻각: 깎다 모질다 cut uppity unaffectionate
銘명: 금석문 metal-print

067. 촛불의 아우성 (반계이윤 좌시아형)

모처럼 필자의 시대, 시국 관련 사건을 다뤄 본다. 시위에 참여는 안 했지만 2017년 나라를 어지럽힌 지도자를 응징하고자 광화문 광장에, 인도의 간디의 철학처럼, 비폭력 평화로운 촛불 시위를 몇 달 동안 지속적으로 하여, 쿠데타가 아닌, 사법적 단죄 분위기가 조성되었다. 과거 보수 정권에서는 비무장 비폭력 데모에 공권력의 폭력적인 진압과는 많이 달라지고, 참여도 과거에는 대학생 위주였으나, 전 연령층으로 폭넓어졌다. 나라 걱정하는 사명감과 투철한 정의감으로 무장한, 몇 사람의 끈질긴 노력으로 국정농단의 실마리를 찾아 그 진상이 만천하에 드러나게 되었다. 힘없는 시민의 함성, 그들이 나라를 바로 세운 공신이리라. 반계와 이윤이 공신이듯이 말이다. 그 공으로 이윤은 아형(고위직 명칭)이라는 재상이 되었으나, 우리의 시민(공헌한 국민)은 어느 직책에도 등용되지 않았다, 역사의 중심이 된 것으로 자부심과 긍지를 가질 만하다. 그 이후에도 끊임없이 반민족 친일수구 기득권 세력은 권모술수로 기웃거린다. 그냥 평범한 국민으로 염려하고 조바심 나고 행복해하면, 민족과 조국을 위하는 것일까.

067. The crying with candles

I finally mention about the situation related important events in my period. I did not participate in the demonstration, but in 2017 we tried to punish the leader who disturbed our country, Like Gandhi's philosophy in India, nonviolent peaceful candle light protests continued for months, which can create an atmosphere of judicial condemnation, not a coup. In the past conservative regimes, the violent suppression of public power was much different from the violent suppression of unarmed non-violent demonstrations, and participation was widened to all ages, although it was mainly college students in the past. Armed with a sense of mission and a sense of justice that worries about the country, with the persistent efforts of some people, the truth of the influence peddling was found in the whole world. The cries of the powerless citizens, they would be the men of merit who set the country straight. As if the Ban-gye and I-yun were merit. With that credit, I-yun became a secretary of ahyeong(the name of high office), but our citizens(the people who contributed) were not enrolled in any position. It is the center of history and deserves pride and dignity. After that, the anti-ethnic pro-Japanese vested interests of the conservative force are constantly snooping around with the trickery. If you are just worried and anxious and happy about a counrty as an ordinary person, is it really for my country?

磻 반	溪 계	伊 이	尹 윤	佐 좌	時 시	阿 아	衡 형
ban	gye	i	yun	jwa	si	a	hyeong
돌	시내	저	다스릴	도울	때	언덕	저울대
dol	sinae	jeo	daseuril	doul	ttae	eondeok	jeouldae
stone	stream	that	govern	help	time	slope	scale

133. 반계(강태공)은 주나라, 이윤은 은나라 황제를 도왔고				134. 그들은 고위관직(아형)에 올랐다			
Bangye (Gang Tae-gong) helped the emperor of Ju state and I-yun helped the emperor of Eun state				They were brought to the rank of high-ranking official (Ahyeong)			

반계磻溪	계곡溪谷	이시伊時	관윤官尹	보좌補佐	시절時節	아첨阿詔	균형均衡
fisherman /angler	valley/ canyon	specific -time	office	assistance /aid	days /season	flatter /adulate	balance/ equilibrium

磻반: 돌화살촉 stone-arrowhead	佐좌: 권하다 advise recommend
溪계: 산골짜기 개천 mountain-valley stream	時시: 세월 엿보다 years time peek
伊이: 이 this	阿아: 구룽 구석 hill corner
尹윤: 바르다 right correct	衡형: 달다 멍에 weigh yoke

068. 상속의 지혜 (엄택곡부 미단숙영)

우리는 부모로부터 귀중한 신체를 물려받았지만, 재산을 상속받기도 한다. 부모의 재력에 따라 많고 적음이 다를 뿐 아무런 노력도 없이 자식이라는 이유로 상속이나 증여 또는 부채를 받는다. 혹여 받기를 바라는 마음이나 욕심은 처음부터 버리는 게 자기 인생 발전에 매우 좋으리라. 자기 것인 몸도 아끼면서 잘 관리하여 건강을 유지하는 것이 효도하는 것이고 본인에게도 이롭다. 혹여 부모는 차등이나 딸 아들 구별 없이 증여, 상속의 도리를 하는 것이 자녀들에게 보여 줄 수 있는 마지막 모범이다. 여유 불문하고, 일정 부분은 공적인 곳에 기부하거나, 자손이 공유하여 대소사 모임 때 활용하면 좋을 듯하다. 옛날 중국 왕조시대며 농경시대일 때, 주나라 성왕이 곡부라는 거대한 땅(차후 노나라가 됨)을 공자가 성현이라 말할 정도의 능력이 훌륭한 주공이라는 사람에게 물려주었다. 주공은 물려받은 곡부 땅인 노나라를 아주 잘 다스려 후세에까지 명성이 자자하다.

068. The wisdom of inheritance

We inherit valuable bodies from our parents, but we also inherit property from our parents. Depending on the financial situation of the parents, children have different situations, thus they receive inheritance, gift or debt. It would be very good if children has self-development from the beginning. It is filial piety and beneficial for me to maintain my health by managing my body well while saving my own body. Parents are the last example that can be shown to their children by giving gifts and inheritance without distinction between sons and daughters. Regardless of the extra, it would be good to donate some parts to public places or share them with their descendants and use them at matters great and small meetings. In the old Chinese dynasty and agricultural era, the King of Zhu Dynasty passed on a huge land called Gokbu(becoming the next No-nation) Confucius calls The Ju-Gong saint to a man who had the ability to be a saint. The Ju-Gong has a good reputation until the later generations by managing his heritage very well, which is the land of the inherited Gokbu.

奄 엄	宅 택	曲 곡	阜 부	微 미	旦 단	孰 숙	營 영
eom	taek	gok	bu	mi	dan	suk	yeong
가릴	집	굽을	언덕	작을	아침	누구	경영
garil	jip	gupeul	eondeok	jakeul	achim	nugu	gyeongyeong
cover	house	bend	slope	small	morning	who	manage

135. 주공이 곡부라는 나라를 잘 다스렸고	136. 단(주공의 이름)이 아니면 누가 잘 다스렸겠는가?
The Lord(Ju-gong) ruled the country of Gokbu	Who would have ruled well if it were not the Dan (the name of Ju-gong)?

엄연奄然	귀댁貴宅	희곡戱曲	구부丘阜	미소微笑	원단元旦	시숙時孰	운영運營
sudden	your home	play /drama	sloping -hill	smile /grin	newyear- morning	time to ripen	manage

奄엄: 문득 다스리다 abruptly control
宅택: 거주하다 reside live
曲곡: 노래 옳지 않다 song music unright
阜부: 크다, 번성 big great prosper

微미: 숨기다 자세하다 hide detail
旦단: 밤새다 all-night
孰숙: 익다 친절 ripe kind
營영: 변명 경작 excuse defense cultivate

155

069. 도덕재무장의 시대 (환공광합 제약부경)

　자주 보는 편은 아니지만, 복싱 경기나 코미디 프로를 보면서 박장대소하고 즐거워하거나 슬퍼한다. 같은 화면을 보는데도 이런 차이가 있다. 스포츠나 오락프로는 엄격한 규칙과 규율에 의한 것으로 뭐라 할 일이 아니다. 사람의 기본 마인드가 화합이 중요하고 측은한 마음 씀씀이가 소중하다. 한없이 이런 태도를 견지할 수 없는 게 사회생활이며 인생이지만, 세상에는 천사도 있지만 악마도 있으며, 어떤 사람은 도움 주면서 행복을 느끼고, 다른 어떤 사람은 고통스러워하는 모습을 보면서 쾌감을 느끼기도 한다. 약한 것을 도와주고 기울어지는 것을 일으켜 세워 주는 것(제약부경)은 사람의 일상적 인간의 정이지만, 안타깝게도 주의해야 하지 않을까. 사회의 양심 다양성을 선택하기보다는 국가와 인류의 무사태평을 위하여, 과거에 깨달은 철학자가 주장하였던 도덕 재무장처럼 더욱 예법 교육을 강화하였으면 하는 마음이다. 이런 주장의 글을 쓰면 구태스런 꼰대 마인드라 할 듯하다.

069. The age of moral rearmament

　I do not often watch TV, but I feel thrilled, happy or sad when I watch boxing games and comedy shows. There is a difference in seeing the same screen. Sports and entertainment are not strictly governed by rules and disciplines. The basic mind of a person is important for harmony and the compassion. It is the life that can not keep this attitude forever. There are angels in the world, but there are demons as well. Some people feel happy while helping, and others feel pleasure when they see pain. It is the daily human nature of a person to help the weak and to raise the tilting, Unfortunately, I should be careful. For the unscathed criticism of the nation and mankind rather than choosing the diversity of conscience in society, I hope that the moral rearmament that the philosophers who have realized in the past will strengthen the education of etiquette more. If you write this argument, it would seem to be an old-fashioned mind.

桓 환	公 공	匡 광	合 합	濟 제	弱 약	扶 부	傾 경
hwan	gong	gwang	hap	je	yak	bu	gyeong
굳셀	벼슬	바를	합할	건질	약할	붙들	기울
gudsel	byeoseul	bareul	haphal	geonjil	yakhal	butdeul	giul
strong	duke	right	unify	rescue	weak	help	decline
137. 제나라 황제, 환공이 천하를 통일하여 많은 장군들을 모아				138. 약한 나라를 구해 주고, 기우는 나라를 도왔다			
Je state Emperor, Hwan-gong, unified the world and gathered many generals				Saved a weak country, helped a leaning country			
환웅桓雄	공연公演	광정匡正	통합統合	경제經濟	약화弱化	부양扶養	경청傾聽
Korean ancestry father	perfor-mance/ concert	correct	unite/ integrate	economy	weaken	support	listen /hear

桓환: 위엄 크다 dignity large big great
公공: 공평 귀인 fair impartiality noble
匡광: 구원 돕다 salvation help aid
合합: 모으다 일치하다 gather coincide

濟제: 구제 나루 건너다 relieve ferry across go over
弱약: 쇠약 날씬 debilitation thin slim
扶부: 도울 받치다 help support prop
傾경: 기울다 탕진 tilt lean dissipate

157

070. 인생의 전환기적 감격의 순간 (기회한혜 열감무정)

내 인생에 감동적인 것은 뭐가 있을까. 이런 계기로 기억 속을 뒤져 보니, 정월 대보름날 전후로 어려서 추위도 못 느낀 채 밤늦도록 불놀이 하다 집에 오니, 어머니가 콩 주머니에 어름 박힌 손발을 넣어 주던 기억, 시골 어린이가 생전 처음으로 냄새도 색다른 도시로, 그것도 뭔가 모를 남다르게 유학 갔던 추운 겨울날의 번쩍했던 깨달음, 중간 기말고사 볼 때 시험지만 보면 답이 툭툭 떠오르던 뿌듯했던 기억과 공부의 즐거움, 가슴 설레며 연애하여 결혼한 감동, 애어른 같은 딸 아들 키우는 보람과 기쁨, 자식들 결혼한 기쁨, 손자들을 낳았을 때의 감동, 가장 최근의 신인상으로 작가 등단한 감동, 강원도 설악산 자락 어느 가을날, 홍천 골자기의 빈틈없는 단풍, 벌어진 입을 다물 줄 몰랐던 단풍 구경 등, 위와 같은 사건들은 생애 최고의 감동으로 떠오른다. 남들에게는 시시하고 별로인 것처럼 보일지라도 그때도 감동적이고, 지나고 보니 더욱 더 필자에게는 감동적인 장면들이고 사건들이다. 그야말로 열렬하게 느끼는 감동(열감무정)이다.

070. The moment of transitional impression in life

What is touching moment in my life? When I was young around a period of the New Year's full moon day, I played with fire late at night, then I came home, my mother put my cold hands and feet into a warm blanket, The flash of a cold winter day when I was a rural child, I went to a city for the first time I smelled with a different smell from the city in my life, I've been studying abroad and don't know disparately anything about that, When I look at the midterm finals, I see the joy of studying and the memories that I was proud of the test answer only came to mind, I am thrilled and married, and I am rewarded and happy to raise my daughter's son like adult, The joy of marriage, the impression of having a grandchildren, I'm impressed by the latest new writer, One autumn day at the foot of Seorak Mountain in Gangwon Province, the tight maple leaves of Hongcheon valley, and the maple leaves that did not know how to shut up. These events are the best impressive moments of my life. It seems to be a trivial for others, but it was touching at that time, and it becomes more and more touching for me. It is a feeling of passion.

綺 기	回 회	漢 한	惠 혜	說 열	感 감	武 무	丁 정
gi	hoe	han	hye	yeol	gam	mu	jeong
비단	돌아올	한수	은혜	기쁠	느낄	호반	고무래
bidan	dolaol	hansu	eunhye	gibbeul	neuggil	hoban	gomurae
silk	return	Han-water	favor	delight	feel	military	rake
139. 네 명(기리계)의 현자가, 한 나라 태자의 지위를 회복시켰고				140. 부열이라는 현인은, 황제 무정을 감동시켰다			
The four (Gi-ri-gye) sages restored the status of Han-state's prince				Buyeol sage moved the Emperor Mujeong			
기언綺言	회복回復	한자漢字	수혜受惠	화성설 火成說	감정感情	무기武器	장정壯丁
flowery language	recovery replace	Chinese character	benefit	vulcanian -theory	emotion -feeling	weapon /arms	strong -man
綺기: 무늬 아름답다 pattern design beauty 回회: 소용돌이치다 swirl curl 漢한: 한나라 Han-nation 惠혜: 어질다 베풀다 benign give bless				說열: 말씀 따르다 talk word follow 感감: 감동 impress 武무: 굳세다 자랑 strong firm proud 丁정: 일꾼 넷째 worker fourth			

071. 정신수양과 호구지책 (준예밀물 다사식령)

필자가 앞에서 말했지만, 언행이 모범인 지식인을 보면 마음도 편안해지고 숙연해진다. 학창 시절 어느 겨울날 원불교 서울 원남지부 교당에 사촌 누이 조효경이 교무선생으로 있는 인연으로 숙식하였다. 깨끗하고 잘 정리된 작은 방에 중년의 남자 원로 교무선생의 단정하고 흐트러짐 없는 자세를 보고, 받은 깊은 감명이 지금도 생생하다. 그는 책을 보거나 서류 정리하거나, 본인의 일만 하고 있을 뿐 아무런 말이 없었다. 원불교 교리, 인과보응의 신앙문에 사요가 있다, 중생에게 요구되는 네 가지로 자력양성, 지자본위(지식인 위주), 타 자녀 교육, 공도자(공공 봉사자) 숭배가 나온다. 지자본위는 공부를 노력해서 많이 하고, 뛰어난 덕과 재주 있는 인재가 리더가 되어, 힘써 일하는 분위기가 되면 참으로 푸근하고 평화로우리라. 즉, 준걸한 인물과 선비가 빽빽하게 많으면 편안하고 얼마나 좋은 세상(다사식령)일까 하는 감탄의 말이다.

071. Spiritual Training and Means of livelihood

As I mentioned before, when I meet an intellectual person who has elegant and neat words and actions, my mind becomes comfortable and mature. One winter day during school days, my cousin, Cho Hyo-kyung's relationship as a teacher, stayed at the Wonnam branch of Won Buddhism Seoul, The deep impression I received from seeing the neat and uncompromising posture of a middle-aged male elder teacher in a clean and well-organized small room is still vivid. He was only looking at books, organizing documents, and doing his job, but he had no words. In Won buddhist doctrine, In the faith text of cause and effect reward, There are four things required by people: self-sufficiency, intellectual-oriented, other children's education, and public service worship. Intellectuals work hard and work a lot, and excellent virtues and talented people become leaders, and when they become working hard, they are very warm and peaceful. In other words, it is an admiration that how comfortable and good for the world can be if there are a lot of excellent people and a lot of scholar people.

俊 준	乂 예	密 밀	勿 물	多 다	士 사	寔 식	寧 녕
jun	ye	mil	mul	da	sa	sik	nyeong
준걸	어질	빽빽할	말	많을	선비	이	편안할
jungeol	eojil	bbaek bbaekhal	mal	manheul	seonbi	i	pyeonanhal
hero	merciful	dense	not	many	scholar	this	comfort
141. 재주와 덕이 뛰어난 인재들이 힘써 일하고				142. 대들보처럼 많은 학자들이 있어, 세상이 참으로 평안하구나			
Excellent people with talent and virtue work hard				There are many scholars like the beam, and the world is truly peaceful			
준재俊才	준예俊乂	비밀秘密	물론勿論	다행多幸	박사博士	식경寔景	안녕安寧
brilliant person	excellent -man	secret	of- course /sure	luckily	doctor /pro	fine -view	hi/hello

俊준: 뛰어나다 높다 excel talent high tall
乂예: 풀 베다 다스리다 cut chop manage
密밀: 자세하다 은밀 detail clandestine
勿물: 아니다 문지르다 no not rub scrub

多다: 뛰어나다 good great excel
士사: 벼슬 무사 officer soldier
寔식: 참으로 두다 truly put let
寧녕: 문안 공손 hello health polite

072. 쉽고 즐거운 것부터 성공의 맛을 (진초경패 조위곤횡)

마중물처럼, 모든 일은 쉽고 즐거운 것부터 접근하여 성공의 맛을 보면 달콤하다. 필자가 넘어져 발목이 삐끗하여 진통으로 한의원 찾고, 정형외과에 가서 엑스레이 검사 후 물리치료 받고, 깁스하고, 보름 정도 지나니 괜찮아져 정상적으로 걸을 수 있었다. 어릴 때는 넘어져 피가 나고 쓰리고 고통스러워도 별로 지장이 없었던 것이, 세월이 흐르고 몸이 굳어지니 고장이 나면 오래 가는 구나. 살다 보니, 어려움과 곤란한 일이 육체적 정신적으로 잊을 만하면 온다. 어찌 하겠는가 역경과 곤경이 일상적인 삶이거늘(조위곤횡), 불평해 봐야 좋아질 리 없으니, 즐기면서 손님대접을 해 줘야 마음이라도 편하리라 (진초경패). 좌절하지 않고, 완급 조절하여 해법을 찾아야 하리라.

072. The taste of success begins by easy and pleasant challenge

Like the priming water, everything is sweet when you approach easy and pleasant challenges and taste the success by them. I fell down and my ankle was twisted, so I went to an oriental clinic with analgesics, I went to an orthopedic surgeon, then I received physical therapy after X-ray examination, gibbs for two weeks. Finally, I was able to walk normally. When I was a child, I fell down, bleeding, bitter and painful, but it did not interfere for me. However, it's going to last long if it breaks down since I became older. Difficulties and troubles come again when I would forget all the pain after all. What should you do? Adversity and plight are everyday life, and it can not be good to complain, so it will be easy to enjoy it and treat the guests. I will not be frustrated, I will have to find a solution by adjusting the suspension.

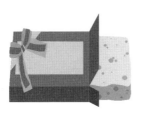

합격과 샴페인

晉 진	楚 초	更 경	覇 패	趙 조	魏 위	困 곤	橫 횡
jin	cho	gyeong	pae	jo	wi	gon	hoeng
나라	나라	바꿀	으뜸	나라	나라	곤할	가로
nara	nara	baggul	eutteum	nara	nara	gonhal	garo
Jin-state	Cho-state	change	chief	Jo-state	Wi-state	difficult	width
143. 진나라와 초나라는 번갈아 권력를 잡았고				144. 조나라와 위나라는 연합 전술 실패로 어려움을 겪었다			
The Jin and the Cho nation alternately took power				The Jo and the Wi nation suffered from the failure of the coalition tactics			
진주晉州	고초苦楚	경신更新	패권覇權	조지훈 趙芝薰	상위象魏	피곤疲困	횡단橫斷
jin-villige	hard-ships	renewal	hege-mony	Korean poet	great palace gate	tired	cross/traverse

晉진: 나아가다 억누르다 go forward, suppress
楚초: 매질 회초리 hit beat, switch whip
更경: 다시 개선 again repair improve
覇패: 우두머리 head leader

趙조: 뛰어넘다 jump over beyond
魏위: 능히 하다 adept
困곤: 가난하다 poor needy
橫횡: 제멋대로=방자 impudence self-indulgence

073. 악법도 법일까 (가도멸괵 천토회맹)

역사 공부를 하다 보면 화나는 일이 하나둘 아니다. 유사 이래 국가 간 전쟁 없던 적이 없었다. 크고 작은 분쟁들이 끝없이 지구촌 각지에서 벌어지고 있다. 민족적 종교적 이념적으로 수천 년에 걸쳐서 앙금이 누적되어 있으니, 긁어 부스럼처럼, 국가 간에도 조금만 건드려도 옛날 감정이 생생하게 살아나고, 북받치니 그럴 수밖에 없으리라. 부모 형제 등 수십만에서 수백만 명이 죽고 희생당하고 불구가 되었으니 세월이 흐른다고 잊혀 지기 어려울 것이다. 심지어 건너편 나라를 멸하러 갈 테니 길 좀 빌려 달라(가도멸괵)는 일까지 벌어지고 있다. 그러니 권모술수 약육강식 거짓과 도둑이 끝이 없고, 정의가 무너져 내리고 있다. 급기야 야구처럼 스포츠에서 조차 도루할 때 못 잡으면 도둑 성공하여 박수 받는 규칙이 만들어지고 있는 실정이다. 사람들의 마인드를 무의식중에 불법의 오묘함 속으로 빠져들게 하는 것이 아닐까. 악법도 법이라는 왕조시대 철학자의 잘못된 유산이 아니었으면 한다.

073. Is evil law a law?

There is nothing mad about studying history. There has never been a war between nations since the same time. Large and small disputes are endlessly happening all over the world. Ethnic religious ideology has accumulated over thousands of years, so even if you touch a little bit between countries, the old feelings will live vividly, and it will have to be done. Hundreds of thousands to millions of people, including parents and brothers, have died, been sacrificed and crippled, so it will be hard to forget that years will pass. Even the other side of the country is going to be destroyed, so I am asking for a road. So, there is no end to the lie and the thief, and justice is falling down. If players can cheat other team even in sports like a baseball game, people attend to a rule to be applauded for the success of the thief. I hope that it is not the wrong legacy of the law.

假 가	途 도	滅 멸	虢 괵	踐 천	土 토	會 회	盟 맹
ga	do	myeol	goek	cheon	to	hoe	maeng
빌릴	길	멸할	나라	밟을	흙	모을	맹세
bilril	gil	myeolhal	nara	balbeul	heulk	moeul	maengse
rent	way	destroy	Goek-state	step on	land	gather	swear
145. 진 황제는 우 나라 길을 빌려, 괵과 우 나라를 멸망시키고				146. 승리 후 천토에 장군들을 모아, 충성 맹세하게 하였다			
Emperor of Jin borrowed the path of U-nation, destroyed Goek and U-nation				After the victory, he gathered the generals in the Cheon-to and made them swear allegiance			
가정假定	용도用途	소멸消滅	괵국虢國	실천實踐	토지土地	회의會議	동맹同盟
suppose/ assume	use	extinc-tion	Goek-state	practice	real-estate	confer-ence	alliance /union

假가: 거짓 교환 false untrue exchange
途도: 도로 road street
滅멸: 멸 끄다 없애다 ruin off eliminate
虢괵: 호랑이발톱자국 tiger-claw-marks

踐천: 짓밟다 이행 tread fulfillment
土토: 뿌리 땅 root ground earth
會회: 모이다 모임 gathering meeting
盟맹: 맹세하다 pledge promise vow

165

074. 법의 헤게모니 (하준약법 한폐번형)

조원선 조부께서 원불교에 귀의하여 창시자 소태산 대종사와 원불교 기반 수립에 기여하고, 원불교 성서인 교전에 대화내용이 수록되어 있다. 자손 대대로 할아버지의 은혜를 입고 있다. 원불교 교리에 사은사요가 있다. 네가지 은혜는 천지은, 부모은, 동포은, 법률은이다. 법률 은혜는 사람으로 태어나 조금만 지내다 보면 많은 혜택을 받음을 몸소 느끼게 된다. 그러나 현실은, 법을 전공하는 사람이 교묘하게 해석하여 이용하는 경우가 너무 많아 선량한 사람이 오히려 억울한 누명을 쓰고 피해를 보고 있다. 인간의 악행은 끝이 없어 보인다. 춘향전에 나오는 악마 사또 스토리처럼 말이다. 선량하고 정의로운 법공무원은 상을 주고, 사악한 법공무원을 단죄할 장치가 있어야 하리라.

074. The hegemony of law

Cho Won-sun of my grandfather returned to Won Buddhism and contributed to the establishment of the foundation of Won Buddhism and the founder of Sotaesan Daejongsa Temple, It contains conversations in the engagement of the Won Buddhism Bible. He is receiving his grandfather's grace for generations of descendants. There is the four graces and four demands to the Won Buddhism doctrine. Four graces are heaven and earth, parents, compatriots, laws. Legal grace is born as a person and feels that you will receive a lot of benefits if you spend a little time. However, the reality is that many people who major in law use it in a clever way, so good people are suffering from unfair accusations. Human evil seems endless, like the evil sato story of Chunhyangjeon. A good and justified law officer should be rewarded and there should be a proper device in order to condemn an evil law officer.

신세대 악마

何 하	遵 준	約 약	法 법	韓 한	弊 폐	煩 번	刑 형
ha	jun	yak	beop	han	pye	beon	hyeong
어찌	좇을	묶을	법	나라	폐단	번거로울	형벌
eojji	jocheul	muggeul	beop	nara	pyedan	beongeoroul	hyeongbeol
how	follow	tie/bind	law	Han-state	abuse	complex	penalty
147. 신하 소하는 간단한 법을 따르고				148. 한비는 복잡하고 매서운 법을 지켜 해를 당했다			
The servant So-ha follows a simple law				Hanbi was harmed by the complicated and harsh laws			
기하학 幾何學	준법遵法	계약契約	법원法院	한인韓人	폐습弊習	번잡煩雜	형법刑法
geome-try	law-abiding	contract /sign	court	Korean -people	bad-habit	comple-xity	criminal law

何하: 꾸짖다 scold
遵준: 따라 배우다 learn-along
約약: 약속 promise
法법: 방법 규정 way rule regulation

韓한: 한국 Korea
弊폐: 악 쓰러지다 해질 vice fall collapse
煩번: 괴롭다 어지럽다 pain dizzy chaotic
刑형: 벌하다 punish penalty

167

075. 보호능력은 지덕체로 (기전파목 용군최정)

군에 입대하여 논산 훈련소에서 본격 훈련 들어가기 전 대기병으로 약 일 주일 정도 머무른다. 그 기간에 해병대 가고 싶은 사람 있으면 나오라든가, 그 시절엔 어떤 대기병을 지목하여 뽑혀 가는 경우도 있었다. 해병대 교육은 안 받아 봤지만 거의 살인적인 훈련이라고 말한다. 쉽게 말해서 인간을 독종으로 만드는 것이다. 어렸을 적에 동네 말썽꾼 술주정뱅이 어른이 있었다. 개판 치며 험하게 행동하는, 저 사람은 군대를 개병대 나왔다고 마을 사람들이 수군거렸었는데, 나중에 알고 보니 해병대 출신이다. 사실 군인은 점잖은 신사가 아니라, 최정예 훈련 받아 전쟁을 해야 하는 것(용군최정)이 최종 임무일 것이다. 국가든 개인이든 보호능력은 지덕체로 튼튼히 뭉쳐야 하리라. 다음 페이지의 시도 용감무쌍한 이야기다.

075. The protection ability contains knowledge, morals, and body

A Korean man joins the army and stays for about a week as an waiting soldier before entering full-scale training at Nonsan Training Center. In that period, if there was anyone who wanted to go to the Marine Corps, there were cases where they were picked up by pointing out some waiting soldiers. I have not received Marine-soldier education, but it is almost a murderous training. In short, it is to make humans poisonous. When I was a child, there was a drunken adult who was a troublemaker in the neighborhood. He's a dog-behavior, rough-headed man, he's got an soldier out of the dog-Marine military, The villagers were talking about him, and later it turned out that he was a Marine soldier military. In fact, soldiers are not decent gentlemen, but it is the final task to be trained to fight the war. Whether it is a country or an individual, the protection ability must be firmly united with wisdom, virtue, and physical strength. The poem on the next page is also about a brave story.

起 기	翦 전	頗 파	牧 목	用 용	軍 군	最 최	精 정
gi	jeon	pa	mok	yong	gun	choe	jeong
일어날	자를	자못	기를	쓸	군사	가장	정밀할
ileonal	jareul	jamot	gireul	sseul	gunsa	gajang	jeongmilhal
rise	cut	unbalance	raise	use	soldier	extreme	finely
149. 백기와 왕전은 진나라, 염파와 이목은 조나라의 뛰어난 장수다				150. 군사훈련과 전략이 가장 치밀하고 능란했다			
Baekgi and Wangjeon are a Jin nation general, and Yeompa and Imok are excellent generals of Jo nation				Military training and strategy were the most detailed and slick			
기원起源	전발기 翦髮機	편파偏頗	목장牧場	이용利用	군인軍人	최고最高	정성精誠
origin/ root	haircut machine	impartial	ranch	use/ utilization	soldier	best maximum	earnest sincerity
起기: 깨어남 출세 awake advancement 翦전: 화살 가위 arrow scissors 頗파: 치우치다 biased lean-toward 牧목: 양치기 shepherd sheep-raising				用용: 용도 도구 use tool 軍군: 진치다 군대 encamp army military 最최: 최상 제일 best first 精정: 찧다 pound			

076. 헌신과 명예라는 선물 (선위사막 치예단청)

강원도 홍천 여행하다 강재구 공원을 우연히 가게 되었다. 지금도 교과목 한 페이지에 있는지 모르지만, 군대서 부하 훈련병이 훈련 도중, 잘못 투척한 수류탄을 온몸으로 덮쳐 주위 병사들을 구했다는 살신성인의 의인이다. 그 후 세월이 흐른 어느 날 동인천의 한 골목길을 가다 창영초등학교에 강재구 모교라고 새겨져 있는 기념석 문구를 보게 되었다. 그래서 강재구 소령이 인천 출신임을 알게 되었다. 자기 고향, 더구나, 자기 학교 출신이다 하면 느끼는 감동이 훨씬 강하여, 그 영향을 많이 받기 마련이다. 다른 관계없는 사람보다는, 그 사람의 행적을 찾아보고 참고할 것이다. 그러면 그 사람과 닮고 싶은 마음이 발동하여 인생의 물줄기가 변화될 수도 있을 것이다. 강재구 그 짧고 굵은 인생의 명예가 교과서와 그림과 동상으로 전국 곳곳에 널리 알려졌다(치예단청, 선위사막). 어려서부터 유적지 여행을 하고, 그곳에 세워진 안내 글이나, 선지자의 자서전 등, 독서를 많이 하여 인생의 귀감으로 삼아 활용하면 좋으리라.

076. The gift of devotion and honor

I went to accidentally Gang Jae-gu's park while traveling in Hongcheon, Gangwon-do. He is a righteous person who saved the soldiers around him by covering the grenades that were mistakenly thrown during the training. After that, one day, I went to an alley in Dongincheon and saw a memorial stone phrase engraved on Changyoung Elementary School as Gang Jae-gu's alma mater. So I learned that Major Kang Jae-gu was from Incheon. If you are from your hometown, especially your school, you will feel much stronger and will be affected by it. Rather than other unrelated people, they will look for and refer to the person's actions. Then, the mind that wants to resemble the person may be triggered and the water stream of life may change. Gang Jae-gu The short and thick honor of life is widely known throughout the country for its textbooks, paintings and statues. It would be good to travel to historical sites in the young age, and it would be good by reading a lot of autobiographic books to find their own role-model.

宣 선	威 위	沙 사	漠 막	馳 치	譽 예	丹 단	靑 청
seon	wi	sa	mak	chi	ye	dan	cheong
베풀	위엄	모래	사막	달릴	기릴	붉을	푸를
bepeul	wieom	morae	samak	dalril	giril	bulkeul	pureul
give	dignity	sand	desert	run	honor	red	blue

151. 앞 명장들은 위엄이, 멀리 사막까지 알려졌고	152. 그들의 초상화를 남겨, 명성이 후세까지 전해지고 있다
The masters were known for their dignity, for distance to the desert	Remaining their portraits, fame is being passed down to later generations

선전宣傳	권위權威	사과沙果	대막大漠	상치相馳	영예榮譽	단풍丹楓	청년靑年
adver- tise	autho- rity	apple	large desert	conflict	honor /glory	foliage	young -man

宣선: 떨치다 알리다 spread inform 威위: 권세 힘 authority power 沙사: 봉황 사막 phoenix desert 漠막: 넓다 아득하다 wide faraway	馳치: 지나가다 pass go past 譽예: 명예 기념 honor remember 丹단: 정성 sincerity earnest 靑청: 무성하다 thick dense

077. 통솔을 위한 조직 (구주우적 백군진병)

학생들을 가르칠 때다. 필자가 과대표와 부대표만 선출하여 통솔하려니, 전혀 진척이 없고, 학생들은 과대표 말도 잘 듣질 않고, 뺄질거리기만 한다. 과대표와 함께, 다섯 조직의 책임자를 지명하여 운영하니, 책임감으로 협력이 잘됨을 알게 되었다. 연구조, 축구조, 청소조, 농구조, 오락조 등, 강제로 조 편성하지 않고, 학생들의 특성과 선호도에 따라 자발적 참여로 구분하였다. 한쪽 쏠림 되는 조는 가위, 바위, 보로 승복하도록 하고, 개월 단위로 재개편하도록 하였다. 그리하니 실적도 좋아지고 화합도 잘되었다. 아래 나오는 시처럼, 아홉 개의 큰 고을과 백 개의 작은 마을로 나눠서 나라를 다스렸다 (구주우적)는 것과 비슷한 개념 아닐까. 그들은 땅 덩어리가 크면 다스리기가 어려우니, 나눈 고을에 조직을 만들어 책임자를 정하여 다스렸음이다. 모세혈관과 같은 마을의 대표와 반장이 있듯이 말이다. 상기와 같은 조직 편성 발상은 몇 권의 조직론을 읽고 참고하였다.

077. The organization for leadership

It was time that I taught students. I had no progress at all, and students did not listen to the leader from thier own classmates and did make a trouble although I elected a class leader and the sub-class leader. With the representative of the class, I appointed the five organizations to be in charge, and I realized that the cooperation was well done with responsibility. The group was not organized by force, there consisted five teams such as research group, soccer team, cleaning team, basketball team, entertainment group, etc., and it was divided into voluntary participations according to the characteristics and preference of students. One side of the group was to be restored to scissors, rocks, and beams, and to be re-configured on a monthly basis. So the performance improved and the harmony was good. Like the poem below, it is similar to the concept of ruling the country by dividing it into nine large towns and a hundred small villages. They are hard to control when the land mass is large, so they have set up an organization in the divided city and ruled the person in charge. Just as the representatives and chiefs of the village, it seems such as capillaries. The idea of organization as described above inspired by several organizational theories.

九 구	州 주	禹 우	跡 적	百 백	郡 군	秦 진	竝 병
gu	ju	u	jeok	baek	gun	jin	byeong
아홉	고을	임금	자취	일백	고을	나라	아우를
ahop	goeul	imgeum	jachwi	ilbaek	goeul	nara	aureul
nine	village	king	trace	hundred	county	Jin-state	manage
153. 진 나라로 통일 후, 아홉 개의 주로 나누어, 통치한 것은 우임금의 업적이고				154. 아홉 개 주를 다시 백여 개의 군으로 나누어 다스렸다			
After unification into the Jin Dynasty, it was divided into nine states, It was the achievement of Emperor U who ruled				Nine states were ruled and divided into more than a hundred counties again			
중구重九	주립州立	우구禹韭	유적遺跡	백화점 百貨店	군수郡守	진시황 秦始皇	병행竝行
Korean holiday =9.9day	built office of state	woogu of grass	ruins/ remains	department store	county headman	emperor jinshi	parallel /both
九구: 모으다 gather together collect 州주: 마을 village town 禹우: 하우씨 Mr. Howe 跡적: 발자국 흔적 footprint step track				百백: 모든 여러 all whole every 郡군: 군청 지역 county office distrct 秦진: 벼 이름 진황 rice name Jin-emperor 竝병: 짝하다 나란히 mate pair side by side			

173

078. 거대함에 대한 인간 심리 (악종함대 선주운정)

고향 연촌마을 앞에, 스님이 바랑(배낭의 불교 언어)을 맨 모습과 닮았다는 중봉산이 있다. 중봉산 능선줄기 따라 이십 여리 가다 보면, 인간의 심리를 압도하는 거대한 불갑산 정상 기암괴석 연실봉이 있으며, 아래로 백제불교 최초 불사로 유명한 불갑사를 품고 있다. 불갑산은 험악하고 인적이 드물어 호랑이가 서식하고 있다는 소문이다. 병풍처럼 둘러진 아름다운 산과 호수 같은 커다란 불갑저수지를 앞에 두고 있다. 고향마을 뒤에는 창령 조씨 북카페 회관과 연촌 마을의 이름을 아우르는 연휴정이라는 정자가 창령 조씨 선산에 아담히 자리 잡고 있다. 연휴정은 창령 조씨 묘량파 종손이며 원광대학교 명예교수 조수현 서예가(대동천자문 참고문헌 참조)의 필체로 현판 하여 기념하였다. 가끔 가는 명절에, 연휴정에서 바라보는 경치는 한 폭의 동양화이며 마음을 힐링하는 안식처다.

078. The human psychology of grandeur

It is the majesty of the greatness that overwhelms human psychology. In front of the rural village in my hometown, there is Jungbong mountain, which resembles the monk with a barang(the Buddhist language of backpacks). If you go along the stem of Jungbong mountain, there is a Bulgap temple famous for Baekje Buddhism's first Buddhist temple, and there is a big mountain called Yeonsilbong behind the temple. It is in front of a beautiful mountain surrounded by folding screens and a large Bulgap-reservoir like a lake. There are a resting platform, calls Yeonhyu-Jeong and a book-cafe, which is for Changryeong-Cho's. They are located in ancestral burial ground at the village of Yeonchon behind the home town. The

Yeonhyu-Jeong(the resting platform) was commemorated by Changryeong-Cho, a descendant of the Myoyangpa, and was commemorated by the handwriting of Emeritus Professor Cho Soo-hyun of Wongwang University. Sometimes I visited my hometown on the vacation of the korean festival days, I watched the scenery in the Yeonhyu-Jeong, it is like a wide oriental paintings and it makes me heal the mind.

嶽 악	宗 종	恒 항	岱 대	禪 선	主 주	云 운	亭 정
ak	jong	hang	dae	seon	ju	un	jeong
큰산	마루	항상	태산	봉선	주인	이를	정자
keunsan	maru	hangsang	taesan	bongseon	juin	ireul	jeongja
large mountain	basis	always	great mountain	ritual	owner	speakl	arber
155. 다섯 개의 산중, 가장 높고 큰 산이 항산과 대산이다				156. 제사는 운운산과 정정산에서 한다			
Among the five mountains, the highest and largest are the Hang-mountains and the Dae-mountains				The sacrifice is held at Unun-mountains and Jeongjeong-mountains			
산악회 山嶽會	종교宗敎	항상恒常	대가岱駕	참선參禪	주제主題	운위云爲	누정樓亭
mountai-neering club	religion /faith	constant	large shape	sit still for meditation	subject /theme	words and behavior	rest-stand

嶽악: 높은 산 high-mountain
宗종: 사당 으뜸 shrine, chief best
恒항: 변함없다 정직 all the time honesty
岱대: 큰 산 large-mountain

禪선: 고요함 좌선 calm sit down and pray hermit
主주: 우두머리 main master host
云운: 운운 말 number of words gossip call
亭정: 조망대 view-stand sightseeing-deck

079. 전통의 매력 (안무자새 계전적성)

필자의 딸, 결혼식을 서울대 입구 낙성대 한국 전통 혼례식장에서 했다. 딸
의 남편이 독일 청년이어서, 한국의 풍습을 보여 주고자 하였다. 전통 결혼식
은 시골에서 보고, 지금까지 구경하기 어려웠는데, 여러 곳에 문의하여 찾아
보니, 서울에 몇 군데 있었다. 모두가 최소 육 개월에서 일 년 전에 예약을 해
야 그나마 토일 등 공휴일에 할 수 있었다. 하루에 한 팀 전통 혼례 행사를 하
였다. 전통 혼례가 아니어도 폐백(한국의 혼례 절차)은 있지만 폐백과 혼례
식 순서에 나무 조각 기러기가 등장한다. 기러기의 세 가지 덕목(안무)인 사
랑의 약속을 영원히 지키며, 멀리 여행하면서도 질서를 지키고 리더가 울면
뒤에서도 따라 화답하는 예를 지키며, 어디에 도착하면 흔적을 분명히 남김
을 본받고자 함일 것이다.

079. The charm of tradition

My daughter, she had a wedding ceremony at the entrance of Seoul
National University in Nakseongdae, it was a traditional Korean wedding
ceremony since her husband is a german man. I tried to show Korean
customs. Traditional weddings were generally seen in the countryside
and it was difficult to see nowadays. I inquired about various places and
found some places in Seoul. Everyone had to make a reservation at least
six months to a year ago so that they could do it on holidays such as
Saturday. A team held a traditional wedding ceremony a day. Even if it is
not a traditional wedding ceremony, there are Pyebaek(korean wedding
procedure: bride's gifts to her parents-in-law), but wooden sculpture geese
appear in the order of the Pyebaek and wedding ceremony, it means

forever keeping the promise of love. If they travel far, so they keep order among groups, and if the leader cries, they keep examples of responding from behind, and if they arrive somewhere, they want to emulate the traces clearly.

鴈 안	門 문	紫 자	塞 새	鷄 계	田 전	赤 적	城 성
an	mun	ja	sae	gye	jeon	jeok	seong
기러기	문	붉을	변방	닭	밭	붉을	재
gireogi	mun	bulkeul	byeonbang	dalk	bat	bulkeul	jae
goose	door	red	marginal	chicken	field	red	wall
157. 안문산과 흙빛 자주색인 만리장성 자새가 있다				158. 만리장성 밖에, 계전과, 한국 지도자 치우가 살던 적성이 있다			
There is Anmunsan and the purple earthy the Great Wall of China of Jasae Village				Gye-jeon, Outside the Great Wall of China, there is Jeok-seong that the Korean leader Chiu resided in			
서안舒鴈	창문窓門	자두紫桃	요새要塞	계란鷄卵	유전油田	적토赤土	성문城門
wild goose	window	plum	fortress	egg	oilfield	red soil	castle gate
鴈안: 가짜 거위 fake goose 門문: 묻다 집안 ask question home 紫자: 자주색 purple violet 塞새: 성채 막다 fortification block				鷄계: 양계養鷄 poultry farming chicken raising 田전: 밭 갈다 field farm garden plow 赤적: 적자赤字 적십자사 deficit the Red Cross 城성: 성벽 castle wall rampart			

080. 사람은, 인연들로 엮여져 (곤지갈석 거야동정)

사람 사는 곳은 인연들로 함께 엮여져 있는 듯하다. 딸이 거주하는 네덜란드에 어쩌다 간다. 옛날이 아니라 몇 십 년 전만 해도 비싼 비용 때문에 전화도 어려웠던 시절이 있었다. 요즘은 시절이 좋아 무료로 언제든 화상 통화까지 할 수 있으니, 감사한 세상이다. 딸집은 3층 같은 2층 집(3개 층 사용)이다. 대부분의 집들이 가든이라는 정원이 있다. 손주 등 아이들이 언제든 안전하게 놀이 할 수 있도록 꾸며져 있었다. 딸의 친구네 도심 아파트에도 가 보니 우리의 테라스 같은 가든이 있었다. 거기서 커피 등 다과와 함께 휴식도 하고 햇볕도 즐기고 있었다. 부부는 생일이라든가 특별한 날은 친구나 동료를 초대하여 가든파티도 하였다. 우리나라 잘 정리된 시골 앞마당 같기도 하다.

080. People, they're tied together by destiny

The place where people live seems to be tied together with relationship. I sometimes went to the Netherlands where my daughter lives. Decades ago, I had a difficult time to call abroad because of the high cost. Nowadays, it is a world of gratitude because it is good to have a good time and can make video calls at any time without costs. The daughter house is a two-story house (using three floors) like the third floor; most houses have a garden. It is decorated so that children, my grandchildren could play safely at any time. I went to my daughter's friend's downtown apartment and there was a garden like our terrace. I was relaxing there with refreshments such as coffee and enjoying the sun. The couple had a birthday or a special day, and they invited friends and colleagues to a garden party, which is like a well-organized countryside front yard in Korea.

昆 곤	池 지	碣 갈	石 석	鉅 거	野 야	洞 동	庭 정
gon	ji	gal	seok	geo	ya	dong	jeong
맏	못	비석	돌	클	들	골	뜰
mad	mot	biseok	dol	keul	deul	gol	tteul
eldest	lake	gravestone	stone	big	field	village	garden

159. 곤지라는 큰 연못과 갈석이라는 큰 산이 있다				160. 거야라는 초원과 동정이라는 호수가 있다			
The Gonji is a large pond, and the Galseok is a large mountain				There is a grassland of the Geo-ya and a lake of the Dong-jeong			
곤충昆蟲	전지電池	석갈石碣	보석寶石	거어鉅魚	야구野球	동굴洞窟	가정家庭
insect /bug	cell battery	tomb- stone	jewel /gem	large fish	baseball	cave cavern	family home

昆곤: 형 자손 older brother progeny	鉅거: 강하다 낚시바늘 strong fishing-hook
池지: 도랑 홈통 ditch gutter	野야: 변두리 시골 marginal outskirts country
碣갈: 선돌 stand-stone menhir	洞동: 골짜기 동네 valley neighborhood
石석: 숫돌 whetstone rubstone grindstone	庭정: 조정 court-garden

081. 희망과 성취의 심리 (광원면막 암수묘명)

노무현 전 대통령을 많은 사람들이 좋아한다. 거짓과 꾸밈이 없다. 소탈한 보통 사람의 이미지가 매력인 듯하다. 대통령이라서 반대편에서는 뭔가 흠을 찾아, 싫어하는 사람도 있으리라. 노대통령은 김해 고향집 앞산들이 드넓고, 바위와 산봉우리가 미묘하며(암수묘명), 아득하고 가물거리는 능선들이, 뱀 능선처럼 보인다며 좋아하였다(광원면막). 산 능선이 용처럼 보인다면 더 이상 오를 곳이 없으니 별로지만, 뱀은 용이나 더욱 큰 봉황이 될 수 있는 가능성에 힘껏 노력의 묘미가 있어 좋으리라는 꿈의 대상이라 하였다.

081. The psychology of hope and achievement

Many people like former president Roh Moo-hyun. He has no lies and decorum. The image of a normal person seems to be attractive. There are people who hate to find faults on the other side because they are presidents. President Roh said, The mountains in front of Gimhae's hometown are wide, the rocks and peaks are subtle, and the ridges that seemed to be distant and lurking, seemed like snake ridges. If the ridge looks like a dragon, there's no place to climb anymore. The snake is a dream object because it has still the charm of effort in the hope of becoming a dragon.

우주선

曠 광	遠 원	綿 면	邈 막	巖 암	岫 수	杳 묘	冥 명
gwang	won	myeon	mak	am	su	myo	myeong
넓을	멀	솜	멀	바위	묏부리	아득할	어두울
neolbeul	meol	som	meol	bawi	moetburi	adeukhal	eoduul
wide	far	cotton	away	rock	summit	faraway	dark
161. 대지는 넓고 멀리 이어져 아득하다				162. 바위와 산봉우리도 깊고 아득하고 어둡다			
The earth is wide and far away				The rocks and peaks are deep, faraway and dark			
광토曠土	원격遠隔	면봉綿棒	막막邈邈	암벽巖壁	암수巖岫	묘묘杳渺	명복冥福
empty& teasing land	remote /distant	cotton -swab	gloomy/ lonely/ lonesome	rockwall /rock face	rock-cave /rock- hole	far-off shape	heavenly bliss

曠광: 멀다 밝다 들판 distance bright field	巖암: 가파르다 낭떠러지 steep cliff precipice
遠원: 선조 하늘 ancestor sky	岫수: 산봉우리 mountain-peak
綿면: 이어지다 connect follow continue	杳묘: 깊숙하다 어둡다 deep dark shadowy
邈막: 아득함 번민 faraway far-off worry	冥명: 밤 night evening

082. 지식축적의 시대 (치본어농 무자가색)

시대가 변하여, 요즘은 주경야독으로, 지식축적이 천하지대본이다. 필자는 농사짓는 사람이 모든 것의 근본이라는 농자천하지대본 인, 농본사회에서 태어나 자라고(치본어농), 산업화 사회에서 가정을 돌보고, 민주화 시대와 정보화 시대를 거쳐, 인공지능화 사회 등 제4차, 제5차 융복합화 시대에 접어들고 있는 시점에서 살고 있는 듯하다. 시대의 변화와 과학의 발달로 그야말로 불가측 시대라 할 만하다. 손주들이 갖고 놀이하는 아이패드나 모바일을 보면 세상이 어찌 변할지 가늠하기조차 어렵다. 예수, 부처, 케인즈, 마르크스, 노벨, 아인슈타인 등 그 누가 헤매고 있는 사람들의 앞길을 안내 할 것인가. 먹고살 수 있으면 평화롭다(무자가색) 했는데, 풀뿌리와 나무껍질을 먹고사는 시절도 아닌(초근목피), 대체로 풍족한 시절에, 도덕적으로 어지러운 세상을 구할 참다운 지도자가 그리워지는구나.

082. The age of accumulation knowledge

The time has changed, so these days knowledge accumulation is the foundation of the world, working by day and studying by night. I was born and raised in a farming society. It seems to live in the era of fourth and fifth fusion in the industrialization society, after taking care of the family, through the democratization era and the information age, and artificial intelligence society. It is a non-available age due to the change of the times and the development of science. It is difficult to even guess how the world will change when we see iPads and mobiles played by grandchildren. Who will guide the way ahead of those who are wandering, such as Jesus, Buddha, Keynes, Marx, Nobel, and Einstein? It is a peaceful time not to worry about hunger, but I miss a true leader who can save a morally dizzying world in a period of abundant times.

AI와 인간

治 치	本 본	於 어	農 농	務 무	茲 자	稼 가	穡 색
chi	bon	eo	nong	mu	ja	ga	saek
다스릴	근본	어조사	농사	힘쓸	이	심을	거둘
daseuril	geunbon	eojosa	nongsa	himsseul	i	simeul	geodul
govern	root	with	farming	try/strive	this	plant	earn
163. 나라를 다스리는 근본이 농사이며				164. 백성에게 심고 거두고, 농사에 힘쓰도록 하였다			
The root of the country is farming				They planted and collected the people, and they worked hard on farming			
통치統治	기본基本	어언於焉	농업農業	업무業務	자자茲者	가동稼動	가색稼穡
rule /reign	basic	short time	agriculture /farming	work /job	now /today	operation	agriculture
治치: 치료 평정 treat cure calm composure 本본: 뿌리 본인 root person 於어: 깨닫지 못하는 사이 unawares 農농: 농부 경작 farmer cultivation				務무: 일 직분 work one's duty 茲자: 무성 더욱 exuberant profuse further 稼가: 농사 벼이삭 farming fallen rice-glean 穡색: 수확 농사 harvest farm			

083. 기술은 평생의 호구지책 (숙재남묘 아예서직)

쌀인 벼 외에 기장, 조, 수수, 잡곡은, 농업사회가 아닌 요즘은 농촌의 들에서 여간해서 보기 어렵다. 그래도 찾아보면 도시나 농촌 어딘가에는 있으리라. 어느 여름날 부천 생태박물관인 자연 생태공원에 갔다. 그곳에는 주위에서 흔히 볼 수 없는 다양한 꽃들과 옛날 시골 영농 도구와 모습들이 많이 갖춰져 있고, 거기다 토끼와 닭, 조랑말, 수억 년 된 커다란 통나무 화석 등도 있어 지루함 없이 구경하기 좋았다. 더구나 기장, 조, 수수 등, 보기 어려운 농작물도 있어 자연 공부하기에 적절한 듯하다. 기장과 조는 전문 농업인이 아니면 구분하기 까다롭다. 기장과 조는 크기와 모양이 거의 같거나 비슷해 보인다. 기장은 찰기장, 메기장, 메조, 차조 등 종류도 다양하다. 이러한 곡식들은 적은 습기에도 잘 자라, 가뭄 들거나 하늘만 바라보는 천수답에 적절한 식물이다. 그래서 그런지 고향 시골 산 가장자리 등 천박한 밭에서 항상 보았다. 옛날 시골은 농기계 등이 발달하지 않아 사람 힘에 의한 순수한 노동력으로 한 농사이니 얼마나 힘든 시대였을까. 농촌에 살았던 어머니는 남편 봉양하고 칠남매 키우느라, 그녀의 손끝이 닳아진 농기구처럼 뭉뚝하였다.

083. Technology is a means of livelihood for a life

It is difficult to see other grains such as rice paddies, millet, glutinous millet, sorghum in rural areas these days. But there must be at somewhere in the city or rural area. One summer day, I went to the Natural Ecological Park, Bucheon Ecological Museum. There were many flowers and old rural farming tools and appearances that are not common around, There were rabbits, chickens, ponies, and large log fossils of hundreds of millions of years old, so it was good to see without boredom. Moreover, there are difficult crops such as millet, glutinous millet, sorghum, and it seems to be suitable for studying nature. The millet and the glutinous millet are difficult to distinguish unless they are professional farmers. The millet and the glutinous millet look about the same size and shape. There are also various types of millet such as chalgijang(glutinous-millet), megijang(millet), mezzo(bright millet), and chajo(bright glutinous millet). These grains grow well in low moisture, and are suitable for drought-stricken or heavenly rice-field. So I always saw it in a shallow field such as the edge of my hometown country mountain. In the old countryside, agricultural machinery and other things did not develop, so how hard it was to be a farmer with pure labor force by human power. My mother, who lived in a rural area, had dull fingertips like a worn farm equipment because she raised her husband and seven children with a tough life.

俶 숙	載 재	南 남	畝 묘	我 아	藝 예	黍 서	稷 직
suk	jae	nam	myo	a	ye	seo	jik
비로소	실을	남녘	이랑	나	재주	기장	피
biroso	sileul	namnyeok	irang	na	jaeju	gijang	pi
finaly	load	south	furrow	i	talent	millet	grass
165. 농부들은 남녘 밭에 농사를 짓고				166. 관리들도 밭에 나가 기장과 피를 심었다			
Farmers farm in the south field				Officials have a knack for planting millet and grass in the fields			
숙장俶裝	연재連載	남부南部	견묘畎畝	자아自我	서예書藝	당서唐黍	사직社稷
prepa-ration	serial-ize	southern	furrow	self/ego	calli-graphy	corn-fruit	ministry/govern

俶숙: 처음 일하다 first work serve
載재: 탈것 운반 vehicle transport fill
南남: 군주 남향 monarch southward
畝묘: 논밭 도랑 rice-field furrow

我아: 아집 고집 egotism stubborn obstinate
藝예: 예술 심다 art artist plant
黍서: 술그릇 bowl of wine
稷직: 기장 농관 millet farm-officer

084. 조직 관리와 조세의무 [세숙공신 권상출척]

직장생활 때 처음에는 봉급 즉 월급을 현금으로 받은 적이 있다. 그러다 월급명세서만 받고 통장으로 이체되었다. 월급 명세서에 보면 각종 세금들이 나열되어 있다. 나라와 사회를 관리하고 유지 발전시켜야 하는데 당연히 국민이 내야 하는 조세 의무리라. 백여 년 전 비교적 최근의 역사인 동학농민혁명은 위정자들의 잘못되고, 세금을 가장한, 폭압적인 수탈에 항거하다, 발생한 것이다. 굶어 죽든 맞아 죽든 같은 것이라며 일으킨 혁명인 것이리라. 얄팍한 지식으로 관직을 맡아 배움이 조금 부족하다 하여 농사를 짓고 있는 농민들의 먹을 죽거리까지 모두 수탈하고. 농민을 모질게 고문하며 죽이니, 농기구와 죽창, 꽹과리를 들고, 스스로 참여한 민초와 전봉준 장군이 일으킨 전쟁이 동학농민혁명이다.

084. Organizational management and tax duties

At first I received a salary in cash, and then later I got salary to a my bank account with a salary statement. The salary statement showed various taxes. It is a duty of taxation that the people must pay to manage and maintain the country and society. A hundred years ago, the relatively recent history of the Donghak Peasant Revolution occurred when the people were wrong, protesting against tyranny, pretending to be taxes. It would be a revolution that caused him to starve or die. With a thin knowledge, he takes over the office and takes all the food of the farmers who are farming because they lack a little learning. The Donghak Peasant Revolution is a war caused by farmers and general Jeon Bong-joon who participated in the war as a leader for their own lives.

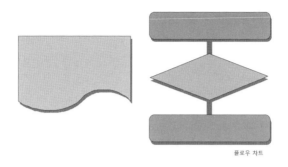

플로우 차트

稅 세	熟 숙	貢 공	新 신	勸 권	賞 상	黜 출	陟 척
se	suk	gong	sin	gwon	sang	chul	cheok
구실	익을	바칠	새	권할	상줄	내칠	오를
gusil	ikeul	bachil	sae	gwonhal	sangjul	naechil	oreul
tax	ripen	offer	new	advise	prize	send	promote
167. 익은 곡식은 세금으로, 햇곡식은 제사에 바치며				168. 임금은 실적에 따라 권하고 상이나 벌주고 칭찬하였다			
Ripe grain is taxed, and the new grain is sacrificed				The emperor recommended, punished, and praised, according to his performance			
세금稅金	성숙成熟	공헌貢獻	혁신革新	권장勸獎	상금賞金	출당黜黨	진척進陟
tax	mature/ ripen	contribute	innova- tion	recommend	prize money	depriva- tion	progress
稅세: 징수하다 관세 조세 levy tariff tax 熟숙: 풍년 곰곰이 good-harvest deeply 貢공: 추천 공물 recommend tribute 新신: 새해 new-year				勸권: 힘쓰다 즐기다 efforts strive, enjoy like 賞상: 주다 찬양 give a prize, celebrate praise 黜출: 쫓다 제거 expel throw-away, remove 陟척: 얻다 gain have get pick up			

085. 지식의 클래식 [맹가돈소 사어병직]

　유교 문화권인 한국 사람은 어려서부터 직간접적으로, 공자 왈, 맹자 왈 소리를 누군가로부터 자연스럽게 들으며 자란다. 그저 우스갯소리처럼, 잠꼬대처럼(꼰대스럽게) 심각하지 않게 듣는다. 뭐 좀 아는 소리 한다든가, 한자가 들어간 말을 하면 또 공자냐고 한다. 다 아는 소리라 시시하다는 것일 수도 있고, 케케묵은 걸 왜 꺼내느냐는 소리 같기도 하다. 일상생활에 별로 도움이 안 되는 걸, 이미 그건 한물간, 시대에 뒤떨어진 필요 없는 것이라는 의미도 있으리라. 그 시절 필자도 너무도 당연한 성현의 말이라서 차라리 귀에 들어오지 않았고, 끊임없이 귀를 물어뜯는 허깨비 소리였던 때가 있었다. 그러나 많지 않은 세월이 흐른 후, 깊숙이 들여다보니 꽤나 기본적이고, 함축적인 효용성이 있음을 깨닫는 시기가 있는 듯하다. 누구든 자기의 발전을 위하여 귓가에서 겉돌던 맹자 왈, 공자 왈을 찾게 되는 시기가 있지 않을까.

085. Classical knowledge

　Korean people, who belong to the Confucian culture, grow up directly or indirectly from their childhood, listening to Confucius and Mencius naturally from someone or a society. However, it's considered not really helpful knowledge for your daily life, and it's already outdated. In those days, I was so natural that I did not come into my ears because of the words of sages, and there was a time when I was constantly biting my ears. But after a lot of years, it seems that there is a time when we realize that there is a fairly basic, implicit utility. I believe if there comes a time when everybody finds Mencius and Confucius Wal(the words of sage) in his ear for his own life development.

도돌이표

孟 맹	軻 가	敦 돈	素 소	史 사	魚 어	秉 병	直 직
maeng	ga	don	so	sa	eo	byeong	jik
맏	수레	도타울	바탕	역사	물고기	잡을	곧을
mad	sure	dotaeul	batang	yeoksa	mulgogi	japeul	godeul
eldest	cart	strength	base	history	fish	hold	upright
169. 맹자의 성선설은, 타고난 착한 본바탕을 돈독하고 소중히				170. 사어는 공직자로, 맡은 일을 살펴서 곧게 지켰다			
Mencius's theory that man's inborn nature is good, in strength and precious				Sa-eo is a public official, look at his job and keep it straight			
맹자孟子	가軻	돈화敦化	평소平素	사료史料	문어文魚	병권秉權	직선直線
mencius	mencius name	serve the people	usual/ normal	historical data	octopus	military power	straight line
孟맹: 처음 맹랑 first firstborn, untrue 軻가: 위험한 수레 dangerous cart 敦돈: 다스리다 정성 govern sincerity 素소: 희다 생명주 white, silk-goods				史사: 사관 history view 魚어: 어류魚類 fishes 秉병: 자루 쥐다 bag grip have 直직: 바르다 정직 right honesty			

189

086. 직업에 따른 품성 (서기중용 로겸근직)

　참 착하고 인간성 좋고 성격 좋은 서울 직장 동료 심 교수가 있다. 볼 때마다 웃으며 인사도 하고 말도 예의 있게 한다. 부지런히 일하고, 겸손하고, 신중하다. 호인이라고들 한다. 또 다른 동료 유 교수는 성격도 까칠하고 잔정이 별로 없고 자기주장이 강하며 타협보다는 밀고 나가는 타입이다. 둘 다 장점과 단점이 있지만, 그들은 필자와 잘 어울리는 편이다. 심 교수는 필자를 심심하거나 일만 있으면 함께 어울리려 불러낸다. 그는 원래 성격도 좋지만 필자와 어울리는 게 그리 좋은 표정이다. 유 교수도 상담하거나 궁금한 것이 있으면 필자와 만나 이야기하고, 등산도 함께하는 일이 더러 있었다. 끼리끼리 모인다던데 필자는 깐깐한 사람인지, 호인 같은 사람인지 아리송하다. 필자는 습관적으로 경청하는 편이다. 연구 스타일이나 책 보는 걸 좋아하는 교수들을 선호하는 것 같다. 뚜렷한 철학과 가치관이 정립되어 있어야 심오한 중용이 몸에서 나오지 않을까.

086. Personality according to occupation

　There is a professor Sim at a Seoul workplace who is very good, humane and personality. He smiles, greets every time he sees me, and makes polite. He works diligently, he is humble, he is careful. He is called a good man. Another fellow professor, Yoo, is a tough personality, lacks little warmhearted, has strong assertiveness, and pushes rather than compromise. Both have merits and disadvantages, but they are well suited to me. Professor Sim calls me to be together if I am bored or work. He has a good personality, but it is a good look to hang out with me. Professor Yoo also talked to me if he had any counselling or questions, and there were some things to do with climbing. I hear that they are gathered together, and I am curious whether they are tough man or good man. I tend to listen habitually. I think that I prefer professors who like to study or read books. I believe if a profound Doctrine of the moderate will come out of the body if you make a clear philosophy and values are established.

庶 서	幾 기	中 중	庸 용	勞 로	謙 겸	謹 근	勅 칙
seo	gi	jung	yong	ro	gyeom	geun	chik
무리	거의	가운데	떳떳할	수고로울	겸손	삼갈	경계
muri	geoui	gaunde	tteottteothal	sugoroeul	gyeomson	samgil	gyeongge
group	almost	middle	honorable	trouble	modesty	humbly	careful
171. 치우치거나 모자람이 없는 중용에 도달하기 바란다면				172. 튀지 말고, 부지런하고 겸손하고 신중하고 경계해야 한다			
If you want to reach a medium-use, biased or lacking				Don't protrusion behavior, be diligent, humble, cautious and vigilant			
서무庶務	기하幾何	집중集中	중용中庸	위로慰勞	겸허謙虛	근정謹呈	칙령勅令
general affairs	how- much /geometry	focus/ concent -rate	middle -use /moderate	comfort	humble/ humility	present	edict/ royal -order
庶서: 여러 제거 several many, remove 幾기: 낌새 가까울 hint nearly approach 中중: 맞을 meet go to meet 庸용: 고용 항상 employ always				勞로: 노력 effort strive work hard endeavor 謙겸: 혐의 족하다 suspect sufficient 謹근: 경계 신중 precautions, caution 勅칙: 조서 protocol record report			

191

087. 부처는 소리도 볼 수 있다 (영음찰리 감모변색)

　아래 시에 음이라는 한자가 있어, 관세음을 빌려 왔다. 관세음보살은 모든 것을 보살피는 자비롭고, 희생적이며, 대중적인 보살이다. 뜻글자인 한자음이 한국으로 건너와 소리글자가 되어 번역해 볼 뿐이다. 음은 음악이 있다. 네 박자 뽕짝 같은 노래는 어쩌다 부르지만, 음악에 대한 전문지식은 별로다. 요즘 유튜브와 기타 교본에 의지하여 기타를 독학으로 익히고 있다. 말소리, 연주 소리를 듣고, 그 사람의 생각을 알고, 얼굴만 봐도 그 사람의 속마음을 읽을 수 있다는 의미를 내포한 아래 시를 보고, 영화 아마데우스가 떠오르고, 연결되는데, 신기할 따름(영음찰리, 감모변색)이다. 어떤 사람의 행동으로 표출되는 여러 소리는 무의식간에 그 사람의 생각이 함축되어 나오리라. 더욱이 얼굴은 사람 마음의 거울 노릇을 하니 만나면 눈빛과 안색부터 보는 것이 아닐까.

087. The Buddha can also see the sound

　There is a Chinese character called "Eum(sound)" in this poem, so that I borrowed a Gwanse-Eum. The Goddess of Mercy, Bodhisattva is a merciful, sacrificial, and popular bodhisattva that takes care of everything. The Chinese character, which is a meaning letter, comes to Korea and translates it into a sound letter. The sound has music. I sing songs like four beats, but I do not have much expertise in music. Nowadays, I am learning guitar by myself by relying on YouTube and other textbooks. I heard the sound of the words, the sound of the performance, I knew the thoughts of the person, I saw the poem below which means that I can read the inside of the person even if I look at the face, The movie Amadeus comes to mind and connects, but it is amazing. The various sounds expressed by the behavior of a person will be included in the unconscious mind. Moreover, the face is a mirror of the mind of a person, so if you meet, you will see other people's eyes and complexion.

聆 령	音 음	察 찰	理 리	鑑 감	貌 모	辨 변	色 색
ryeong	eum	chal	ri	gam	mo	byeon	saek
들을	소리	살필	이치	거울	모양	분별	빛
deuleul	sori	salpil	ichi	geoul	moyang	bunbyeol	bit
hear	sound	look	reason	mirror	shape	prudent	light
173. 목소리를 듣고 말하고자 하는 이치를 그대로 알고				174. 얼굴빛을 보고 속마음을 분별한다			
I know the way I want to hear and speak				Man see the light of a person's face and he discern his heart			
연령年齡	발음發音	경찰警察	원리原理	감상鑑賞	용모容貌	변명辨明	색채色彩
age /years	pronun- ciation	police	principle /theory	impre- ssion	appea- rance	excuse /defense	color /tint
聆령: 깨닫다 따르다 realize follow 音음: 음악 그늘 music shade 察찰: 감시 밝히다 observe reveal find 理리: 다스리다 도리 manage reason justice				鑑감: 살피다 look see check 貌모: 얼굴 외모 face appearance 辨변: 판단 judge recognize 色색: 꾸미다 decorate make-up			

088. 간절하면 영감이 응답한다 (이궐가유 면기지식)

필자가 천자문 에세이를 쓰게 된 계기가 자식들은 이미 성장하여 가정을 꾸리고 있어 나름대로 인격이 형성되어 있는 것으로 보이며, 손주들과 후손에게 대대로 한 가닥 존경 받을 수 있는 지적 성장과 발전에 도움을 주고자 함이다. 꽃피는 어느 봄날 용인 자연농원(현, 에버랜드)에 구경하러 간 적이 있다. 자가용으로 산 고개를 넘어 골짜기에 그럴듯한 놀이 공원과 잘 꾸며진 각종 식물원과 오솔길, 주변에는 향기 나는 각종 꽃들이 있어 데이트하기에 안성맞춤이다. 최신 시설의 건물에 멋있는 유니폼으로 단장한 종업원들, 먹음직한 한식당, 양식당과 진한 커피향의 카페는 호기심 많은 관광객들을 즐겁고 흡족하게 하였다. 한참 후에 알게 된 소식으로, 꿈의 유원지 디즈니랜드라든가 세계 유명놀이 공원이 여러 비판과 비관적 예측과는 달리 인기를 끌어 성공하였음을 알았다. 이후 여러 나라에서 벤치마킹하여 용인 자연농원도 그중 하나인 듯하다. 필자가 시대에 맞춰 개선 적용한 영어천자문 에세이처럼 아름답고 좋은 교훈을 물려주고, 올바름을 찾아 꽃피우도록 노력했으면 하는 바람이다.

088. When you are eager for something, the inspiration from you responds at the end

The reason why I wrote this essay is that my children grow already up and have their own family, and I think that their personality is already formed in their own way. I want that this book can help my grandchildren and descendants for the intellectual growth and development that can be respected for generations. One spring day, when I bloomed, I went to Yongin Natural Farm (currently, Everland). It is a perfect place to date because there are a plausible amusement park, a well-decorated botanical garden and a trail across the mountain hill with a car, and various flowers with fragrance around it. Employees dressed in stylish uniforms in the latest facilities, Korean restaurants, aquaculture and dark coffee cafes made curious tourists happy and satisfactory. In the news that I learned after a while, I knew that Disneyland, a dream amusement park, and world famous play parks were popular and successful, unlike many criticisms and pessimistic predictions. Since then, it has benchmarked in many countries and Yongin Natural Farm seems to be one of them. Like the poems that I have improved and applied to the times, I hope passing on beautiful and good lessons to my grandchildren and they can try to find the right way and bloom by reading this book.

貽 이	厥 궐	嘉 가	猷 유	勉 면	基 기	祗 지	植 식
i	gwol	ga	yu	myeon	gi	ji	sik
끼칠	그	아름다울	꾀	힘쓸	그	공경	심을
ggichil	geu	areumdaul	ggoe	himsseul	geu	gong gyeong	simeul
affect	that	pretty	wit	efforts	it	respect	plant
175. 민족을 위하여 아름답고 좋은 교훈을 물려주고				176. 그 올바름을 꽃피도록 노력한다			
Transfer you beautiful and good lessons for your people				We try to bloom the rightness			
이훈貽訓	돌궐突厥	가행嘉行	대유大猷	근면勤勉	기초基礎	지경祗敬	식물植物
message /moral	Turkish nomadic countries	good-behavior	grand -plan	diligent /industry	basic /base	very -respect	plant

貽이: 남기다 주다 remain give hand-down
厥궐: 궐나라 Gwol-state
嘉가: 경사 기쁘다 congratulation happy
猷유: 그리다 draw paint picture

勉면: 시도 권하다 격려 try offer advise encourage
基기: 그것 기본 that fundamental
祗지: 삼가다 polite
植식: 초목 기둥 지키다 vegetation post keep

089. 오만과 교만은 인생을 망친다 (성궁기계 총증항극)

찌는 듯이 더운 어느 여름날 강원도 백운계곡으로 가족 동반 피서를 간적이 있다. 작은 계곡이지만 텐트치고 물놀이도 하고, 수영도 하고, 캠프파이어도 하며 노래도 부르고, 수박 참외 등 먹거리도 아쉬운 대로 별미였다. 아이들은 더욱 더 신나 하고 물에서 나올 줄을 몰랐고, 그들은 너무 오랜 물놀이에 더위 보다는 추워서 아이들 입술이 덜덜거렸다. 부모들은 물속 작은 바위에서 발만 담근 채 아이들 물놀이 구경하고 있다. 귀여운 아이들 하면서 함께 즐겨 놀아 주니 아이들이 버릇이 없어진다. 어른들이 자기 친구인 양 좋아하면 좋으나, 머리 위(상투 끝)에서 놀 듯하니, 귀엽기보다 불쾌해지기 마련이다. 그들이 큰 사랑(총애), 즉, 귀여움을 너무 과분하게 받으면 애 어른 할 것 없이 오만함이 극에 달하니(총증항극), 스스로 교만하지 말고, 경계하고 반성해야 하리라. 아이들은 템포(완급)를 조절하여 적절하게 귀여워해 줘야 하리라.

089. Arrogance and haughtiness ruin the life

One extreme hot summer day, I went to Baekun Valley in Gangwon Province as a family travel. It is a small valley, but it was a delicacy to eat watermelon, to stay in a tent, a water play, a swimming, a campfire and to sing a song. The children were more excited and did not know they would come out of the water, and they were so cold in the water for too long that their lips were rattling. Parents watch children's play and have their feet dipped in small rocks in the water. Children are spoiled because they play with cute children. It is good for adults to like their friends, but they seem to play on their heads, so they are more unpleasant than cute. If they are too much love, that is, cuteness, they will have to be careful and reflect on themselves, not to be proud of themselves, because arrogance is at its peak. The children should be appropriately deserved by adjusting the tempo of love.

省 성	躬 궁	譏 기	誡 계	寵 총	增 증	抗 항	極 극
seong	gung	gi	ge	chong	jeung	hang	geuk
살필	몸	나무랄	경계할	고일	더할	겨룰	다할
salpil	mom	namural	gyeong gehal	goil	deohal	gyeoreol	dahal
check	body	scold	wary	favor	add	compete	finish
177. 몸을 잘 살피어 스스로 꾸짖고 조심하고				178. 총애가 좋을수록 오만함이 없도록 잘난 체 말라			
You look at yourself, you scold yourself, you watch out				The better the favor, the better the way you are			
성묘省墓	궁행躬行	기롱譏弄	계명誡命	은총恩寵	증가增加	항의抗議	적극積極
holy-grave/observe	do one's work	fun /kidding /tease	command-ment/discipline	bless/grace	increase	protest	positive

省성: 추석 Korean Thanksgiving Day
躬궁: 몸소 행하다 do one's own work
譏기: 원망하다 resent blame
誡계: 훈계 admonish

寵총: 은혜 사랑함 favor mercy benefits love
增증: 얻다 겹치다 gain overlap
抗항: 다투다 fight argue dispute
極극: 극진하다 very kind cordial

090. 마음과 올바른 마무리 (태욕근치 임고행즉)

요즘은 사업자가 아닌 봉급생활자의 형태가 다양하다. 정부 관료나 대기업의 중역 임원직은 의사 결정권자라서 파워가 상당히 크다고 할 수 있다. 필자는 평범한 사람이지만, 어느 정도 성공하여 이목이 집중되는 방석에 앉게 되면, 그에 따른 즐거움과 역경이 뒤 따른다. 사람의 속마음을 알기 어려우므로, 윗사람에게는 경계의 눈초리를 받게 되고(저 사람이 회장이나, 사장한테 잘 보여 내 자리를 넘볼까!?), 부하에게는 시기와 미움의 대상이 될 수도 있다(학벌, 언어 구사 능력, 인물, 집안 등 여러 가지, 보아하니 크게 잘난 것도 없는 상사라는 등). 직장인으로서 자기의 본분이 정점에 올랐다 싶으면, 명예로운 물러남도 고려할 수 있겠다. 부귀영화 다음에는 위태로움이 따를 수 있으므로(태욕근치), 숲이 있고 시냇가 언덕의 한가로운 곳, 소위 말하는 전원주택 같은 곳(임고행즉)에서 말년을 여유롭게 보내면 어떨까 하는 옛날이야기다. 요즘 실버 세대는 여러 편의시설과 병원시설이 갖춰진 도심을 선호하는 듯하다.

090. The mind and the proper finish

Nowadays, there are various types of salaried workers, not business operators. Executive officers from government officials and top management from large corporations are decision-makers, so they have a lot of power. I am an ordinary person, but when I succeed to some extent and sit on a cushion where attention is focused, the pleasure and adversity follow. It is difficult to know the inside of a person, so the boss can be alerted to the wariness(He's good to the president, the boss, and I'll take my place!?), and the subordinate can be subject to the jealousy and hatred(There are many things such as academic background, language ability, character, family, etc., and it seems that it is a boss who does not have much good work). If you want to be at the peak of your job as an employee, you will consider honorable retreat. It is an old story about how to spend the late years in a place like a forest, a leisurely place on a stream hill, a so-called garden house, because the danger can follow after the wealth and prosperity. Nowadays, the silver generation seems to prefer a city center with a hospital close to various facilities.

殆 태	辱 욕	近 근	恥 치	林 림	皐 고	幸 행	卽 즉
tae	yok	geun	chi	rim	go	haeng	jeuk
위태할	욕될	가까울	부끄러울	수풀	언덕	다행	곧
witaehal	yokdoel	gaggaul	buggeureoul	supul	eondeok	dahaeng	god
dangerous	dishonor	near	shy	forest	hillside	fortunate	at once
179. 부귀영화 다음에는 위태로움이 따르기 쉬우므로				180. 숲이 있는 시냇가 언덕 전원주택에서 한가롭게 독서하라			
After the rich prosperity, it is easy to follow the precarious				Read leisurely in a forested stream hill house			
태반殆半	모욕侮辱	근처近處	염치廉恥	밀림密林	고복皐復	행복幸福	즉석卽席
near-half	insult/affront	close/around	sense of shame	jungle forest	three-call of dead-name	happy/welfare	instant/imme-diate
殆태: 거의 두려움 near fear afraid 辱욕: 더럽히다 dirty taint soil 近근: 친척 near[distant] relative 恥치: 수치심羞恥心 shame				林림: 들 유림儒林 field plain, Confucian-scholars 皐고: 못 늪 pond marsh swamp 幸행: 사랑 혜택 love benefit favor 卽즉: 즉시 immediate soon			

091. 군대의 민주화와 변화 (양소견기 해조유핍)

오래 전 군대 생활할 때, 선임 병들의 말이 지금은 군대도 아니다. 그들은 군기가 엄한 시기에 군 생활을 했는데, 세상 정말 좋아져서 구타도 없고, 규율도 약하고, 내무반에 티브이도 있고, 군 생활이 편해졌다. 사실 필자는 거의 모든 병사가 매년 받는 유격훈련 일주일 외에는 사적이건, 단체건, 줄 빳따나 기합 같은 가혹행위를 당한 적이 없었다. 구성원 몇 명이 군기가 빠졌다고, 완전 장비(군장) 후 운동장(연병장) 오십 회 쯤 훈련(얼차려) 하였던 것 같다. 선임과 후임 병이 서로 도와 가며, 병영생활을 즐겁게 했다. 그런데 수십 년이 흐른 요즘은 더욱 개선되어 좋아졌을 것으로 보이는데도, 군대에 구타와 각종 문제가 발생하여, 매스컴에 나오는 걸 보면 의아한 생각이 든다. 사회와 격리되고, 군영에 얽매이고, 자유로움이 부족한 것은 군생활의 기본이다. 공휴일은 보초 서는 거 외에는 거의 자유시간이여서 계획이 서 있는 사람은 기회를 잡아 자기개발하고 싶은 것을 많이 하고 성취하기도 했었다. 요즘은 휴일도 많아졌다. 각종 자격시험 준비도 가능할 수 있다. 짐작컨대, 요즘 군기문란은 병영생활이 너무 편하고, 자유시간이 많아서 발생하는 것이 아니기를 바랄 뿐이다.

091. The democratization and change of military

When I was in the army a long time ago, there was a saying of the senior soldiers that the army training became now so comfortable. They lived in the military during a severe period of military discipline, and the world of the military society got really better, so there was no beating, weak discipline, there is TV in the sleeping place. In fact, I have never been subjected to harsh acts such as private, group, line-beat, or strike, except for a week of military training that almost all soldiers receive every year. Some of the members seemed to have lost their discipline, and they trained about 50 times in the playground after the full equipment. Senior and successors helped each other and enjoyed barracks life. However, even though it seems to have improved and got better more decades later, it is strange to see that the army has been hit by beatings and various species problems, and it appears in the media. It is the basis of military life that is isolated from society, is suppressed by military camp, and lacks freedom. Public holidays were almost free time except for guarding, so those who had a plan had a lot of opportunities to take advantage of and achieve what they wanted to develop. Nowadays, there are more holidays. Preparation for each type of qualification test can be possible. I guess, nowadays, the military discipline is just too easy to live in barracks, and I hope it does not happen because of the free time.

兩 량	疏 소	見 견	機 기	解 해	組 조	誰 수	逼 핍
ryang	so	gyeon	gi	hae	jo	su	pip
두	섬길	볼	틀	풀	끈	누구	핍박할
du	seomgil	bol	teul	pul	ggeun	nugu	pipbakhal
two	serve	see	frame	solve	string	who	pressure

181. 황제 인척인 소광과 소수는 미리 낌새를 느끼고				182. 인연의 끈을 풀고 떠나 시골집으로 가니 누가 핍박하리오			
So-kwang and So-su of the emperor's relative feel premonition				They left the bond and went to the country house, and who is persecuted?			

천냥千兩	소통疏通	견해見解	기회機會	해결解決	조직組織	수하誰何	핍박逼迫
thousand /much- money	communi -cation	view/ opinion	opportunity /chance	solution/ untie	organize	who/ anyone	persecu -tion

兩량: 짝 단위 pair unit measure
疏소: 소통 understanding talk
見견: 나타나다 appear come out
機기: 실마리 상황 clue condition

解해: 깨닫다 realize find
組조: 짜다 weave
誰수: 묻다 ask
逼핍: 다그치다 push urge impel

092. 옛날이나 지금이나 [색거한처 침묵적요]

경인선 전철을 타고 동암역 부근을 지나다 보면 산꼭대기 정상에 누각(정자)이 있다, 가족과 단양팔경을 구경하다 보니 호수 한가운데 누각이 아슬아슬하게 보인다. 전설 같은 사실로, 단양팔경에서 유년시절을 보냈다는 유명한 삼봉 정도전(1337~1392)과 김홍도(1745~?), 이황(1501~1570) 등은 화폭같이 아름다운 곳이라고 시를 읊고 찬사를 하였다. 같은 시대에 활동한, 절친 정몽주(1342~1398)와 정도전은 시대의 변환기에 적이 된다. 과거의 인간세상도 선악을 구별하기 어려울 정도로 서로 간에 가치관, 이념, 잇속의 갈등속에서 독야청청 쉽지 않았으리라. 정보 홍수시대요, AI시대인 현대의 갈등은 거친 진흙탕에 뒹굴고 있는 시대다. 악화가 양화를 축출한다는 경제 논리처럼, 악이 선량한 사람을 농락하는 기술을 부리고 있다. 오십보백보 하면서 말이다. 옛날처럼, 누가 풍경 좋은 산꼭대기 정상에 한가로운 거처를 찾아, 자연의 멜로디를 들으며, 홀로 떨어져, 아무 말도 필요 없이, 조용히, 한가롭게, 한적하게 지내는 걸 싫어할까, 호구지책만 있다면 말이다. 현대는 진흙탕에서 빠져나오기도 쉽지 않은 세상 아닐까. 그래도 인간은 스치는 바람에도움츠리며 떨리는 양심의 소리를 많은 사람이 듣길 바랄 뿐이다.

092. In the past or now

When you pass the Gyeongin Line train near Dongam Station, there is a pavilion on the top of the mountain. When you look at the family and Danyang Eight scenery, the pavilion in the middle of the lake looks breathtaking. As a legend, Sambong Jeong Do-jeon, Kim Hong-do, and Lee Hwang, who are famous for having spent their childhood in Danyang Eight scenery, praised the poem as a beautiful place like a canvas. In the same era, his best friends, Chung Mong-joo and Jeong Do-jeon, became enemies in the transition period of the times. The human world of the past was not easy to distinguish between good and evil in the conflict between values, ideology, and conflicts. The era of information floods, the age of AL, is the era of modern conflict, which is rolling in rough mud. Like the economic logic that deterioration expels quantification, evil is a skill to exploit good people. Like in the old days, who would hate to find a leisurely place on the top of a landscaped mountaintop, listen to the melody of nature, fall alone, and stay silent, idle, and quiet without needing to say anything. It is not easy to get out of the mud, but we can only hope that many people will hear the trembling conscience of human beings even when they are brushed.

索 색	居 거	閑 한	處 처	沈 침	默 묵	寂 적	寥 요
saek	geo	han	cheo	chim	muk	jeok	yo
찾을	살	한가	곳	잠길	잠잠할	고요할	한적할
chateul	sil	hanga	got	jamgil	jamjamhal	goyohal	hanjeokhal
find	live	leisure	place	sink	silent	quiet	secluded
183. 벼슬(고위급관직)에서 물러나 한적한 곳에 살고 있으니				184. 근심 걱정 없이 한가롭고 편안하구나			
He is out of high-level office, living in a quiet place				He is relaxed and comfortable without worrying			
탐색探索	거실居室	한담閑談	처리處理	침묵沈默	묵념默念	적막寂寞	적요寂寥
search	living- room	chat/ idle-talk	treat- ment	silence/ quiet	silent prayer	lone- liness	lonely &quiet
索색: 구하다 save rescue 居거: 있다 be lie take place stand 閑한: 자유 고요 우아 free still elegance 處처: 머무르다 stay remain				沈침: 물에 빠지다 fall into the water 默묵: 조용 어둡다 quiet dark 寂적: 편안 열반 comfortable nirvana 寥요: 쓸쓸하다 lonesome forlorn			

203

093. 건강과 산책 (구고심론 산려소요)

거의 매일 이곳저곳으로 산책을 간다. 쇼핑백에 물과 커피나 쥬스, 네다섯 조각 든 작은 크래커 한두 봉지나 약과 한두 개, 견과류 준비하여, 걱정일랑 멀리멀리 흘러보내고, 한가로이 산보도 하고, 커피도 마신다. 도심 둘레 길에 잘 만들어 놓은 아름다운 뉴 모델 쉼터에 머물기도 하고(산려소요), 가끔 편의점 파라솔 의자에 기대어 아이스크림을 먹기도 한다. 지나간 추억을 속닥거리고(구고심론), 손주들 커 가는 걸 생각하며, 지난날 언젠가 보았던 듯한, 풀꽃 위를 맴돌고 있는 나비와 벌, 잠자리들 구경과 하늘 위 다양한 모양의 구름들을 보고 그림을 그리기도 하니, 시간 가는 줄 모르고 즐겁구나. 우리는 신체 사이클에 적합할 때, 때때로 가끔 나라에서 베풀어 준 무료 전철표로 가까운 곳에 가서, 가볍게 식도락하면 기분전환도 되는 듯하다.

093. Health and taking a walk

I go for a walk almost every day. I have a shopping bag with water, coffee, juice, a small bag or two of four or five pieces of creckers, a medicine or two, nuts, and get away from worrisome. I stay in a beautiful new designed shelter that is well built on the streets around the city center, and sometimes I lean on a parasol chair at a convenience store and eat ice cream. I think about the memories of the past, thinking about the grandchildren growing up, seeing butterflies and bees hovering on grass flowers, watching dragonflies, and seeing clouds of various shapes on the sky. I'm glad you don't know how long it's going. When we are fit, sometimes we go somewhere with for free train ticket that we have given in the country, and a light gourmandism there seems to be a diversion.

별과 구름과 해 그리고 잠자리

求구	古고	尋심	論론	散산	慮려	逍소	遙요
gu	go	sim	ron	san	ryeo	so	yo
구할	옛	찾을	의논할	흩어질	생각	노닐	노닐
guhal	yet	chateul	uinonhal	heuteojil	saenggak	nonil	nonil
find	old	search	debate	scatter	think	stroll	stroll

185. 공직에서 물러나 욕심 없이 한적한 곳에서 옛 현자의 책을 보며 의논하니	186. 선지자와 생각을 주고받으니 한가롭고 흐뭇하구나
He is out of office and in a quiet place without greed, I discuss the book of the old sage	He is so relaxed and happy to exchange ideas with the prophet

추구追求	고전古典	추심推尋	결론結論	산책散策	배려配慮	소요逍遙	요망遙望
search/ pursue	classic	collect	conclu- sion	walk /stroll	consider	wander/ saunter	look far away

求구: 탐내다 찾다 covet find 古고: 오래되다 former ancient past 尋심: 평소 usual normal everyday 論론: 말하다 토론 say discussion	散산: 비틀거리다 reel stumble stagger 慮려: 염려 근심 concern anxiety 逍소: 거닐 get around roam 遙요: 멀 서성거리다 far hover walk

094. 바쁘게 돌아가는 세상 (흔주누견 척사환초)

　사람들은 모두가 어디로 가는지도 모르고 바쁘기만 한 것처럼 보인다(사실 인생의 목표와 목적, 장기와 단기 계획, 연간, 월간 계획대로 실행하는 사람들도 꽤나 많이 있다). 필자도 참 바쁜 것처럼 보인다. 독서도 하고, 집필도 해야지, 핸드폰 속 뉴스, 날씨, 유익한 정보도 스와핑하고, 각종 쥬스와 영양제도 먹어야지, 청소도 해야지, 취미생활도 해야지, 이처럼 모두가 바쁘다. 어린 손주들도 아주 바쁘다. 장난감 놀이, 아이패드, 유튜브, 동화책 보기, 블록놀이, 놀이터에서 미끄럼틀 타기, 시소 타기, 그네 타기 놀이 등 바쁘다. 조금 여유만 생겨도 "심심혀." 하면서 조른다. 이러한 모든 것이 기쁨이 아닐까. 기쁨은 불러와 알리고, 번뇌로 얽어 맨 족쇄는 멀리 보내거라(흔주누견). 속세에 살고 있는 우리는 쉽지 않은 환경이다. 탐내고, 미워하고, 못 배워 우매함(탐진치)을 극복하면 성현이 되는 길이라 한다. 독서하며 한 없이 노력하는 중이다. 기쁨이 몰려오면 슬픔은 사라진다(환초척사). 또한 기쁨을 나누면 배가 되고, 슬픔을 나누면 작아진다 하더라. 바쁨은 짜임새 있는 계획으로 여유 시간을 만들어 실천하면, 바빠 허둥대는 마음을 줄일 수 있다.

094. A busy world

　People seem to be busy, not knowing where everyone is going (and in fact, there are quite a few people who do it according to their goals and purposes, long-term and short-term plans, annual and monthly plans). I am also very busy. I have to read, write, swap news, weather, useful information on my cell phone, drink juice and nutrition, clean a room, and have a hobby, likewise everyone is so busy. Young grandchildren are also very busy, such as toy play, iPad, YouTube, fairy tale book viewing, block play, slide rides on playgrounds, seesaw rides, swing rides, and so on. Even if children have a little time, they will scream with "boredom." I wonder if all of this is joy. Bring joy, let it know, and send the bare shackles away with the agony. We live in a world where it is not easy. It is said that if you overcome the foolishness by coveting, hate, and not learning(Tamjinchi is buddhist terminology), it is a way to become sages. I am trying hard to read. When joy comes, sadness disappears. And when joy is shared, it becomes doubled, and when sorrow is shared, it becomes smaller. With a structured plan, that can reduce the busy scrambling mind by creating and practicing spare time.

欣 흔	奏 주	累 루	遣 견	感 척	謝 사	歡 환	招 초
heun	ju	ru	gyeon	cheok	sa	hwan	cho
기쁠	아뢸	근심	보낼	슬픔	사례할	기쁠	부를
gibbeul	aroel	geunsim	bonael	seulpeum	sarehal	gibbeul	bureul
pleasure	say	worry	send	sad	reward	happy	call

187. 은둔 선비의 마음가짐, 즐거움이 모이면 근심은 사라지고				188. 슬픔이 물러가면 기쁨이 밀려온다			
The mindset of the hermit scholar, the anxiety disappears when the joy is gathered				When grief recedes, joy comes upon it			
흔희欣喜	합주合奏	정루情累	파견派遣	척우慼憂	감사感謝	환영歡迎	초대招待
fun& joyful	concert/ ensemble	feelings -drag	send/ dispatch	worry/ trouble	thank/ gratitude	welcome	invitation

欣흔: 기쁘다 glad delightful 奏주: 연주 play perform recital 累루: 묶다 곤란 괴로움 tie up, distress 遣견: 선물 gift futures present	感척: 근심 친척 concern fear care relative 謝사: 물러나다 back resign leave 歡환: 즐거움 pleasure joy enjoyment 招초: 손짓 gesture signs motion

095. 고향 산천 (거하적력 원망추조)

봄이 되면 선산 북카페 앞 배롱나무(백일홍)는 붉게 물들어 또렷이 빛나고, 여름 되면 연휴정 위 잡풀이 죽죽 뻗어 우거진다. 선산 창조공원에서 바라보는 시골 마을은 한가롭고 평화롭기 그지없다. 인구 감소와 도시 집중화로 소멸되어 가는 시골 연촌마을에 농공단지가 조성된다니 아주 기쁜 소식이다. 이러한 농공단지는, 농촌 살리기 운동이며, 또한 우리나라에서 알아주는 큰 불갑 저수지가 있어, 물이 풍부하고, 비교적 교통이 편리한 시골이라는 입지적 이유일 수도 있다. 불갑 저수지에서 천년 고찰 불갑사까지 관광의 명소가 되고 있다. 상사화 군락지와 천년방아라는 국내 최대 규모 물레방아는 그중 유명 상징물이다. 모든 것은 마음이 만들어 내는 것이라 하듯이, 익숙한 고향이라 스쳐 지나가던 것들이 소중해 보인다. 평소에는 하찮고, 대수롭지 않던 것들이 새롭게 보이는 것(거하적력 원망추조)은 눈을 움직이는 마음이 달라졌음이리라.

095. Home mountain stream

In spring, the barley tree (Baek Il-hong) in front of the our ancestral burial mountain book-cafe(sacrifice-house) is reddish and bright, and in summer, the grass on the Yeonhyu-pavilion stretches out. The rural village seen from the our ancestral burial mountain Chang-Cho Park is leisurely and peaceful. It is very good news that an agricultural complex will be built in rural village, which is disappearing due to population decline and urban concentration. These agricultural complexes are rural revitalization campaigns, and there is also a large Bulgap reservoir that is known in Korea, which may be a reason for the fact that it is rich in water and relatively convenient to traffic. It is becoming a tourist attraction from the Bulgap Reservoir to the Millennium Bulgap old temple. The largest water mill in Korea, the Lycoris Community site and the Millennium waterwheel, is a famous symbol. As everything is made by mind, the things that have passed by became precious. What is usually trivial and worthless is that new things are seen, that means that the mind that moves the eyes must change.

渠 거	荷 하	的 적	歷 력	園 원	莽 망	抽 추	條 조
geo	ha	jeok	ryeok	won	mang	chu	jo
도랑	연꽃	과녁	지냄	동산	풀	뽑을	가지
dorang	yeonggot	gwanyeok	jinael	dongsan	pul	bbopeul	gaji
ditch	lotus	target	stay	garden	grass	pick	branch

189. 벼슬에서 물러나 욕심 없이 세상을 보니, 도랑의 연꽃이 환하게 빛나고	190. 동산의 잡풀들도 우거져 보기 좋다
When he is out of office and look at the world without greed, the lotus flowers of the ditch shine brightly	The weeds of the garden are good at the lush

구거溝渠	하역荷役	목적目的	학력學歷	정원庭園	초망草莽	추첨抽籤	조건條件
small ditch	load& unload	purpose/ aim/goal	education -level	garden	lush/pile -grass	lottery	condition /terms

渠거: 개천 open-stream rivulet streamlet
荷하: 꾸짖다 scold reprimand chide
的적: 밝다 표준 bright standard
歷력: 이력서履歷書 personal history

園원: 밭 별장 field villa country-house cottage
莽망: 거칠다 덮다 rough tough cover
抽추: 당기다 추상화 pull draw abstraction
條조: 줄기 규범 stem trunk rule

096. 마당에 홀로 선 오동나무 (비파만취 오동조조)

　시골 앞마당 귀퉁이에 오동나무가 있었다. 옛날에는 아들을 낳으면 소나무나 잣나무를 심고, 딸을 낳으면 주로 오동나무를 심었단다. 앵두나무 옆, 오뉴월이면 초롱 같은 꽃, 보라색 오동나무꽃 고요히 피어, 잡힐 듯 사라질 듯 은은한 향기를 뿜는다. 오동나무는 고급 장롱 소재나 보배같이 귀한 나무라 한다. 오동나무는 쟁반같이 넓은 잎과, 곧게 뻗은 기둥 같은 나무와 줄기들, 오동나무로 만든 가야금은 천 년이 지나도 가락을 잃지 않는다 한다. 가을 소식을 가장 먼저 알려준다는 오동나무(오동조조), 어느 날 잎이 뚝뚝 떨어지는 날이 가을이다. 오동나무의 뾰쪽한 혼중 혹 계란 모양의 열매는 초겨울에 들어서면서 둘로 갈라지고 안에 들어 있던 날개 달린 열매들은, 차갑지만, 고마운 겨울바람에 실려, 오동나무 씨앗은 민들레처럼 멀리 멀리 온 세상 곳곳에 자손을 남기려 어디론가 정처 없이 님 찾아 가겠지.

096. Alone oak tree in the yard

　There was a oak tree in the corner of the front garden in my old house in the countryside. In the old days, when parents give birth to a son, then they planted pine trees and korean-nut pine trees, and when they give birth to a daughter, then they mainly planted oak trees. Next to the cherry tree, in May and June, the flowers like lanterns, the purple oak flowers bloom quietly, and the fragrance that seems to disappear as if caught. The oak tree is said to be a precious tree like a high-quality wardrobe material or treasure. The oak tree does not lose its broad leaves like a tray, straight columns and stems, and its rhythm after a thousand years. The oak tree is the first to tell the news of autumn, and one day the day the leaves fall sharply is autumn. The pointed fumigation black egg-shaped fruit from the oak tree is divided into two when it enters the early winter, and the inside of winged fruit is cold, but it is carried in a grateful winter wind. The seeds of the oak tree will go somewhere far away in order to make their descendants all over the world as faraway as dandelion.

枇 비	杷 파	晚 만	翠 취	梧 오	桐 동	무 조	凋 조
bi	pa	man	chwi	o	dong	jo	jo
비파나무	비파나무	늦을	푸를	오동나무	오동나무	일찍	시들
bipanamu	bipanamu	neujeul	pureul	odongnamu	odongnamu	iljjik	sideul
loquat	loquat	late	green	paulownia	paulownia	early	wither
191. 물러난 학자가 보는 계절, 비파나무는 늦게까지 푸르고				192. 오동나무는 가을되면 일찍 시든다			
The season of the retreating scholar, the loquat tree is blue until late				The paulownia fades early in the fall			
비파枇杷	죽파竹杷	만찬晚餐	취옥翠玉	오하梧下	자동刺桐	조기早起	조락凋落
loquat	farm equip-ment	dinner/ banquet	emerald	respect	Kalopanax -pictus	get up early	fall early/ withering

枇비: 수저 참빗 spoon&chopsticks brush
杷파: 시파柴杷 farm-equipment
晚만: 저물다 노년 grow-dark, old-age
翠취: 비취색 jade-green

梧오: 거문고 기둥 Korean-harp, column
桐동: 거문고 Korean lute
무조: 새벽 아침 dawn daybreak morning
凋조: 슬퍼하다 feel-sad grieve sorrow

097. 김소월의 시「부모」(진근위예 낙엽표요)

계절을 잊은 어느 날, 떨어진 단풍잎 하나에 가을, 뒤뜰 텃밭 흙에 서린 서릿발 하나에 겨울이 다가옴을 느낀다. 늙은 뿌리 말라 시들고(진근위예), 낙엽이 차가운 바람에 나부낄 때(낙엽표요), 어머니가 생각나, 김소월「부모」라는 시를 읊어 본다. 가요로 대중화 되어 귀에 익숙한 시다. "낙엽이 우수 떨어질 때, 겨울의 기나긴 밤 어머님하고 둘이 앉아, 옛 이야기 들어라 나는 어쩌면 생겨 나와, 이 이야기 듣는가, 묻지도 말아라, 내일 날에, 내가 부모 되어서 알아보리라" 무엇을 보면, 그와 연관된 지난 일이 떠오르기 마련이다. 모차르트 피아노 음악과 레오나르도 다빈치의 모나리자 그림 같은 감동스런 것만 떠오르면 좋은데, 불쾌하고 무서움이 아른거리면 몸속의 혈액조차 파랗게 놀랄 수 있다. 소위 정신적 상처라는 트라우마다. 그러나 필자의 에세이『어머니 향기』처럼 아무거나 떠올라도 조금의 슬픔은 있지만, 언제나 기쁨이 도사리고 있다.

097. Kim So-wol's Poetry 「Parents」

When I forgot the time, I felt autumn approaching one of the fallen maple leaves, and I feel winter when I saw one of the frost columns in the back garden soil. When the old roots are dried and the leaves are cold in the wind, my mother reminds me of the poem 「Parents」 by Kim So-wol. It is popularized as a song and is familiar to the ears. "When the leaves fall, The long winter night, I and my mother sit together, Listen to the old story. I may come up, listen to this story, Don't ask, tomorrow, I'll be a parent and I'll find out." In a way, the past associated with it comes to mind. It is good to come up with Mozart piano music and Leonardo da Vinci's Mona

Lisa picturesque touching. If you are uncomfortable and afraid, even the blood in your body can be surprised. The trauma of what we call a mental wound. But there is a little sadness in my essay 『Mother's Scent』, but there is always a bit joy as well.

陳 진	根 근	委 위	翳 예	落 락	葉 엽	飄 표	飀 요
jin	geun	wi	ye	rak	yeop	pyo	yo
묵을	뿌리	맡길	가릴	떨어질	잎	나부낄	나부낄
mukeul	bburi	matgil	garil	tteoleojil	ip	nabuggil	nabuggil
old	root	entrust	cover	fall	leaf	flutter	flutter
193. 가을이 가고 겨울이 오니, 늙은 뿌리는 시들고				194. 떨어진 나무 잎이 바람에 뒹굴며 휘날리는 구나			
Fall is going and winter is coming, old roots withered				The fallen leaves are rolling and blowing in the wind			
진열陳列	근본根本	위원委員	원예圓翳	등락騰落	엽서葉書	표락飄落	표요飄飀
display/ showcase	foun- dation	committee -member	macular	up&down rise&fall	postcard	leaf is scattered	flounder or flying shape

陳진: 늘어놓다 펴다 extend spread open
根근: 근본 능력 basis ability capacity
委위: 쌓이다 자세하다 stack pile details
翳예: 방패 양산 shield sunshade parasol

落락: 탈락 몰락 drop fail eliminated lose
葉엽: 세대 책 generation book
飄표: 떠돌다 돌풍 wander float gust
飀요: 질풍疾風 whirlwind swiftly

098. 인간이 바라는 파랑새 (유곤독운 능마강소)

자식 키워 보면 혼자서 자기 할 일만 잘해 줘도 너무 고맙고 대견스러운 일이며 효도하는 것임을 느낀다. 아기 때는 아장아장 걷기만 해도, 대소변만 가려도, 밥만 잘 먹어도, 얼마나 좋은지. 어린이집, 유치원, 초등학교 다닐 때는 등하교가 부모 몫이다. 중고등학교 때는 말썽 부리는 사춘기 때니 신경을 곤두세워야 한다. 이때까지만 잘 보살피고, 애어른처럼 행동한다면 한결 좋으리라. 그렇게 할 수 있는 나이가 몇 살 정도인지는 누가 알까. 그렇더라도, 물가에 내놓은 새끼마냥, 부모는 사실 죽을 때까지 자식 걱정하기 마련이다. 위와 같은 현실(사바)세계는 상상의 거대한 봉황새(곤)가 해 뜨는 붉은 동녘하늘(강소)로 유유히 치솟는 영화 같은 장면 속, 아래 시는 인간이 바라는 파랑새일까.

098. The bluebirds that a man wants

When I see my child, I feel that it is very grateful, proud and filial piety if he does his own work well. When you are a baby, even if you walk in a toddler, even if you go to the toillet, you eat well. As a parent you are happy when the child attending daycare centers, kindergartens, and elementary schools. Picking up from the school is up to parents. In middle and high school, you have to be nervous because children are a troubled adolescent. It would be better if you were only taking care of it until this time. Who knows how old you should take care of them? Parents actually worry about their children until they die. It is a poem below a blue bird that human beings want the above real world in a movie-like scene where the imaginary giant phoenix rises to the red east sky?

요술피리와 파랑새

遊유	鯤곤	獨독	運운	凌릉	摩마	絳강	霄소
yu	gon	dok	un	reung	ma	gang	so
놀	물고기	홀로	운전	능가할	문지를	붉을	하늘
neul	mulgogi	holro	unjeon	neunggahal	munjareul	bulkeul	haneul
play	fish	alone	driving	exceed	rub	red	sky
195. 크기가 몇천 리나 되는 상상의 물고기며 봉황인, 곤은 홀로 움직이며				196. 해가 떠오르는, 붉게 물든 동녘 하늘을 날아간다			
The imaginary fish, phoenix, which is a few thousand sizes, moves alone				The sun rises, flying through the reddish east sky			
유학遊學	곤붕鯤鵬	독립獨立	운동運動	능인凌人	안마按摩	강홍絳紅	중소中霄
studying abroad	imaginative -fish -phoenix	indepen -dent	exercise /motion	ice-man	massage /masseur	dark -red	middle of the sky

遊유: 여행 travel trip journey tour
鯤곤: 상상 속 북극물고기 giant fish in imagination
獨독: 고독 외롭다 solitude isolation
運운: 돌다 turn go-round circle

凌릉: 업신여기다 disgrace despise slight
摩마: 갈다 grind sharpen scrub
絳강: 진홍 dark-red
霄소: 닮다 resemble look-like similar

215

099. 환경을 극복하고 (탐독완시 우목낭상)

어린 학창시절 세상일에 제대로 안목이 있겠는가. 잡기나 소일로 시간을 보내는 친구들이 많았다. 가정이 너무 어려워 도시락도 없는 친구는 눈에 불 키고 공부를 하여 장학금으로 학비를 조달하였다. 매우 친했던, 점수라는 친구는 집에도 자주 놀러왔다. 어느 날 친구가 여러 날 결석하여, 담임이 필자와 그 친구와 장학생 라이벌인 상원이라는 친구와 가정 방문할 것을 권하였다. 공부로 학비는 가능하나, 가족 생계는 어려웠다. 그 친구는 어려운 환경에서 공부하여 교사로 가족을 보살피게 되었으니 얼마나 다행인가. 어떤 사람이 시장 구석에서 구두닦이를 하면서 사법시험에 합격했다(탐독완시)는 뉴스를 봤다. 새나 동물도 둥지를 떠나 자립하듯, 발달이 늦은 인간일지라도, 고등학교 졸업 후는 자기가 인생을 스스로 개척하여 일어남이 자연의 이치 아닐까. 요즘은 복지제도와 장학제도도 많고, 고등학교까지 학비가 무료화된다 하니 얼마나 좋은 세상인가. 돈이 없어도 공공도서관, 무료 도서관, 대형서점에 가면 공짜로 책을 볼 수 있으며, 꿈만 있으면 되니, 젊음의 혈기를 조금 자제하고, 게으름 피지 말고 꿈 실현을 위해 움직여, 자신의 인생에 대한 예의를 가꾸면 되리라.

099. Overcome the environment

Do you have a good eye for the world during childhood? Many friends spend time for miscellanies or for doing a small task. A friend who had no lunch box because the family was too difficult to study, and he raised his tuition by scholarship. A friend who was very close, Jeomsu came to my home often. One day, a friend was absent for several days, and the charge teacher recommended that we visit the house with a friend of the author and his friend and a scholarship rival, the Sangwon. Studying allows tuition, but family livelihoods were difficult. How fortunate that he studied in a difficult environment and took care of his family as a teacher. I saw the news that someone passed the judicial examination while washing shoes in the corner of the market. Even if birds and animals are self-reliant, even if they are late to develop, after graduating from high school, they will pioneer their own lives and become natural. Nowadays, there are many welfare systems and scholarships, and how good a world is it because the tuition is free to high school. Even if you do not have money, you can go to public libraries, free libraries, large bookstores and you can read books for free. You will refrain a little from the temptation of youth, do not be lazy, move to realize your dreams, and cultivate your courtesy of your life.

耽 탐	讀 독	翫 완	市 시	寓 우	目 목	囊 낭	箱 상
tam	dok	wan	si	u	mok	nang	sang
즐길	읽을	갖고 놀	저자	붙일	눈	주머니	상자
jeulgil	ilkeul	gatgonol	jeoja	butil	nun	jumeoni	sang
enjoy	read	play-with	market	stick	eye	pocket	box
197. 왕충이라는 학자는 가난하여, 시장에 진열된 책을 읽었고				198. 기억력이 뛰어나 한번만 보아도 내용을 주머니나 상자에 넣은 것과 같았다			
The scholar Wang Chung was poor, and read a book on the market				If he looks at it once with excellent memory, It was like putting the contents in a pocket or a box,			
탐독耽讀	독서讀書	설완褻翫	시내市內	우화寓話	목표目標	배낭背囊	소상巢箱
avid reading	reading	close-up viewing	city-town	(Aesop's) fables.	goal/ target/aim	backpack/ rucksack	beehive
耽탐: 빠지다 indulge 讀독: 독자讀者 reader 翫완: 구경하다 watch toys 市시: 시장 marketplace				寓우: 머무르다 보내다 stay spend send dispatch 目목: 보다 요점 see look point gist 囊낭: 포대자루 sack pouch bag 箱상: 옆방 side or next or adjoining room			

217

100. 새와 쥐와 담장에 귀가 있다 (이유유외 속이원장)

우리는 세상을 살다 보면, 자기밖에 모를 것 같은 비밀스런 일을 어느 누군가가 알고 있음을 경험하게 된다. 나쁜 일이든 좋은 일이든 그렇더라. 낮에 하는 말은 새가 듣고, 밤에 하는 말은 쥐가 듣는다 하고, 담장에도 귀가 달렸다(속이원장) 한다. 자라면서 이런 말을 많이 들었던 기억이 있다. 실제로 사람 말을 쥐와 새가 듣는 것으로 믿기도 했다. 그도 그럴 것이 옛날 시골에 살 때, 밤에 천정에서 쥐가 뛰어 다니는 소리를 가끔 들었고, 참새들은 초가지붕 처마 끝 지푸라기 틈새에 집을 짓고 살고 있었기 때문이다. IT시대인 요즘은 도청기가 너무 발달하여 사생활이 노출되는 위험한 환경이 되었다. 사람이 말을 함부로 하면, 누구든 실수를 저지르게 마련이니, 우리는 누가 보지 않는다고 남을 헐뜯거나 비웃지(이유유외) 말아야 할 것이다. 우리는 언제나 좋은 일, 올바른 행동을 하도록 노력하면서 지내야 하리라, 언젠가는 자기에게 다시 돌아오는 경우가 있다.

100. Birds, Rats and Fences also have ears

Everybody has an experience that someone knows some secrets that we did not share before. It does not matter with bad or good secrets. The day is said to be heard by birds, the night is heard by rats, and the ears are on the fence. I remember hearing a saying of this as I grew up. I actually believed that mice and birds were listening to people's word. It would, too, because I sometimes heard rats running on the ceiling at night when I lived in the old countryside, and sparrows lived in houses at the end of the eaves of the roof. Nowadays, in the IT era, eavesdropping devices have become so advanced that privacy has become a dangerous environment. If a person speaks out, anyone will make a mistake, so we should not scold or laugh at others that no one sees. We must always try to do good things, to do right things, and someday it will come back to us.

易 이	輶 유	攸 유	畏 외	屬 속	耳 이	垣 원	墙 장
i	yu	yu	oe	sok	i	won	jang
쉬울	가벼울	바	두려울	붙일	귀	담	담
swi	gabyeoul	ba	duryeoul	butil	gwi	dam	dam
easy	light	thing	fear	stick	ear	fence	wall
199. 쉽고 가볍게 보일지라도, 헐뜯거나 비웃으면 원한을 부른다				200. 속담에 담장에도 귀가 있다고 한다			
It may seem easy and light, but if you scold or laugh, you call a grudge				The proverb says that the fence has ears			
무역貿易	유차輶車	유연攸然	경외敬畏	소속所屬	이목耳目	원장垣牆	판장板墙
trade/ commerce	light -cart	nonchalant -shape	honor &fear	belong	eye&ear attention	tree&grass -fence	plank -fence
易이: 바꾸다 change turn transform 輶유: light lightweight mild 攸유: 곳 위태 scene spot dangerous 畏외: 꺼리다 reluctant avert hesitate				屬속: 붙다 동아리 stick attach club circle group 耳이: 듣다 hear act listen 垣원: 토원土垣 soil-fence wall 墙장: =牆 경계 boundary border			

101. 호의호식과 식도락가 (구선손반 적구충장)

학창 시절, 친구 가족이랑 익산에 있는 원불교 동산선원에 간 적이 있다. 둘러 보다 점심시간이 되어, 기다란 밥상이 놓여 있는 좌식 식당으로 갔다. 세속의 가정식과 별반 다르지 않았으나, 기름진 것보다 나물 종류의 초식성 반찬으로, 적절하면서 간편하고 깔끔하게 마련되어 경건한 마음으로 기도하고 식사 후 그릇까지 식수로 돌려 깨끗이 마셨다. 수도 생활은 허례허식 없이 식사와 행동 등 모든 것이 감사요, 절제요, 기도였다. 아래 시처럼, 고른 영양을 위해 반찬(선)을 갖추어, 물에 밥 넣어(손반) 먹고, 입에 맞아(적구), 배 채우는 것(충장)으로 만족하고 감사하면서 세속의 모범을 보여주는 듯하다. 기름지고 맛있는 것으로 잔뜩 배 채울 때는 그럴 듯하게 좋지만, 좀 지나면 가볍고 산뜻한 느낌보다 몸에 부담 느끼는 경우가 많다. 어린 성장기나 혈기 왕성한 젊은 시절을 포함하여, 되도록 작은 양의 식사가 좋다는 연구 결과를 여러 미디어에서 발표하고 있다.

101. Dressing well and faring richly and Epicure

During my school days, I went to Won Buddhism Dongsan Seonwon(believer training institute) in Iksan with my friend's family. I looked around here and there and went to a sedentary restaurant where a long table was placed. It was not much different from the secular family, but It is a herbaceous side dish of herb rather than oily, and it is prepared with appropriate, simple and neat, praying with a pious heart, and after eating, it turned to drinking water and drank it cleanly. The monasticism was all gratitude, discipline, prayer, and all things such as eating and acting without any hesitation. Like the poem below, it seems to show a model of worldliness by satisfying and grateful for having a side dish for even nutrition, eating in water, filling your mouth, filling your stomach. It is plausible when you fill your stomach with oily and delicious things, but after a while, you often feel burdened by your body rather than feeling light and fresh. There have shown in many studies that small amount of meals is good, including during childhood and a period of vigorous youth.

具 구	膳 선	飧 손	飯 반	適 적	口 구	充 충	腸 장
gu	seon	son	ban	jeok	gu	chung	jang
갖출	반찬	저녁밥	밥	맞을	입	채울	창자
gachul	banchan	jeonyeok bap	bap	majeul	ip	chaeul	changja
repare	sidedish	dinner	rice	fitting	mouth	fill	intestine
201. 반찬을 갖추어 밥을 물 말아 먹되, 고전에 말하기를 배부른 것을 구하지 말고				202. 학자는 입에 맞아, 주린 배를 채우는 것으로 만족하라			
Do not get a lot of eating to say in classics, but eat water rice with a side dish				A scholar is fit in the mouth, satisfied by filling the stomach			
가구家具	선물膳物	옹손饔飧	조반朝飯	적성適性	인구人口	충족充足	위장胃腸
furniture	gift/ present	breakfast &dinner	breakfast	aptitude /fitness	population	satisfy /fulfill	stomach& intestine

具구: 그릇 함께 bowl with together
膳선: 선사膳賜 give-thing
飧손: =飧≒湌=餐 밥말 eat water-rice
飯반: 밥먹다 eating-meal&rice

適적: 알맞다 편안 right affordable comfort
口구: 입구入口 entrance gate entry
充충: 가득차다 fill-up packed rich
腸장: 창자 마음 자세 bowels mind posture

221

102. 시장이 반찬이더라 (포어팽자 기염조강)

사회생활과 군대 훈련 생활의 가장 큰 차이는 상명 하복과 규칙적인 생활도 있지만, 식사인 것 같다. 훈련은 육체적인 훈련이다. 아침 허겁지겁 먹고 쉴 틈도 없이 모여서 강도 높은 훈련이 시작된다. 구보와 제식 훈련, 쪼그려 뛰기, 선착순 달리기, 기합, 이런 훈련은 점심때까지 계속된다. 점심도 각자의 밥그릇에 부족한 듯한 양을 주는 대로 먹어야 한다. 점심 휴식도 번쩍 지나가고, 집합하여 훈련이 계속된다. 군대 식사를 짬밥(잔밥)이라 하는데, 잠시 후면 배고파진다. 강도 높은 훈련 때문인지, 몇 년 전에 생산된 군량미 때문인지는 모르지만, 훈련병들은 후자처럼 부실한 군량미라서 영양가가 별로 없다고들 말한다. 저녁에는 거의 그로기 상태에서 식사하게 된다. 사회에서는 배부르게 먹어, 맛있는 소고기나 찜 요리도 남기는데(포어팽자), 군대서는 배고파서, 돼지에게 주는 찌꺼기 밥을 먹는(기염조강) 훈련병도 있었다. 훈련병은 소지한 작은 용돈으로 군대 매점(피엑스) 빵을 구매하여 화장실에서 눈치껏 먹기도 한다. 혈기 왕성한 젊은 시절, 배고픈 백성을 마구 잡아들이는 조선시대 경찰(포도청) 같은 목구멍이여, 불쌍한 훈련병이여.

102. The hungry is a best appetite

The big difference between a social life and a military training life is that there are absolute orders and the subordinate obeys but having a meal as well. Training is physical training. The mornings are full of food and no breaks, and the intense training begins. Lunch should also be eaten as you give the amount that seems to be lacking in your own rice bowl. Lunch breaks flash past, and the training continues in groups. Military meals are called Janbap, and after a while I am hungry. It may be due to intense training or the military rice produced a few years ago, but the trainees say that they are poor military rice like the latter and have little nutrition. In the evening, we shall eat almost in a groggy state. In society, they eat full, leave delicious beef or steamed dishes, and the military is hungry, and there were trainees who ate discarded rice for pigs. The trainees buy the army canteen bread with the small money they have and eat it in the toilet. It is pity to see there are a poor trainee in their youth.

飽 포	飫 어	烹 팽	宰 재	飢 기	厭 염	糟 조	糠 강
po	eo	paeng	jae	gi	yeom	jo	gang
배부를	배부를	삶을	재상	주릴	싫을	지게미	겨
baebureul	baebureul	salmeul	jaesang	juril	salmeul	jigemi	gyeo
full	full	boil	premier	hungry	hate	dreg	chaff
203. 배부르면 삶은 고기도 먹기 싫고				204. 배고프면 술지게미처럼 형편없는 것도 찾는다			
If the stomach are full, Man don't want to eat boiled meat				If you're hungry, you find something as bad as scraps			
포식飽食	어사飫賜	팽란烹卵	주재主宰	요기療飢	염증厭症	주조酒糟	조박糟粕
eat full	give grant	boiled egg	take care of the work	allay -hunger	inflam- matory	wine -lees	residue

飽포: 실컷 먹다 eat a lot
飫어: 포식 eat a lot
烹팽: 익힌 요리 boiled cook haute cuisine
宰재: 다스리다 control govern manage

飢기: 흉년 기아 bad-year hunger starvation
厭염: 염세厭世 pessimism weariness of life
糟조: 찌거기 residue left after rice wine is drained
糠강: 쌀겨 chaff rice-bran

103. 식성은 다양하다 (친척고구 노소이량)

우리는 나이에 따라 먹는 음식의 종류와 양도 다르다.

아기는 당연 모유와 분유를 먹는다. 어쩌다 처가에서 식사하다 보면 할아버지 할머니 밥상은 조그만 상에 밥과 간장, 들기름, 된장국이나 나물국 또는 미역국, 김치 등 간소하게 따로 주고, 또한 가루 영양식 등이 항상 곁에 있다. 그녀의 부모와 우리는 조부모보다는 좀 화려한 듯 멸치볶음, 고기와 생선 등이 추가 된다. 누가 보기엔 차별적 상차림처럼 보이지만, 세심한 배려가 있는 듯하다. 동성끼리도 다르며, 남녀 간에도 식성에 따라 다르겠지만, 보편적으로 보면 음식 양과 종류도 조금씩 다른 듯하다. 어린이와 젊은 사람, 나이 많음에 따라 음식도 달리함(노소이량)이 좋을 듯하다.

103. Taste from each person is varied

We have different types and amounts of food to eat depending on age. The baby naturally eats mother's milk and milk powder. When I eat at my wife's house, her grandfather's grandmother's table is a small table, it's a simple separate, giving rice, soy sauce, perilla oil, miso soup, herb soup, seaweed soup, kimchi etc, also, powder nutrition is always around. Her parents and we add anchovy, meat and fish, rather than grandparents. It seems to be a discriminatory table, but it seems to have careful consideration. Same sexes are different, and between men and women, depending on their diet, but universally, the amount and type of food seem to be slightly different. For children and young people, depending on their age, it will be nice to adjust the sorts and amounts of food.

팥죽과 비빔밥

親 친	戚 척	故 고	舊 구	老 로	少 소	異 이	糧 량
chin	cheok	go	gu	ro	so	i	ryang
친할	거레	옛	옛	늙을	젊을	다를	양식
chinhal	gyeorae	yet	yet	neulkeul	jeolmeul	dareul	yangsik
friendly	relative	old	old	old	young	different	food
205. 친척과 옛친구를 접할 때, 소화능력에 따라				206. 늙고 젊음에 따라, 음식을 달리 해야 한다			
When you encounter your relatives and old friends, according to digestive capacity				Depending on your age and youth, you have to change your food			
부친父親	외척外戚	고국故國	구식舊式	원로元老	소량少量	이국異國	식량食糧
father	mother-relative	homeland/native-country	old-fashion	elder/veteran	small&little amount	other country	food/provisions

親친: 화목 harmony concord	老로: 늙은이 old person aged-person elder
戚척: 가깝다 close near more like	少소: 조금 bit some little
故고: 연고지 based hometown located	異이: 구분하다 distinguish classify
舊구: 오래되다 long-ago for a long time	糧량: 군량미軍糧米 military food

104. 없어져야 할 관습과 차별 (첩어적방 시건유방)

　서구 유럽과 한국 등 선진국은 형식상으로 남녀 차별이 없어진 지 오래다. 아들 딸, 남녀 의식하지 말고 자기 꿈과 희망과 목표와 뜻을 펼치도록 끊임없이 노력함이 마땅하다. 이번 시는 남녀 차별적 옛날 전설 같은 문장이다. 단순히 한자 익히는 것으로 만족해야 할 듯하다. 뜨개질 하듯, 옛날 수공업으로 천을 짜던 시절(적방)에서 탈피하여, 요즘은 세계적으로 방직문화가 발달하여 옷으로 몸 가리는 역할과 신분의 차이를 벗어나, 패션의 가치와 미적 표현의 상징이 된 듯하다. 더구나 화장실 문화가 발달하여 사시사철 냉온수가 나오고, 세탁기가 있어 향기 나는 수건이 항상 즐비하다. 후진적인 나라, 세계 도처에 아직도 여성을 가볍게 보는 나라가 많아 안타깝다. 다시 말하지만, 여성들은 좌절 말고 용기가 매우 필요하다. 한국은 신분이 귀하고 천함에 따라, 수건을 들고 화장실 문 앞에서 기다리는 일이 오래 전에 사라졌다(시건유방).

104. Custom and discrimination to be eliminated

　In developed countries such as Western European countries and South Korea there is no discrimination between men and women long time ago. It is necessary to constantly try to spread your dreams, hopes, goals and wills without being conscious of son and daughter, men and women. This poem is a male-female, old-fashioned legend. It seems to be satisfied with simply learning Chinese characters. As knitting, we're off the old handicrafts weaving cloths, Nowadays, the textile culture has developed worldwide, and it seems to have become a symbol of the value of fashion and aesthetic expression, escaping the difference between the role and status of covering the body with clothes. Moreover, the toilet culture has developed, and cold and hot water comes out, and there is a washing machine, so there are always fragrant towels. It is a pity that there are many countries that still look lightly at women all over the world. Again, women need very much courage, not frustration. The habit according to the identity to wait in front of the bathroom door with a towel disappeared a long time ago.

妾첩	御어	績적	紡방	侍시	巾건	帷유	房방
cheop	eo	jeok	bang	si	geon	yu	bang
첩	모실	길쌈	길쌈	모실	수건	장막	방
cheop	mosil	gilssam	gilssam	mosil	sugeon	jangmak	bang
mistress	serve	spin	spin	serve	towel	tent	room
207. 옛 남성 문화에 따라, 처와 첩은 옷을 만들고				208. 커튼 친 방문 밖에서, 수건을 들고 기다린다			
According to the old male culture, the wife and concubine make clothes				Outside the curtained door, wait with a towel			
처첩妻妾	어용御用	성적成績	방적紡績	시중侍從	수건手巾	박유薄帷	주방廚房
wife& handmaid	bad-intel lectual	grade /score	spinning	care/serve	facecloth washcloth	thin- insignia	kitchen/ cookroom

妾첩: 하녀=몸종 lady's maid handmaid
御어: 섬김 거느리다 attend have lead
績적: 잇다 이루다 join link, realize achieve
紡방: 실 잣다 thread spin take a thread

侍시: 기르다 care raise grow
巾건: 헝겊 cloth
帷유: 휘장揮帳 덮개 insignia curtain cover
房방: 집 아내 home house-wife

227

105. 전통의 새로운 변신과 탄생 (환선원결 은촉위황)

필자가 옛 시골 농촌에서 호롱불로 지냈던 마지막 세대인 듯하다. 그릇에 석유를 넣고, 무명실 심지를 담근다. 그 심지에 불을 켜는 호롱불이다. 호롱불이 운치가 있어, 요즘은 호롱불 전구로 만든 장식품으로 카페나 레스토랑에 걸어 분위기를 살리고 있다. 호롱불보다 발전한 것이 촛불이다. 촛불은 그을음이 나오지 않고 더 밝다. 단지 더 비싸므로 부자 집에서나 사용했다. 요즘도 고급 식당이나, 사찰 교회 등 종교시설에서 사용한다. 자기를 태워 주위를 밝혀 주는 살신성인의 상징이라 이용하는 듯하다. 호롱불 전구처럼 촛불 전구가 분위기 장식용으로 시판되고 있다. 귀족과 절대 군주의 상징인 옛 궁궐에는 은빛의 촛불이 빛나고(은촉위황), 비단으로 만든 둥근 부채(환선원결)로 시녀들이 서비스 하고 있는 모습을 영화에서나 볼 수 있으리라.

105. New transformation of tradition

It seems to be the last generation lived with a holong fire that I have been in the old rural area. It is a holong fire that puts oil in a bowl, soak cotton thread wick, and turns on the light at the wick. There is a holong fire, and nowadays it is a decoration made of holong fire light bulb, and it is walking in cafes and restaurants to make the mood good. The candle is more advanced than the holong fire. The candle is brighter without soot. It is only more expensive, so it is used in rich houses. It is used in religious facilities such as high-level restaurants and temple churches. It seems to be used as a symbol of a sacrifice oneself to preserve one's integrity saint who burns himself and illuminates his surroundings. Like a holong fire bulb, candlelight bulbs are being marketed for mood decorations. The old palace, a symbol of the nobility and absolute monarch, will be able to see in the movie.

紈 환	扇 선	圓 원	潔 결	銀 은	燭 촉	煒 위	煌 황
hwan	seon	won	gyeol	eun	chok	wi	hwang
흰비단	부채	둥글	맑을	은	촛불	빛날	빛날
huinbidan	buchae	dunggeul	malkeul	eun	chotbul	bitnal	bitna
white silk	fan	round	clear /pure	silver	candle-light	shine	shine
209. 흰 비단으로 만든 부채는 둥글고 깨끗하며				210. 은빛 같은 촛불은 밝게 빛난다			
The white silk fan is round and clean				The silvery candles glow brightly			
빙환氷紈	원선圓扇	원불교	청결淸潔	은행銀行	화촉華燭	위어煒如	황성煌星
smooth silk	round fan	圓佛教 won-buddhism	clean/ cleanse/ purify	bank	colored candle	very bright shape	shining star

紈환: 겹치다 overlap	銀은: 돈 money cash fund
扇선: 선동 incite agitate instigate	燭촉: 초 비추다 candle light shine
圓원: 동그라미 하늘 circle sky heaven	煒위: 빨갛다 밝다 red bright
潔결: 깨끗 바르다 fresh right correct	煌황: 황황히煌煌 flashing brightly

106. 왕조시대 권력자 실상과 현재 [주면석매 남순상상]

독서도 좋아하지만 가끔 영화도 본다. 편안히 휴식하고, 비용이 저렴한 주로 실버 극장의 흘러간 추억의 영화다. 처음 보는 것과 과거에 봤던 것이 더러 있다. 영화에서 볼 수 있는 절대 군주의 상징인 대궐 왕실의 쪽빛 죽순과 코끼리가 그려진 침대(남순상상)에 걸쳐 앉아, 옆에는 하녀가 선녀형 묶음 머리를 하고, 오색 깃털 부채 바람결에 눈을 깜박 거리며 졸고, 밤에는 잠자고 있는 군주의 모습(주면석매), 그야말로 사람의 귀천이 태어나면서 결정되는 왕정시절의 모습이다. 잘못된 제도로 무시 받는 세상, 평범한 집안에서 태어나, 성장하면서 보고 듣고 하늘의 이치를 깨달은 사람이 많았으리라. 그러한 제도를 탓하며, 그 사람들이 자기의 신분에 대해 너무 억울하게 생각 했으리라. 그러한 것이 동서고금 불문하고 의적과 반란이 끊임없이 발생하게 된 이유 중 하나가 아닐까. 억울해했던 사람이 혁명에 성공하여도 앞선 제도와 비슷하거나 조금 변혁된 경우가 대부분이라는 것이 문제고, 그처럼 반복 되는 역사의 수레바퀴라는 것이 아이러니하다. E. H. Carr(Edward Halleat Carr, 1892-1982)의 『역사란 무엇인가』의 지적처럼 "역사는 반복되는 것처럼 보이지만, 나사처럼 전진한다."는 통찰력에 의지해야 하니 안타깝다.

106. The reality and present of the powers in the dynasty

I like reading books, but sometimes I like watching movies. It is a memorable movie of silver theater, which is comfortable and cheap. There are some things I have seen for the first time and what I have seen in the past. Sitting across a bed with a picture of the royal indigo and elephants, the symbol of the absolute monarch seen in the movie, Next to him is a maid with a bundle of angel's hairstyle, a monarch who sleeps at night, blinking and blinking in the wind of a five-color feather fan, It is a figure of the monarchy that is determined by the birth of high and low. Many people would have been born in a world that was ignored by the wrong system, a normal family, and realized the reason of heaven by seeing and hearing it as they grew up. They would have blamed such a system and thought too unfairly about their identity. Is that one reason why the rituals and rebellions constantly occur regardless of the all ages and countries? It is ironic that the person who was unhappy is mostly similar to or slightly transformed from the previous system even if he succeeded in the revolution, and it is the wheel of history that is repeated like that. As E. H. Carr's 『What is history』 points out, history seems to repeat itself, but it is a pity that we have to rely on the insight of advancing like a screw.

晝 주	眠 면	夕 석	寐 매	藍 람	筍 순	象 상	床 상
ju	myeon	seok	mae	ram	sun	sang	sang
낮	졸	저녁	잘	쪽	죽순	코끼리	평상
nat	jol	jeonyeok	jil	jjok	juk	koggiri	pyeongsang
day	nap	evening	sleep	violet	bamboo	elephant	bench
211. 은퇴한 공직자는 걱정 없이, 낮에는 졸고, 밤에는 자는데				212. 푸른 대나무와 코끼리를 그려 장식한 침대를 사용한다			
Retired officials doze during the day, sleep at night, without worrying				The bed which decorates with the blue bamboo and elephant is used			
주야晝夜	수면睡眠	추석秋夕	몽매夢寐	가람伽藍	죽순竹筍	기상氣象	책상冊床
day& night	sleep	Korean Thanksgiving -Day	dream in sleep	buddhist temple	bamboo shoot	natural pheno- menon	desk/ table
晝주: 주경야독 work by day and study by night 眠면: 쉬다 졸다 rest break doze 夕석: 밤 night 寐매: 잠자는 미녀(사자) sleeping beauty(lion)				藍람: 쪽빛 indigo deep-violet blue 筍순: 가마 여린 대나무 kiln soft-bamboo 象상: 조짐 추상적 sign abstract 床상: =牀, 온상溫床 warm floor(bed)			

107. 신분을 떠나 여흥은 즐겁다 (현가주연 접배거상)

나이트클럽 밤 문화가 일시적으로 유행하던 시절, 낭랑 악극단의 곡예사들의 연극처럼 중앙 무대에서 흥을 돋우어(현가주연) 볼 만했다. 훤칠한 키의 남성과 볼륨감 넘치는 여성이 등장하여 팬터마임(pantomime)같은 형식으로 이십여 분 진행된, 다이나믹하고 과격한 동작은 관중들 시선을 집중시켰다. 팬터마임 연극이 끝난 후, 그들이 의상을 벗고, 관중에게 인사하는데 둘 다 남성이어서 폭소를 터트리고, 다행이다 싶었다. 이후 가수가 등장하여 두세 곡 노래하고, 품바 팀의 각설이 타령과 신명난 코미디로 관객을 흥분시켰다. 학교 대강당처럼 큰 영동 나이트클럽에 사람들이 발 디딜 틈 없이 꽉 차, 앉을 자리가 없을 정도다. 과일과 마른안주, 병맥주로 건배하고 부딪치며, 마시면서 모처럼 흥미롭게 구경했다(접배거상).

107. Apart from our identity, the entertainment is always pleasant

In the days when nightclub was popular, it was as exciting as the acrobats of the recital theater group, and it was worth watching it on the central stage. A tall man and a voluminous woman appeared, and they made the dynamic and radical movements, which was carried out for twenty minutes in a pantomime-like form, got an attention of the audience. After the pantomime play, they took off their costumes and greeted the crowd, both of them were men, so they wanted to laugh and be glad. Since then, the singer has appeared and sang two or three songs, and the Pumba team has excited the audience with a singing beggar ballad and a exciting comedy. People are packed in a big Yeongdong nightclub like the school auditorium,

and there is no place to sit. We cheered and bumped with drinks such as a
bottle of beer, and enjoyed the atmosphere with people.

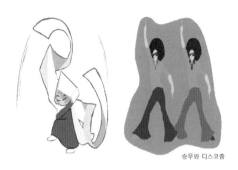

승무와 디스코춤

絃 현	歌 가	酒 주	讌 연	接 접	杯 배	擧 거	觴 상
hyeon	ga	ju	yeon	jeop	bae	geo	sang
줄	노래	술	잔치	접할	잔	들	잔
jul	norae	sul	janchi	jeophal	jan	deul	jan
string	song	alcohol	feast	contact	cup	enter	cup
213. 거문고를 타고, 노래하며, 술잔치를 하는데				214. 잔을 서로 채우고, 술잔을 들어 권한다			
We're playing strings, singing, and having a drink party				Fill each other with glasses, lift them and recommend them			
현악絃樂	가수歌手	맥주麥酒	주연酒宴	대접待接	건배乾杯	선거選擧	옥상玉觴
string music	singer/ vocalist	beer/ lager	feast& drink	treat/ receive	toast/ drink to / cheers	election/ campaign	glass cup of jade
絃현: 현악기 string-instrument strings 歌가: 가곡歌曲 lyrical song by adding poem 酒주: 포도주葡萄酒 wine vinous-liquor 讌연: =醼 환담하다 chat with confabulate				接접: 사귀다 잡다 make friend date-hold catch 杯배: =盃 축배祝杯 celebratory drink toasting 擧거: 권하다 올리다 offer advise raise lift 觴상: 술잔 wineglass goblet winecup			

108. 유흥의 속성 (교수돈족 열예차강)

영동 나이트클럽에 구경하러 동료교수와 간 적이 있다. 어렸을 적 야외 가설 유랑극단 내용과 비슷하다. 나이트클럽은 낭랑 악극단 구경처럼 술 마시며 구경하는 재미로 가는 곳이다. 그 이후 가라오케나 노래방이 들어와 친구들과 노래 부르며, 소규모 모임 하는 것으로 변화한 듯하다. 요즘은 그러한 곳이 많이 변질된 것으로 매스컴에 보도되고 있어 안타깝다. 음주하며, 손을 놀리며, 발을 구르고, 춤을 추는 모습(교수돈족)은 가라오케 문화다. 혈기 왕성한 젊음을 발산하는 과정이라 본다. 생애주기별 정서에 따라, 열광 하면서 춤추고, 기쁘고, 즐거우며, 흥겨우리라(열예차강).

108. The attribution of entertainment

I went to a nightclub in Yeongdong with a fellow professor. It is similar to the outdoor theater when I was a child. Nightclubs are places where you go to the fun of drinking and watching like a sonorous musical troupe. Since then, karaoke or singing rooms has come in, singing with friends, and seems to have changed into small gatherings. It is a pity that such a place has been reported in the media these days as a lot of deterioration. Drinking, teasing your hands, rolling your feet and dancing is a karaoke culture. I think it's a process of exuding a vigorous youth. We enjoy dancing with a passion, and delight, and enjoyment, depending on the emotions of each life cycle.

矯 교	手 수	頓 돈	足 족	說 열	豫 예	且 차	康 강
gyo	su	don	jok	yeol	ye	cha	gang
바로잡을	손	조아릴	발	기쁠	미리	또	편안할
barojapeul	son	joaril	bal	gibbeul	miri	tto	pyeonanhal
correct	hand	deep-bow	foot	please	before	again	comfort
215. 손을 굽혔다 펴고, 발을 구르며, 덩실덩실 춤을 추니				216. 기쁘고 즐거우며, 마음이 편안하다			
Guests bent and spread my hands, rolled my feet, danced in lively				They are joy and happy, and at ease			
교정矯正	가수歌手	정돈整頓	발족發足	희열喜悅	예산豫算	차치且置	건강健康
revision correct	singer/ vocalist	arrange	inaugu-ration/ start	joy delight	budget/ finances	unproble-matic	health/ fit
矯교: 거짓 핑계 false excuse pretense 手수: 손가락 팔 finger arm 頓돈: 두드리다 tap knock bang 足족: 지나치다 만족 too excessive over-satisfy				說열: =설, 소설가小說家 novelist fiction writer 豫예: 즐기다 joy pleasure enjoyment 且차: 도마 kitchen board cutting-board 康강: 화목 harmony concord peace			

109. 제사, 현재와 미래의 변화 (적후사속 제사증상)

요즘은 남녀 평등시대다. 부모로부터 상속도, 장남, 둘째 아들, 남녀 구별 없다. 법과 제도가 바뀌고 있어, 당연한 현상인데도 아직도 옛날 풍습의 경직된 마인드가 있는 부모들이 더러 보여, 갈등이 표출되고, 가족적 사회적 지탄을 받는 사례가 있다. 자손들의 화목이 더 중요하다. 하루 속히 모든 차별은 없어져야 하리라. 같은 형제, 남매라 해도 천성에 따라 붙임성과 싹싹한 사람이 있는 반면 노력해도 무뚝뚝하고 잔정이 부족한 형제가 있기 마련이다. 이러한 것도 감안하고 주의하여 형제들 간에 희생과 양보하는 정신으로 잘 협의하여 각 가정형편에 따른 책임과 의무도 함께 해야 하리라. 꼰대 같은 시절은 지나가고 있지만, 세상 살면서 관혼상제는 누구에게나 당연 있는 일들이라고 볼 수 있다. 허나 요즘은 가치관이 많이 변하고 있어 재검토가 필요한 시점이기도 하다. 혼인과 제사가 많이 흔들리고 있다. 대세는 결혼임에는 분명하지만 소수도 중요한 면이 있다. 변화의 단초를 보여 주기 때문이리라. 그중 제사가 어찌 보면 가장 중요하다. 봄 여름 가을 겨울 등 계절별(제사증상)로, 여기다 삼년상까지 있었던 시절에 비하면, 요즘은 많이 단순해지고 절차가 생략되어 가고 있다. 제사의 기본 취지와 정신은 조상에 대한 예법을 기회로 삼아, 가족 간의 왕래와 친목 도모 및 우애다. 많은 세월이 흐르더라도, 인간이라는 것과 삶의 근본을 생각해 볼 때, 그 중요성은 유지하고 발전되어야 할 기본 도리가 아닐까.

109. Ancestral rites, Change between the present and future

These days, it is the age of equality between men and women. There is no distinction between inheritance, eldest son, second son, and man and woman from parents. Laws and systems are changing, and even though it is a natural phenomenon, there are cases where parents who still have rigid minds of old customs are seen, conflicts are expressed, and family social grievances are received. The harmony of the offspring is more important. All discrimination should be eliminated as soon as possible. The same brother and sister have a brother and a brother who are blunt and lacking in calm, while there are people who are close and spooky depending on nature. Considering this, we should be careful and consult with the spirit of sacrifice and concession among the brothers, and we should also take responsibility and obligation according to each family situation. Nowadays, it is becoming simple and the procedure is being omitted. The basic purpose and spirit of the sacrifice is the opportunity to make a courtesy of the ancestors, and it is to visit family, to promote friendship, and to be friendly. Even after many years, when we think about the human being and the fundamentals of life, the importance of sacrifice is the basic principle to be maintained and developed.

嫡 적	後 후	嗣 사	續 속	祭 제	祀 사	蒸 증	嘗 상
jeok	hu	sa	sok	je	sa	jeung	sang
정실	뒤	이을	이을	제사	제사	찔	맛볼
jeongsil	dwi	ieul	ieul	jesa	jesa	jjil	matbol
wife	back	succeed	succeed	ritual	memorial	boil	taste
217. 옛날 법에, 맏아들이 뒤를 이어 가계를 계승하고				218. 조상에게, 겨울제사(증) 가을제사(상)로 계절마다 지낸다			
In the old law, the eldest son succeeded the family				It is seasonally given winter sacrifices (jeung) and autumn sacrifices (sang), for the ancestors			
정적正嫡	오후午後	후사後嗣	계속繼續	축제祝祭	참사參祀	증기蒸氣	상미嘗味
wife	after-noon	son of the generation	continue	festival	attend the sacrifice	steam/vapor	taste before-hand
嫡적: 적종嫡宗 only lasted for the firstborn 後후: 늦다 late slow 嗣사: 상속자 후임자 successor heir 續속: 연속連續 successive continuous				祭제: 문화제文化祭 cultural festival 祀사: 제사상祭祀床 sacrificial table 蒸증: 겨울제사 덥다 winter sacrifice, hot 嘗상: 가을제사 미리 autumn sacrifice, before			

110. 반가움의 표시 (계상재배 송구공황)

학창 시절 지리과목 고 선생이 수업 시간에 재치 있는 일화를 소개하였다. 옛날 왕정시대의 전설 같은 시절, 상감마마(왕)를 찾아가 인기척을 해도 아무런 움직임도 안 보이고, 눈 감고 있는 듯하여, 한 번 큰절하고 엎드려서 얼핏 보니, 아직도 미동도 없는 듯하여, 절하는 걸 보지 못했다 싶어, 다시 큰절을 올리니, 대뜸 네 이놈 어찌 산 사람한테 두 번이나 절 하느냐고 호통치는 바람에, 큰 코 다쳤구나 하며 망설이다, 기지를 발휘하여, 네, 상감마마 이제 물러가고자 하는 절입니다, 라고 말하여 위기를 벗어났다는 일화다. 그 시절은 임금 눈 밖에 나면 목숨이 걸려 있던 때이니, 어찌 두렵지 않겠는가. 송구스럽고 두려워하며, 머리를 조아리며 두 번 절(송구공황, 계상재배)하노라. 세계화 된 요즘은 인사하는 방법이 다양화되었다. 또한 코로나19 시대가 되어, 지역과 신분과 남녀노소 불문하여 악수가 아닌 주먹인사가 세계적 추세가 된 듯하다. 인사 예절의 평등화, 아직 좀 어색하긴 하다.

110. The sign of pleasure

During my school days, a geography teacher introduced a witty anecdote in the class. In the legendary days of the old monarchy, when a retainer visited a king, he could not see any movement of the king, and it seems that the king's eyes were close. It seemed that the king did not see him bow, He raised the big bow again to the king, then the king said that the retainer had a big problem because he bowed twice to the alive person, it means that the king died. It was an anecdote that he however escaped the crisis by saying that he was now bow to say goodbye to the king to go out from the room. It is a time when the life was at stake when the king was out of sight, so how could he be not afraid? He was ashamed and afraid, and he was twice with giving a deep bow with his head. Nowadays, the way of greeting has been diversified. In addition, in the Corona 19th era, it seems that the fist greetings, not handshakes, have become a global trend regardless of region, status, and age, young and old, men and women. Equalization of greeting etiquette, it is still a bit awkward

稽 계	顙 상	再 재	拜 배	悚 송	懼 구	恐 공	惶 황
gye	sang	jae	bae	song	gu	gong	hwang
조아릴	이마	두	절	두려울	두려울	두려울	두려울
joaril	ima	du	jeol	duryeoul	duryeoul	duryeoul	duryeoul
bend	forehead	twice	bow	fear	fear	fear	fear
219. 제사 때, 땅에 이마를 대며 두 번 절하고				220. 위계질서를 위해, 송구하고 두렵고 황송한 태도를 취한다			
At the sacrifice, He bowed twice with my forehead on the ground				For hierarchy, he takes a remorse, a fearful, and a perplexed attitude			
계류稽留	박상博顙	재생再生	세배歲拜	송한悚汗	경구敬懼	공황恐慌	경황驚惶
stay in guest-house	broad forehead	renewable /recycle	greet one's holiday	sweating in fear	honor and fear	panic	startled, panicked scurry
稽계: 생각 검토 think review consider				悚송: 송구悚懼 afraid and uncomfortable			
顙상: 머리 head				懼구: 의구심疑懼心 doubtful&fearful mind			
再재: 반복 거듭 repeat again				恐공: 염려하다 concern worry care fear			
拜배: 굽히다 bend forward bend-over bow				惶황: 당황 perplexed panic			

111. 기다림과 편지의 간절함 (전첩간요 고답심상)

편지 쓴 지가 너무 오래되어 언제였는지 가물가물하다. 아이들 엄마에게 연애편지는 아직도 기억에 또렷하다. 지금처럼 모바일 등 통신시설이 발달하지 않던 시절, 까마득한 옛날처럼 느껴진다. 그녀는 우체부 아저씨 오기만 기다렸다니, 가히 짐작이 간다. 우체부 아저씨만 봐도 설레던 시절이다. 지나고 나니 참 좋은 추억이다. 요즘은 이메일도 이미 가고, 핸드폰 카톡이나 문자가 편지를 대체하고 있는 듯하다. 연애편지는 있는 감정, 낭만 찾아 보내느라 비교적 장문이다. 요즘은 장문은 없고 단답식 한 줄이나 외마디, 그것도 이모티콘으로 감정을 전달하는 신호시대로 변하고 있다. 복잡한 것을 싫어하고, 단순하고 명쾌한 것을 좋아하는 시대 상황과 다르지 않다. 아래 나오는 시도 요즘 세대 마인드와 같다. 윗사람이나 친구에게 보내는 편지의 장문은, 해석상 오해가 발생될 여지가 있어, 요점만 간단 명료(전첩간요)하게 하고, 답장은 좌우전후를 잘 살피어 신중함(고답심상)이 서로에게 정성이리라.

111. Waiting and eagerness of a letter

It's been so long since I wrote a letter. The love letter to the mother of my children is still clear in my memory. It feels like a long time ago when communication facilities such as mobile were not developed like now. She can only imagine waiting for the postman to come, I can guess. It was a thrilling time to look at the postman. It is a good memory after passing. Nowadays, e-mails are already gone, and cell phone katoks and texts seem to be replacing letters. The love letter is relatively long because it is a feeling and romance. Nowadays, there is no long sentence, and it is changing to a signaling time to convey emotions to a single line or a single word, and emoticons. It is not different from the times when I hate complex things and like simple and clear things. The poems below are like the mindset of the generation these days. The long text of a letter to a superior or a friend, there is room for interpretation of misunderstanding, thus you should make a point simple and clear, and you should look at the left and right before and after of a reply from the letter, and the prudence will be careful to each other.

牋 전	牒 첩	簡 간	要 요	顧 고	答 답	審 심	詳 상
jeon	cheop	gan	yo	go	dap	sim	sang
편지	편지	간략할	중요할	돌아볼	대답	살필	자세할
pyeonji	pyeonji	ganryakhal	jungyohal	dolabol	daedap	salpil	jasehal
letter	letter	simple	important	review	answer	look	detail
221. 편지는 간단히, 중요한 것만, 간추려서 적어야 하고				222. 답장은 오해가 생기지 않도록, 잘 살펴서 자세히 한다			
Letters should be written simply, only important, in a brief way				The reply is carefully examined and detailed so that no misunderstanding occurs			
투전鬪牋	청첩請牒	간이簡易	필요必要	고객顧客	답변答辯	심사審查	상보詳報
gambling -tool	wedding invitation	easy to use	need necessity	customer	answer	judge/ screen	report in detail

牋전: 종이 채전彩牋 paper poetry colored paper
牒첩: 공문서 official document
簡간: 간이역簡易驛 simple station
要요: 요구하다 demand require claim

顧고: 고려하다 consider think over
答답: 해답解答 보답 solution reward
審심: 주심主審 chief(head) umpire
詳상: 속이다 trick cheat deceive fool

112. 문화생활 변화에 인간의 적응 (해구상욕 집열원량)

요즘은 욕실 문화요 화장실 문화라는 단어가 나올 정도다. 보편적으로 깔끔하고 편리한 구조다. 필자는 피부가 안 좋아 집근처 지하철 선릉역 부근 병원을 가니, 의사가 진찰 다 하고, 동물은 목욕을 자주 하지 않도록 태어났으니, 사람도 목욕을 가끔 해야 한단다. 사람도 그에 따라야 좋으리라는 요지였다. 어려서는 명절에 한 번씩, 일 년에 두세 번하는 목욕이다. 욕실이 없던 시절, 부엌에서, 설 전날 가마솥에 물을 끓여 큰 통에 적당한 온도로 만든 목욕물(집열원량)에 찌든 때를 벗겨야(해구상욕) 했다. 큰형이 도왔는데, 때가 너무 많아 까마귀가 깍깍거리겠다며, 문지르면 피가 나오는 듯 고통스러웠던 기억이 솔솔 난다. 그러다 많은 세월이 흐른, 요즘은 거의 매일 하는 샤워, 세면하듯 습관적으로 목욕을 한다. 사실 안 할 수가 없는 환경이 된 듯하다. 매일 아침에 자가용 지붕을 보면 공해먼지가 시커멓게 앉아 있다. 와이셔츠나 칼라도 단 하루 만에 목둘레에 검은 자국이 보인다. 귀지도 검은색이다. 몸도 꺼림칙해서 머리 샴푸와 바디샤워를 해야 그나마 상쾌한 기분이니 어찌하겠는가. 요즘은 공기 중 미세먼지와 환경오염 방지를 위하여 청정에너지 정책 등 전 세계적으로 노력하여 많이 개선되고 있어 다행이다.

112. Human adaptation to cultural life

These days, there is a word as a bathroom culture and a toilet culture in common. It is generality a clean and convenient structure. I went to a hospital near Seolleung Station near my house because my skin was not good, and the doctor was doing his examination, and he said that an animal is born with taking a bath not frequently, thus people have to take baths sometimes. The point was that people would be good accordingly. It is a bath once a Korean holiday, two or three times a year. In the kitchen, the day before the New Year, I had to boil water in the cauldron and peel off the bath water made of suitable temperature in a large barrel. The older brother helped me, but there are so many times that the crow will be clicked, and I remember that it was painful as if blood came out when he rubbed me. Then, after many years, nowadays, I take a shower almost every day, and I take a bath as if I were washing. In fact, it seems to have become an environment that can not be done. Every morning, when I look at the roof of the car, the pollution dust sits black. The shirt and collar also show black marks on the neck in just one day. The ear is black. I feel uncomfortable, so I have to wash my hair with shampoo and take a shower, so I feel refreshed. Nowadays, it is fortunate that many countries put a lot of efforts for the invironment such as a clean energy policy in order to prevent from fine dust in the air and environmental pollution.

骸 해	垢 구	想 상	浴 욕	執 집	熱 열	願 원	涼 량
hae	gu	sang	yok	jip	yeol	won	ryang
뼈	때	생각	목욕할	잡을	더울	원할	서늘할
bbyeo	ttae	saenggak	mokyokhal	japeul	deoul	wonhal	seoneulhal
bone	dirty	think	bath	hold	hot	wish	cool
223. 맹자 성선설에, 몸이 더러우면 목욕을 생각하듯이, 잡념에서 벗어나 마음도 깨끗이 하라				224. 뜨거운 것을 만나면, 시원한 것을 원한다			
In Mencius' theory, If you are dirty, just as you think about bathing, get out of your idle thoughts and clean your mind				When you meet something hot, you want something cool			
잔해殘骸	치구齒垢	사상思想	좌욕坐浴	집필執筆	열정熱情	염원念願	청량淸涼
debris/ wreckage	dirty stuff	thought/ thinking	sit bath	write/ author	passion /desire	hope/ wish /desire	clear& cool
骸해: 형해화形骸化 only form no value&meaning 垢구: 먼지 찌꺼기 dust residue waste 想상: 구상構想 plan conception plot of a novel 浴욕: 해수욕장海水浴場 bathing resort beach				執집: 잡다 집념執念 take catch, tenacity of purpose 熱열: 열망熱望 aspiration desire yearn 願원: 소원所願 desire make a wish 涼량: 돕다 help support aid assist			

243

113. 자연과 함께, 즐거웠던 시절 (려라독특 해약초양)

 필자의 에세이 『어머니 향기』에도 나오는 풍경이다. 내 고향 마을 앞 불갑 저수지 상류는 여름 농사를 다 짓고 나면, 물이 거의 다 소모되어 물놀이하기 좋은 개울이 된다. 드넓은 들판은 한 폭의 그림처럼 그라스 필드가 되어 어린이와 젊은 사람들의 휴식처가 된다. 필자는 송아지 딸린 어미 소(독특)의 먹이 장소로 아침부터 운동장 수십 배 이상 크기의 저수지 필드로 간다. 코 뚫은 어미 소는 풀 좋은 곳을 골라, 기다란 줄 달린 말뚝 박아 동여매 놓는다. 송아지는 놀란 노루마냥 갑자기 멈췄다 이리 뛰고 저리 뛰고(해약초양), 멀어질 듯 가까워지고, 넘어질 듯 유턴하여 어미 곁을 맴돈다. 그리고 필자는 개울에 물고기 저장용 물웅덩이를 만든다. 이리 저리 다니며 이끼 속, 자갈 속, 바위 속을 뒤져 작은 붕어, 송사리, 피라미를 잡아 웅덩이에 넣어 두고, 이놈들이 편안히 쉬도록 돌멩이를 놓고, 작은 풀들로 덮고 헤엄치는 것을 지켜보는 재미로 시간 가는 줄 모른다. 지루하면 들에 뛰노는 메뚜기 잡기놀이 한다. 메뚜기 입에서 나오는 검은 진액으로 손이 진득진득하여 느낌이 별로다. 잡은 메뚜기는 강아지풀을 끈으로 하여, 메뚜기목에 끼워 염주처럼 만든다. 어떨 때는 구워서 먹기도 하는데, 구수하기도 하지만, 벌레 같아 찜찜하기도 하다. 요즘은 보양식으로 고급식당에 등장하기도 한다. 개울 물고기 웅덩이 가 보니, 모래가 흩어지고 물고기는 어디론가 사라져 버렸다. 물고기들아, 그래 잘 갔구나. 다 놔줄려는 생각이었단다.

113. With nature, when it was fun

 It is also a landscape in my essay 『Mother's Scent』 The upper part of the Bullgap Reservoir in front of my hometown village is a good stream to play water after almost all summer period. The vast field becomes a beautiful field like a picture, making it a resting place for children and young people. I go to a reservoir field that is dozens of times the size of the playground from the morning as a food place for a calf-fed mother cow. The pierce cow's nose mother cow picks a good place to grass, and puts it in a long line of stakes. The calf suddenly stops like a surprised roe. It jumps and jumps, gets closer to the distance, and makes a U-turn as if falling and circles around the mother. And I make a fish storage pool in the stream. I wander around, searching in moss, in gravel, in rocks, catching small carp, pine, and pyramids in puddles, putting stone blinds to rest them comfortably, I do not know how to go to the fun of watching the small grass cover and swim. I play grasshoppers in the fields when I'm bored. I feel bad because my hands are full of black essence from grasshopper mouth. The grasshopper caught is made of a puppy grass to string, It fits in the grasshopper neck and it makes like the rosary. Sometimes they bake and eat, but they are like worms. Nowadays, they appear in a luxury restaurant as a recreational ceremony. When I went to the pool of stream to catch fish, the sand was scattered and the fish disappeared somewhere. Fishes!, yes, good to see you. I was going to let you go.

驢 려	騾 라	犢 독	特 특	駭 해	躍 약	超 초	驤 양
ryeo	ra	dok	teuk	hae	yak	cho	yang
나귀	노새	송아지	수컷	놀랄	뛸	넘을	달릴
nagwi	nosae	songaji	sukeot	nolral	ttwil	beomeul	dalril
donkey	mule	calf	cow	surprise	run	over	dash

225. 농민의 형편을 가축수로 평가했다, 나귀 노새 송아지 황소	226. 오경 중 예기의 기록, 놀란 듯 뛰고, 넘고, 달린다
The farmers' situation was evaluated as the quantity of animals raised at home, the donkey mule calf bull	The record of the Yegi(etiquette-record) in the O-gyeong(The Five Book of Confucianism), astonishedly, runs, jumps-over, dash

청려青驢	나려騾驢	독우犢牛	특집特輯	해거駭擧	활약活躍	초과超過	용양위 龍驤衛
dark-blue donkey	mule& donkey	cow's baby	special feature	mischievous &thing	play a role	exceed /over	military organize

驢려: 해려海驢 marine animals&donkey	駭해: 해연駭然 shocking&amazing to be so strange
騾라: 노새 baby of a mule and a mare	躍약: 빠르다 fast quick rapid
犢독: 지독지애舐犢之愛 mother-cow licking a calf	超초: 넘어달리다 jump run rush
特특: 특별特別 special particular unique	驤양: 머리를들다 lift one's head

245

114. 한국문화를 소개하다 (주참적도 포획반망)

유럽에서 온 딸 시부모와 함께, 사촌 형인 조수현교수 안내로 익산 원불교 총부를 구경하고, 고향 영광을 거쳐, 구례 한옥마을과 남원 광한루 유원지로 여행 갔다. 한국의 전통을 보여 줄 겸, 의미 있는 전설 내용도 있어 선택하였다. 오작교도, 광한루도 둘러보고, 체험관에서 이 도령과 성춘향이 한복도 입어 보고, 축 늘어진 수양버드 나무 아래서 사진도 찍어 보고, 맛있는 한국식 피자, 파전, 김치전, 녹두전과 전통술 막걸리 한 사발 마시기도 했다. 독일 사돈이 광한루 동동주 맛있다 하여 기념품으로 선물하였다. 그곳 관청에는, 탁 트인 큰 마루(필자 프로필 사진 배경임), 나무 인형들로 만든 사또가 죄인을 주리 틀어, 나무 벤치에 올려 엎드리게 한 후 병사들이 긴 봉으로 엉덩이를 내리치고 있었다. 네 이놈, 배반하고 도망하여 사로잡았노라(포획반망). 역적이고 남의 물건을 훔친 도적(적도)이니, 너희들의 목을 베어 죽여야(주참) 하나, 엉덩이 백 대 때리는 것으로 하노라. 엉덩이와 허벅다리를 매우 쳐라. 사또가 이러한 형벌을 집행하고 있는 듯하다. 광한루에 나오는 변 사또는 서민들을 괴롭히고, 사리사욕만 챙기는 폭정의 관리로 춘향전에 기록되어 있다.

114. Introduce Korean culture

I traveled to my daughter's parents-in-law from Europe, We visited the Iksan Won Buddhism General as a guide to my cousin, Professor Cho Soo-hyun, and traveled to Gure Hanok Village and Namwon Gwanghanru Amusement Park through my hometown Yeonggwang. I showed Korean tradition and have meaningful legends to them. I also visited Ojakgyo and Gwanghanru, and at the experience center, I-doryeong and Seong-chunhyang try on hanbok(Korean clothes), and took pictures under the drooping beard tree, and drank delicious Korean pizza, green onion-jeon(Green Onion Pancake), kimchi-jeon, mung bean-jeon, and a bowl of traditional wine makgeolli. The German in-laws were presented as souvenirs because they were delicious in the Guanghanru Dongdongju. There, in the government office, the soldiers were hitting their hips with long sticks after a large open floor(The background of my profile picture), a Sato(a high-ranking official name) made of wooden dolls, turned a sinner, put him on a wooden bench and lay down. Your man, betrayed and fled, and captured him, It is a bandit that steals a person's goods, so I have to kill you by cutting your neck, but I will hit your buttocks. Hit your buttocks and thighs very much, Sato seems to be enforcing these sentences. It is recorded in Chunhyangjeon that the Byeon-Sato harassed his people, and he took care of only self-interest.

誅 주	斬 참	賊 적	盜 도	捕 포	獲 획	叛 반	亡 망
ju	cham	jeok	do	po	hoek	ban	mang
벨	벨	도둑	훔칠	잡을	잡을	배반	도망
bel	bel	doduk	humchil	japeul	japeul	baeban	domang
kill	kill	burglar	steal	catch	catch	betray	escape
227. 국가 질서로, 살인자와 도둑은 사형시키고				228. 정부를 배반하거나, 나쁜 짓을 한 자는 사로잡았다			
In the national order, murderers and thieves are executed				The government has been betrayed, or the bad thing has been captured			
천주天誅	참신斬新	도적盜賊	도난盜難	포수捕手	획득獲得	반군叛軍	존망存亡
sin of heaven	new& fresh	thief	stolen	catcher	gain/ acquire	rebel army	survival& destruction

誅주: 주복誅服 Scold for his sins and obey
斬참: 참형斬刑 sentence to cut his throat
賊적: 해치다 hurt harm damage
盜도: 도청盜聽 wiretapping

捕포: 체포하다 arrest apprehend
獲획: 얻다 get pick up catch
叛반: 반란군叛亂軍 rebel army(troops)
亡망: 멸망滅亡 collapse destroy

115. 한민족의 소질과 성취 (포사료환 혜금완소)

우리나라의 양궁은 올림픽에서 매번 세계를 제패하고 있다. 대회를 지켜보면 아슬아슬한 게임도 있어, 가슴도 조이고, 긴장도 한다. 마지막 한두 발에 승부가 결정되는데, 그게 한국의 승리인 경우가 대부분이다. 한마디로 우리 선수들은 신들린 궁사(포사)들이다. 그래서 우리는 올림픽이나 양궁대회 하면 믿고 설레며 관심을 갖게 된다. 세계 여러 나라들은 한국을, 수천여 년 전부터 활 잘 쏘는 동쪽 나라 민족이라고 하였다. 고구려 안시성 전투에서 양만춘 장군이, 까마득히 먼 거리의 갑옷을 입은 적군, 당나라 왕, 태종의 눈을 명중시켜 승리한 역사는 유명하다. 또한 축구, 야구, 배구, 농구 등 공놀이도 뛰어난 실력을 발휘(료환)하고 있다. 뛰어난 피아니스트, 세계적 지휘자, 유명한 성악가, 한류바람을 일으키는 대중 가수 등 연예인들도 지구를 흔들고(혜금완소) 있다. 유명 미래 예측가들은 세계 역사 중심축이 한국이 될 거라고 예언하고 있다.

115. The potential characteristics and achievement of Korean nationals

Our archery is winning every time at the Olympics. There are exciting games when we watch the competition, we are nervous to watch. After the final round or two the result is decided, and most of the time, it was a victory for Korea. In short, our players are gifted archers. So we believe in the Olympics or archery competitions and become excited and interested. Many countries around the world have called Korea a nation of eastern countries that have been shooting well for thousands of years. In the battle of Anshi-castle in Goguryeo, General Yang Man-chun is famous for his victory by hitting the eyes of the enemy, Dang Dynasty king, and Taejong in armor far away. In addition, ball games such as soccer, baseball, volleyball, and basketball are also performing well. Celebrities such as outstanding pianists, world-renowned conductors, famous vocalists, and pop singers who are causing the Korean Wave are also shaking the earth. Famous future forecasters predict that Korea will be the center of world history.

布 포	射 사	遼 료	丸 환	嵇 혜	琴 금	阮 완	嘯 소
po	sa	ryo	hwan	hye	geum	wan	so
베	쏠	멀	둥글	산이름	거문고	성	휘파람
be	ssol	meol	dunggeul	sanireum	geomungo	seong	hwiparam
cloth	shoot	far	round	mountain	harp	familyname	whistle
229. 가문을 잘 꾸려 가려면, 여포의 활쏘기, 료의 공놀이				230. 혜강의 거문고, 완적의 휘파람처럼 기술을 익혀야 한다			
To make a good family, archery of Yeo-po, ball play of Ryo				Like the harp of Hye-gang, the whistle of the Wan-jeok, you have to learn the technique			
폭포瀑布	주사注射	료하遼河	탄환彈丸	혜산嵇山	풍금風琴	오완五阮	소영嘯詠
waterfall	injection	river name	bullet	mountain name	organ	five-wan name	read a poem

布포: 포교布教 보시 missionary almsgive
射사: 맞히다 반사反射 hit reflex
遼료: 느슨하다 소료완少遼緩之 relaxed
丸환: 알 환약丸藥 egg ball pill

嵇혜: =嵆 하남성河南省에 있는 산 henan castle mountain
琴금: 가야금伽倻琴 Korean instrument with 12 strings
阮완: 관문이름 gatedoor name
嘯소: 꾸짖다 scold

116. 마인드도 개발할 수 있다 (념필류지 균교임조)

필자는 학부에서 기계공학과, 대학원에서 공업교육을 전공한 공학도이다. 다양한 인재를 양성하는 한국폴리텍대학의 교수였다. 직제 상 박사 레벨인 기능장(독일은 마이스터라 함)이기도 하지만, 다방면으로 독서하여 인문학적 사고력을 갖추려 노력하고 있다. 자랑하고자 함이 아니라, 거친 원재료로 아름다운 작품을 직접 만들어 본, 공학도인 필자의 마인드가 있다. 별것도 아닌 것, 쓸모없는 것, 고장 나 버려지는 것도 유용하게 만들 수 있는 엔지니어이면서 과학자적 자세, 정신 자세가 있지 않은가 함이다. 불교에서, 존재와 허상의 구별이 없고(유가 무요, 무가 유다.), 세상에는 더러운 것도, 깨끗한 것도 없다. 부처가 과학적 지식이 있었는지는 모르지만, 만물의 이치를 깨달으니, 모두가 동질적인 원리로 관통 하였으리라. 분자와 원자, 원자의 음이온 양이온 등을 분석하면, 하나의 물질 즉 원자는 더러움과 깨끗함의 구분이 없음이 짐작되리라. 바다 속 해초로 먹는 김을 만들 듯이, 풀과 나무, 또는 폐지를 잘게 파쇄하고, 물에 풀어 종이를 만들 수 있으리라(염필류지). 공장에서 녹슬고 더러운 재료를 가공하여 빛나는 장식품을 만들기도 하는데, 낡고, 곰팡이 있고, 지저분한 물품을 수리하고, 갈고, 닦아 새것처럼 할 수도 있으리라.

116. Minds can be developed

I studied engineering which is in mechanical engineering in the university and industrial education in the master course. I worked as a professor at Polytechnic University, which nurtures a variety of talent. Although it is also a functional director (Germany is called Meister), who is a doctoral level in the office, I am trying to have a humanistic thinking ability by reading in various fields. I do not want to boast, but I have a mindset of my engineer who has made beautiful works with rough raw materials. It is an engineer who can make it useful to be nothing, useless, broken or abandoned, and has a scientific attitude and a mental attitude. In Buddhism, there is no distinction between existence and fiction. There is nothing dirty or clean in the world. The Buddha may have scientific knowledge, but when he realized the reason for everything, everyone would have penetrated it with homogeneous principles. Analyzing molecules, atoms, and anionic cations of atoms, you can imagine that a substance, atoms, has no distinction between dirt and cleanliness. As you make seaweed(eating laver) in the sea, you will be able to crush grass, trees, or waste paper, and release it in the water to make paper. They're also made of rusty, dirty materials in the factory to make shiny ornaments, which can be done like new ones by repairing, grinding, and wiping old, moldy, dirty items.

恬 념	筆 필	倫 륜	紙 지	釣 균	巧 교	任 임	釣 조
nyeom	pil	ryun	ji	gyun	gyo	im	jo
편안	붓	인륜	종이	서른근	교묘할	맡길	낚시
pyeonan	but	inryun	jongi	seoreungeun	gyo	matgil	nakksi
comfort	brush	moral	paper	thirty	skillful	entrust	fishing
231. 집안을 일으키려면, 넘이 붓 만들고, 륜이 종이 만들고				232. 균이 나침판 만들고, 임이 좋은 낚시대 만들었듯이, 그들처럼 따라하라			
To raise the house, Yeom made a brush, Ryun made a paper				Gyun makes a compass, Im makes a good fishing rod, follow them like they do			
염담恬淡	수필隨筆	오륜五倫	편지便紙	도균陶鈞	기교技巧	책임責任	조선釣船
clean&cool without greed	essay	five ethics of confucian	letter/ mail	pottery -shelf	technical skill	respon- sibility /liability	boat used to fish

恬념: =염 조용 quiet silent calm peace
筆필: 쓰다 write
倫륜: 삼강오륜 three bonds and the five moral
紙지: 지갑紙匣 wallet purse pocketbook

釣균: 저울 scale
巧교: 아름답다 beautiful pretty
任임: 맡다 임무任務 keep duty task job
釣조: 구하다 save rescue

117. 연구가 취미고 오락이다 (석분이속 병개가묘)

 과학자들은 연구와 집념이 취미고 오락이다. 문화 행사나 콘서트보다 일반적, 세계적, 대중적으로 접하기 쉬운 것이 영화일 것이다. 영화 「파리인간」을 보면, 남다르고, 영리하고, 집요한 천재 과학자 이야기다. 그 영화는 모든 물질의 상호 이동을 과학을 통하여 실질적으로 구현하는, 획기적인 인류발전을 위한, 한 인간의 집념을 이야기하고 있다. 지칠 줄 모르는 끈질긴 노력이다. 보통 사람 눈에는 안쓰러운 인생이기도 하지만, 그러한 과학자들의 덕택에 인류는 끊임없이 발전하리라. 장영실, 우장춘처럼 우리나라에도 유명한 과학자가 많지만, 인류에 지대한 영향을 끼치고 역사의 물줄기를 바꾼 유명한 과학자, 에디슨, 노벨, 아인슈타인, 빌게이츠 등 많이 있다. 불편함과 어려움과 궁금증을 풀어 주고, 세상을 편리하게 한 집념의 사람들이다(석분이속). 보는 사람에 따라 칼처럼 양면성이 있겠지만, 힘의 지렛대를 만들어 이용하는 보통 사람들에게 편리하고 발전적인 영향을 끼쳤음을 깨닫고, 시시때때로 몸소 감사할 따름이다.

117. Research is a hobby and entertainment

 Scientists like research as a hobby. It would be easy to access to watch a film to the general, global, and public than watching cultural events and concerts. If you look at the movie 「fly-human」, it is a story of a different, clever, persistent genius scientist. The film tells of a human commitment to breakthrough human development, experimentally implementing the mutual movement of all materials through science. It is a tireless and persistent effort. It is a sad life for ordinary people, but thanks to such scientists, mankind will continue to develop. There are many famous scientists in Korea like Jang Young-sil and Woo Jang-chun, but many famous scientists such as Edison, Nobel, Einstein, Bill Gates, etc., have had a great influence on mankind and changed the water stream of history. People who are uncomfortable, difficult, curious, and comfortable with the world. Depending on the viewer, it seems maybe like ambivalence like a knife, but I realize that it has had a convenient and developmental effect on ordinary people who make and use a lever of power, and I am grateful sometimes.

釋 석	紛 분	利 리	俗 속	並 병	皆 개	佳 가	妙 묘
seok	bun	ri	sok	byeong	gae	ga	myo
풀	어지러울	이로울	풍속	아우를	다	아름다울	묘할
pul	eojireoul	iroul	pungsok	aureul	da	areumdaul	myohal
solve	dizzy	beneficial	customs	embrace	almost all	beautiful	odd
233. 앞 구절, 포 료 혜 완의 기술과 념 륜 균 임의 능력은, 어렵게 살아가는 사람들을 이롭게 하고				234. 그들의 모든 재주가 아름답고 훌륭하고 탁월하다			
The previous passage, the technique of Po, Ryo, Hye, Wan and Yeom, Ryun, Gyun, Im's ability, they're going to benefit people who live hard				All their talents are beautiful, excellent and outstanding			
석가釋迦	분실紛失	승리勝利	속담俗談	병행竝行	거개擧皆	가향佳香	묘기妙技
Buddha	lost/ miss	win/ victory	saying/ proverb	parallel/ both	mostly	good scent	tricks/ stunt
釋석: 기뻐하다 happy glad excited 紛분: 섞이다 mixed blended shuffled 利리: 이익 profit interests benefit gain 俗속: 세속世俗 common customs world				並병: =竝 함께 together combination 皆개: 개근상 perfect attendance 佳가: 가인佳人 beautiful woman beauty 妙묘: 뛰어나다 great excel outstanding			

118. 인간 눈에 보이는 것의 모순 (모시숙자 공빈연소)

요즘 일부 지식자 간에 남녀 차별적 이슈가 좀 있긴 하다. 미스코리아, 미스춘향, 미스월드 등 미인선발 대회 보면, 보는 사람과 심사위원에 따라 다르지만, 균형 잡힌 사고력과 얼굴, 정숙하고 아름답고 맑고 깨끗함이야 모두 다 좋다고 인정하리라(모시숙자). 찡그리는 모습도 어딘가 모르게 매혹적이고, 얼굴에 난 점도 신기하게도 매력 덩어리처럼 보이기도 한다(공빈연소). 사람은 간사하고 변덕스러워 익숙함 뒤에 숨겨진 이면이 드러나면, 일순간에 추하게 보일 수 있다는 것이 안타까울 뿐이다. 영웅호걸이 누구며, 절색가인이 누구란 말인가. 인간은 허상을 보고 살아가는 것일지도 모른다. 호수 위에서 우아한 모습으로 헤엄치는 거위의 힘겨운 발짓은 우리 눈에 보이지 않을 뿐이다.

118. The contradiction of what is visible to humans

There are some gender-discrimination issues among some intellectuals these days. Miss Korea, Miss Chunhyang, Miss World, etc., according to the viewer and the judge, we will admit that it is all good, with balanced thinking and face, quiet, beautiful, clear and clean. The frown is fascinating somewhere, and the fact that it is on the face is strangely attractive. It is unfortunate that if a person is exposed to the back of familiarity and immutability, it can look ugly at a moment. Who is the hero and great man, who is the excellent beautiful woman? Human beings may be living by the illusion. The strenuous gesture of a geese swimming gracefully on the lake is only invisible to us.

요술과 인어공주

毛 모	施 시	淑 숙	姿 자	工 공	頻 빈	妍 연	笑 소
mo	si	suk	ja	gong	bin	yeon	so
털	베풀	맑을	자태	장인	찡그릴	고울	웃을
teol	bepeul	malkeul	jatae	jangin	jjigril	goul	uteul
hair	give	clear	figure	craftsman	frown	beautiful	smile
235. 오나라 모장과 월나라 서시는 맑고 아름다웠다				236. 서시는 찡그리는 모습도 매력적이고, 미소는 우아했다			
O nation Mo-jang, Wol nation Seo-si, They were clear and beautiful				Seo-si was charming in frowning, and the smile was elegant			
모발毛髮	시설施設	숙녀淑女	자세姿勢	공예工藝	빈발頻發	연려妍麗	미소微笑
hair	facilities /infrast- ructure	good- lady	attitude /stance	crafts/ artifacts	occur- frequently	pretty and fine	smile /grin

毛모: 모포毛布 fur blanket rug
施시: 은혜 grace favor mercy benefits
淑숙: 착하다 good
姿자: 맵시 shapeliness smartness

工공: 교묘하다
頻빈: 자주 빈번히頻繁 often frequent
妍연: 예쁘다 pretty beautiful
笑소: 폭소爆笑 laughing voice burst of laughter

119. 태양은 언제나 밝게, 인생은 화살처럼 (년시매최 희휘랑요)

애들 외조 할머니에게 구십 나이쯤까지 어찌 사셨나요, 물으니, "아침 먹고 저녁 먹고 어릴 때 소꿉놀이처럼 지내다 보니 이 나이가 되었다네." 어쩌다 주말에 가게 되면, 한결같이 파, 시금치 등 나물을 다듬고 있었다. 어느 책을 보니 꼼지락 건강법이 있었다. 하드 트레이닝도 좋지만, 매일매일 움직여 주는 가벼운 일거리, 즉, 꼼지락거리는 운동이 건강 유지에 매우 중요한 듯싶다. 여자들이 좀 더 오래 사는 이유는 다양한 원인이 있겠지만, 평소 가볍게 움직여 주는 사소한(허드레) 일이 그중 하나 아닌가 싶다. 세월은 화살처럼 사람을 늘 재촉하는 걸(년시매최), 모든 사람들이 한 번쯤은 절실하게 알게 되리라. 또한, 사람은 사라져도 아침 해는 찬란히 떠오른다(희휘랑요). 즐거운 예술은 짧고, 노력하며 살아야 할 인생은 생각하는 것보다 길다. 매일매일 밝은 태양이 동쪽에 떠오르듯이, 자연과의 즐거움과 휴식을 가끔 만들고, 짧은 예술이라도 조금씩 쌓고, 가꾸면 좋지 않을까.

119. The sun is always bright, life is like an arrow

How did you live to the age of about ninety to the grandmother of the children? I asked her, "I ate breakfast, ate dinner, and I was like a house play when I was young." When I went to the weekend, I was constantly refining herbs such as green onions and spinach. One book showed a wiggling health law. Hard training is good, but the light work that moves every day, that is, the wiggling exercise, seems to be very important for health maintenance. here are various reasons why women live longer, but I think it is one of the minor things that usually move lightly. All the years will always urge people like arrows, and everyone will know desperately once. Also, even if a person disappears, the morning sun rises brilliantly. The pleasant art is short, and the life to live in is longer than you think. Just as the bright sun rises to the east every day, it would be nice to make pleasure and relaxation with nature sometimes, to build up a little bit of short art, and to cultivate it.

年 년	矢 시	每 매	催 최	義 희	暉 휘	朗 랑	曜 요
nyeon	si	mae	choe	hui	hwi	rang	yo
해	화살	매양	재촉할	복희	빛	밝을	빛날
hae	hwasal	maeyang	jaechokhal	bokhui	bit	balkeul	bitnal
year	arrow	always	fly	name	light	bright	shine
237. 모장과 서시 아름다움도, 화살처럼 흐르는 세월에, 무상하고				238. 변함없이 빛나는, 아침 햇살이 아름답구나			
The beauty of Mo-jang and Seo-si, In the years that flow like arrows, the fleeting				The morning sun is beautiful, shining in constant light			
청년靑年	효시嚆矢	매년每年	개최開催	복희伏義	석휘夕暉	명랑明朗	요일曜日
youth	begin- ning	every year	host/ open	designer of astrology	dnner- sun	pleasant& cheerful	day
년: 청소년靑少年 teenagers 시: 궁시弓矢 bow and arrow 매: 매일每日 every day daily 최: 일어나다(발생하다) occur happen				희: 내쉬는숨 exhaling breath 휘: 여휘餘暉 at sunset 랑: 소리높이 sound height 요: 빛 일주일 light ray a week			

120. 하늘의 달과 별과 구름에 꿈 실고 (선기현알 회백환조)

유럽의 딸 집, 한국의 아들 집에 어쩌다 방문한다. 주택은 전국, 세계 어디나 외관만 서양식 한옥식 다를 뿐, 비슷한 구조와 인테리어로 되어 있다. 내부 장식 또한, 나라의 전통과 습관과 취향과 정서에 따라 다른 듯, 같은 듯하다. 거실, 안방, 작은방, 주방의 커튼들이 화려하다. 사용자의 개성에 맞추어 커튼을 장식한다. 유럽은 우리의 방등, 거실등 같은 천정 등이 별로 없고 사이드 조명등이나 갓등을 주로 사용한다. 작은 아기 방 커튼은, 북두칠성과 잔잔한 별들, 초승달, 그믐달이 떠 있다. 곧 사라질 듯 이슬을 머금은 그믐달은 여인의 진한 눈썹처럼 가냘프기도 하다. 불 꺼진 방 공중에는 천체 같은 둥근 굴렁쇠나, 불가사리 모양의 회전 장난감이 귀여운 토끼, 강아지, 파랑새, 딸랑이 등이 매달려 어린이 경음악과 함께 잔잔히 움직이고 있다(선기현알). 어둠 속에서 방 안의 천체가 손주를 비추고 있다(회백환조). 환경의 변화로, 하늘의 반짝이는 별구경, 달에서 토끼가 방아 찧는 모양 구경하기 어려운 요즘 시절, 아기들은 인공장식을 보며 무슨 꿈을 꾸고 있을까.

120. Dreaming in the moon, stars and clouds of heaven

I visit my daughter's house in Europe, my son's house in Korea. The house is similar in structure and interior, with only the appearance of the western style, Hanok style different from the whole country and the world. The interior decorations also seem to be different, the same according to the tradition, habits, tastes and emotions of the country. The curtains in the living room, the main room, the small room, and the kitchen are gorgeous. It gives an order with the personality of user and the curtain is decorated. European houses do not have many ceilings such as our lamps, living rooms, etc., and mainly uses side lights and hat lights. The baby room curtains in the small room, there are the Big dipper and the calm stars, the crescent moon in the sky, the moon floats. The moon, which is dewy as if it will soon disappear, is as thin as a woman's dark eyebrows. In the air of the turned-out room, a celestial round hoop or starfish-shaped rotary toy is still moving with a child's music with cute rabbits, puppies, bluebirds, and rattles hanging from the air. In the dark, the universe of the room is shining on the grandchild: the changes in the environment, the sparkling star scape of the sky, the rabbit-fighting moonlight, In these days, it is difficult to see the shape of rabbits on the moon. What are babies dreaming with watching artificial decorations?

璇 선	璣 기	懸 현	斡 알	晦 회	魄 백	環 환	照 조
seon	gi	hyeon	al	hoe	baek	hwan	jo
구슬	구슬	매달	돌	그믐	어두울	고리	비칠
guseul	guseul	maedal	dol	geumeum	eoduul	gori	bachim
bead	bead	hang	turn	lastmoon	dark	ring	shine

239. 천문기구인 선기는, 공중에 매달려 돌고	240. 그믐달은 빛 없이 돌면서, 어두운 둘레를 비춘다
The astronomical instrument, the Seon-gi, hanging around in the air	The old moon turns without light, illuminating the dark perimeter

선율旋律	천기天璣	현안懸案	알선斡旋	월회月晦	기백氣魄	환옥環玉	조명照明
melody /tune	third-star	pending issue	media-tion	last day of the moon	spirit/soul	ring jade	lighting

璇선: =璇 옥구슬 jade bead	晦회: 어둡다 dark night a moonless night
璣기: 작은 구슬 small bead	魄백: 넋 soul spirit ghost departed soul
懸현: 현상懸賞 prize reward	環환: 돌다 물러나다 rotate resign retreat
斡알: 관리하다 manage	照조: 볕 sunshine sun

259

121. 덕과 복을 쌓으라, 영광이 영원하리라 (지신수우 영수길소)

필자 시집『가고파도』의「장작열정」이라는 시를 소개한다. "소나무 장작, 사계절 푸름 뽐내던 나무, 억겁 모습 생생함이로다, 인간 세계 문명으로 내 운명 지키지 못하네, 초야 풀들 내 운명과 달리 쉽게 불사르지만, 구들 짝 아궁이 신세는 어이 같노라, 불쏘시게 노릇 잡풀들, 속삭이듯 작은 소리 지르네, 소나무 장작개비 수류탄 터지듯 요란스럽노라, 장작 개비된 소나무, 항온동물 인간들 소모품 소나무, 온갖 쉬이 타는 풀 원망하랴, 시커먼 무쇠 솥 녹일 듯 욕정의 혀 날름거리네" 복을 쌓는 것은 손가락의 정성으로 잡풀을 태워 장작불을 지피는 것과 같이, 통나무를 태우듯, 몸뚱이를 불 태워 세상을 살아가는 것이리라(지신수우). 장작불은 한 번 불이 붙으면, 불쏘시게 풀처럼 쉽게 꺼지지 않고, 다른 장작을 도와주며, 영원히 따뜻하고 편안히 쉴 수 있도록(영수) 하는 힘이 있다. 덕과 복이 자손 대에까지 이어지는(길소), 장작 열정이 아닐까.

121. Build virtue and blessing, Glory will be forever

If you build virtue and blessing, glory will last forever to the progeny. I introduce the poem 「Passion of Firewood」 in my poem 『Gagopado』. "Pine firewood, the tree that showed off the four seasons of blue, It's the vividness of the billion years, I cannot keep my fate from human world civilization, The grasses are easily burned, unlike my fate, I'm sorry, I'm the same one who owes your fuel hole, Fire them, weeds, You whisper a little, It's like a pine firewood grenade, Pine tree, firewood, The thermo-animal human consumable pine, You blame all the grass burn easily, "It's like a black iron pot melted, and it's a tongue of lust." Building your blessing would be like burning logs, burning the body like burning a fire, like burning a weed with the care of a finger to burn a firewood. Once a fire is lit, the firewood does not easily turn off like grass, it helps other firewood, and has the power to keep it warm and comfortable forever. I wonder if virtue and blessing are the firewood passion that leads to the descendants.

指 지	薪 신	修 수	祐 우	永 영	綏 수	吉 길	邵 소
ji	sin	su	u	yeong	su	gil	so
손가락	나무	닦을	복	길	편안	길할	이름
songarak	namu	dakkeul	bok	gil	pyeonan	gilhal	ireul
finger	tree	learn	fortune	long	peace	lucky	name
241. 장작불은 꺼지지 않고, 다른 장작에 불을 전하듯, 복을 쌓으면				242. 오래도록 편안함과, 행운이 장작불처럼 자손한테 전해진다			
The firewood does not go out, but when we build our blessings, as if to spread fire to other firewood				Long-comfortable, lucky is passed on to the subsequent generations like a firewood			
반지半指	적신積薪	연수研修	행우幸祐	영원永遠	수정綏定	길일吉日	성소姓邵
ring	firewood trees	training /study	joy& satisfac -tion	eternity/ immor -tality	peace& stability	lucky day	last- name

指지: 지휘자指揮者 orchestral-conductor
薪신: 풀 grass
修수: 수양하다 꾸미다 cultivate decorate
祐우: 돕다 help support aid assist

永영: 영구적永久的 permanence perpetuity
綏수: 수안綏安 in peace calm
吉길: 좋다 good fine nice
邵소: 고을 이름 village name

122. 고난, 피하기보다 도전 (구보인령 부앙낭묘)

군 생활 시절, 보직의 종류나 장교에 따라 다르지만, 보통의 장병은 매년 유격훈련을 받는다. 체력 단련과 정신무장의 이론이 있으리라. 우리들은 너무 힘들어, 일 년 농사라 부르기도 한다. 보직 좋은 말년 병사는 여러 경로를 통해 빠지려고 손을 쓰는 경우도 있다. 사실 빠지기도 하지만, 인생을 위해 바람직하지 않을 듯하다. 단단히 각오하고, 자신을 위해 도전해 보면 달콤한 맛이 있다. 다른 훈련도 힘들지만, 행군은 더욱 힘들다. 한여름 뙤약볕에 완전군장(가득 찬 배낭에 탄알 없는 소총과 수통, 모포 등 몇십 킬로그램 무게)하고 수십 킬로미터 거리 이상을 행군한다. 쉽게 보면 안 된다. 한가롭게 걷는 게 아니라, 빠른 발걸음이다. 힘이 넘치는 젊은 병사도 쓰러지는 경우가 있다. 사회에서의 등산과는 차원이 다르다. 무거운 방탄 철모는 구보할 때 흔들리지 않고, 착 달라붙도록 턱에 끈을 질근 묶는다(구보인령).

122. Hardship, more challenging than avoiding

During military life, it depends on the type of position or officer, but ordinary soldiers receive guerrilla training or ranger training every year. There will be physical training and theory of mental armament. We are so hard, we sometimes call it year-round farming. A good late-life soldier may use his hand to get out of several routes. In fact, I'm actually missing, but I'm not going to be desirable for life. You are determined and you have a sweet taste when you challenge for yourself. Other training is hard, but marching is even harder. In the summer, he is fully armed in the sun and marches more than a few hundred kilometers away(A full backpack weighs dozens of kilograms including bulletless rifles, water canisters and blankets). You can't see it easily. It's not a leisurely walk, it's a quick step. Young soldiers with power sometimes fall. It is different from climbing in society. Heavy bulletproof iron helmets do not shake when canter, and tighten the straps to the chin to stick together.

矩 구	步 보	引 인	領 령	俯 부	仰 앙	廊 랑	廟 묘
gu	bo	in	ryeong	bu	ang	rang	myo
법	걸음	이끌	옷깃	구부릴	우러를	행랑	사당
beop	geoleum	iggeul	otgit	guburil	ureoreul	haengrang	sadang
law	walk	lead	collar	bend	respect	doorroom	shrine
243. 걸음걸이는 흐트러짐 없이 걷고, 옷차림을 바르게 하며				244. 궁궐에서는 겸손하고, 종묘를 우러러보아야 한다			
Walking without disorder, dressing properly				The palace should be humble and look up to the government			
구척矩尺	행보行步	인상引上	요령要領	부시俯視	신앙信仰	화랑畵廊	사묘四廟
right-angler/ square	step/ walking	increase/ raise	know-how /tact	look down	faith/ belief	gallery	shrine of the four ancestors
矩구: 네모 square four-cornered 步보: 행하다 진보進步 do act progress 引인: 잡아당길 pull retracts 領령: 거느리다 lead head command				俯부: 겸손 앙부仰俯 modest look down&up 仰앙: 의지하다 우러러볼 rely on look up 廊랑: 복도 사랑채 corridor love-room 廟묘: 빈소 mortuary			

123. 복장에 따른 정신과 마음의 변화 (속대긍장 배회첨조)

아침에 눈 뜨고 욕실부터 간다. 먼저 거울 속 얼굴을 보며, 건강 상태를 관찰하고 체크한다. 세면과 머리를 다듬은 후, 하고자 하는 일거리에 맞도록 옷을 선택하여 입는다. 우리의 옷맵시는 언제나 중요하다. 겸손하고 장중하게, 긍지와 자신감 있게 혁대를 단단히 동여맬 때(속대긍장), 마음도 정신도 따르게 되리라. 아침에 간단한 선식을 하고, 운동이나 조깅하러 둘레 길을 돌면서 주위를 관찰한다. 여기저기에 긴요한 운동기구들이 갖춰져 있다. 하고 싶은 것, 아무거나 골라 어깨를 돌려 보고, 다리를 좌우로 움직여 보고, 줄을 팔로 당겨 오십견을 예방해 본다. 우리는 다시 거닐면서 인적이 드문 고층 아파트 모양새와 상가들, 깔끔한 저택, 주차장에서 차를 타고 쉥 나가 버리니, 사람 보기도 어렵다. 가끔 지나치는 조깅 맨들, 진한 울샴푸 향기 여운이 스친다. 코로나19로 안면 마스크하고 돌아다니니 얼굴 보기가 어렵다. 거기다 선글라스까지 하면 형체가 더욱 우주인 같다. 보기에 친근감보다 거북하다. 사실 모두가 무표정하고, 무관심한 듯하다. 그래서 그런지 운동하는 사람 수가 많이 줄었다. 거의 복면 수준이니, 거닐면서도, 바라보는 것도, 사람들에게 오해나 방해가 되지 않도록 예의(배회첨조)가 있어야 하리라.

123. Changes in the spirit and mind according to how to wear

I wake up in the morning and go to the bathroom. First, I look at the face in the mirror, and I observe and check my health. After finishing the wash my face and hair, I choose clothes to fit the work I am going to do. The type of what I wear is always important. When you are humble and dignified, proud and confident, and firmly tied to the belt, your body will follow your mind and spirit. In the morning, do a simple raw meal, and observe the surroundings as you walk around to exercise or jog. There are important exercise equipments here and there. I want to do anything I can see, thus I pick anything, turn my shoulder, move my legs from side to side, pull the string with my arm to prevent the fifty shoulders. We walk again and get out of the rare high-rise apartment, shopping malls, clean mansions, parking lots, and it is hard to see people. Sometimes jogging men with the thick wool shampoo scent, are passing. It is currently difficult to see a face when you walk around with a face mask with Corona 19. And then the sun glasses make the shape even more cosmic. It feelsl more awkward than friendly. In fact, everyone seems expressionless and indifferent. So the number of people exercising has decreased a lot. It is almost masked, and while walking, looking at it, there must be courtesy to prevent misunderstandings or interruptions to people.

束 속	帶 대	矜 긍	莊 장	徘 배	徊 회	瞻 첨	眺 조
sok	dae	geung	jang	bae	hoe	cheom	jo
묶을	띠	자랑	엄숙할	배회할	배회할	볼	바라볼
mukkeul	tti	jarang	eomsukhal	baehoehal	baehoehal	bol	barabol
tie	belt	proud	solemn	loiter	wander	see	look
245. 궁궐에서는, 긍지와 자신감 있게 혁띠를 매고				246. 거닐거나 바라보는 것도 예의 있게 한다			
In the palace, you wear a belt with pride and confidence				It makes polite to walk or look			
결속結束	연대連帶	긍지矜持	별장別莊	배회徘徊	저회低徊	앙첨仰瞻	조망眺望
binding/ solidarity /bond	solidarity	pride/ dignity	villa/ cottage	wander /stray	heads down&think back&go	respectful look up	view/ prospect

束속: 약속約束 promise pledge
帶대: 두르다 붕대繃帶 wear bandage
矜긍: 자긍심自矜心 가엾다 pride sad
莊장: 씩씩하다 bravely valiantly vigorously

徘배: 어정거리다 stroll ramble walk leisurely along
徊회: 머뭇거리다 hesitate
瞻첨: 첨례瞻禮 worship service
眺조: 살피다 look study see check

124. 내 인생에 대한 예의 (고루과문 우몽등초)

필자의 수필집 『에세이 부동산 여행』 중 '공부는 내 인생에 대한 예의다'라는 내용이 있다. 요즘은 과거와 교육환경이 다르지만, 가난하여 스승도, 배움을 줄 만한 그럴 듯한 친구도 없는 사람은 배움이 부족할(고루과문) 수밖에 없으리라. 어깨 너머로 보거나, 홀로 독학하여 터득해야 하니, 평균적 사고에서 벗어나 창조적 사고로 전환이 쉽지 않았다. 학식 높은 스승은 좋은 제자 만나는 걸 가장 큰 복이라 하거늘, 그런 기회를 접하기가 어려우리라. 따라서 홀로 이루고 깨달았다는 생각으로, 고루 중생 독학자는 아집과 편견에서 벗어나기가 어려우니 스스로 폭 넓은 사고에 힘써야 하지 않을까. 참다운 스승 만나기가 어렵고, 참다운 친구 만나기가 어렵지만, 요즘은 참 좋은 책은 매우 많다. 노력만 하면, 어디서든 무료로 볼 수 있으니 참다운 스승으로 삼아 존경하여야 하리라. 배우지 못하면 어리석고 무지 몽매하여 뭇 사람에게 꾸지람을 들을 수 있으니(우몽등초), 한 번뿐인, 내 인생에 대한 예의를 갖추도록 함이 어떨까.

124. Attitude for my life

Among my essay book 『Essay Real Estate Travel』, 'Studying is a courtesy to my life'. The environment between the current are different, but those who are poor and have no good friends do not have a little chance to learn. It was not easy to shift from general thinking to creative thinking because I had to look over my shoulder or learn it by myself. A high-skilled teacher is the greatest blessing to meet a good student, and it is difficult to meet such an opportunity. Therefore, with the idea that it was realized alone, it is difficult for a unclear self-taught scholar in order to escape from egotism and prejudice, so should he try to think widely by himself? It is difficult to meet a true teacher and it is difficult to meet a true friend, but nowadays luckily there are many good books. If you try, you can see it free of charge anywhere, so you should respect it as a true teacher. If you do not try, you can be foolish and ignorant and can be scolded by many people, so why not make sure you have the courtesy of my life.

孤 고	陋 루	寡 과	聞 문	愚 우	蒙 몽	等 등	誚 초
go	ru	gwa	mun	u	mong	deung	cho
외로울	더러울	적을	들을	어리석을	어릴	같을	꾸짖을
oeroul	deoreoul	jeokeul	deuleul	eoriseokeul	eoril	gateul	ggugiteul
alone	dirty	small	hear	foolish	young	equal	scold

247. 스승이 없는, 독학자는 보고 듣는 것이 부족하고, 자기도취에 빠져, 균형 감각이 떨어지기 쉽다.				248. 배움이 부족한 자는 어린아이와 같이, 어리석어 꾸짖음을 받기도 한다. 폭 넓은 정신수양을 해야 한다.			
Without a teacher, a self-taught scholar lacks to see and hear, and is in a self-indulgence, and is likely to lose his sense of balance				Those who have little learning, like children, are foolish and scolded, and should have a wide range of mental training.			

고독孤獨	벽루僻陋	다과多寡	신문新聞	우문愚問	계몽啓蒙	평등平等	초책誚責
solitude /lone	mountain -village	a lot& little	news- paper	stupid question	enlighte -ning	equally/ impartially	scold

孤고: 고아원孤兒院build[establish] orphanage 陋루: 좁다 narrow small 寡과: 약하다 weak poor mild flimsy 聞문: 소문所聞 rumor gossip hearsay	愚우: 바보 foolish silly stupid 蒙몽: 우매하다 ignorant stupid silly 等등: 등급 동아리 grade level club 誚초: 초양誚讓 scolding for wrong things

125. 도움 받기보다 도움 주려는 마인드 (위어조자 언제 호야)

학창시절 교통사고로 절름발이 된 친구와 선천성 꼽추 친구가 있었다. 장애인 단체에 가면 비장애인이 오히려 이상한 사람일 수가 있다. 단순히 생각하면 서로가 다른 구조의 신체로 차별하는 건, 안경 쓴다고 비난하는 것과 같지 않을까. 사리분별 부족하고, 철없던 시절이지만, 그들에게 가까이하고, 하는 말을 잘 들어 주는 역할을 많이 하였다. 이러한 것이 그들에게 도움이 되었는지는 모르겠다. 졸업하고 서른 살도 안 된 어느 날, 우연히 다른 친구를 만났는데, 몇 년 전에 그들 중 한 명이 어찌 되었다는 말을 전해 들었다. 참으로 안타까웠다. 세상살이가 편견과 따돌림에 의한 괴로움, 외로움에 얼마나 어려웠을지, 꿋꿋하게 살아 줬으면 좋았으련만, 도와 줄 때가 보람 있고 가장 행복한 것이 아닌지. 말과 언어에도 도와주는 글자(위어조자, 언제호야)가 있거늘 안타깝기만 하다.

125. Rather than getting help, mind to help

During my school days, I had a friend who was lame in a traffic accident and a friend who was born.

During my school days, I had a friend who was lame in a traffic accident and a congenital hunchback friend. If you go to a group of people with disabilities, non-disabled people may be strange people. If you think simply, discriminating against each other with different structures of bodies is like accusing them of wearing glasses. It was a time when it was lacking in self-discipline and it was a time of immatureness, but I played a lot of roles to get close to them and listen to them. I don't know if this has helped

268

them. One day after graduation, less than thirty years old, I happened to meet another friend, and a few years ago I was told what had happened to one of them. I was so sorry. How hard it must have been for prejudice and ostracism, for bullying, for distress, for loneliness, I wish I had lived firmly, but I am worth and happy to help. There are letters that help in words and languages.

謂 위	語 어	助 조	者 자	焉 언	哉 재	乎 호	也 야
wi	eo	jo	ja	eon	jae	ho	ya
이를	말씀	도울	놈	어찌	어조사	그런	어조사
ireul	malsseum	doul	nom	eojji	eojosa	geureon	eojosa
say	word	help	guy	how/why	particle	such	particle

249. 문장의 토씨로, 이야기와 말을 돕는 글자가 있다. 이렇듯, 세상은 평범한 사람이 없다면 유지될 수 없고, 보잘 것 없는 모든 풀 하나도 중요하다. 천자문의 매듭을 어조사로 한 것은 참으로 심오하다	250. 언제호야 네 글자가 있다, 백두문 사언고시가 어조사다 (이 외에 어조사는 이야여의혜: 而耶歟矣兮가 있다)
In the sentence, the words that help you talk and speak. The world cannot be maintained without ordinary people, and every single insignificant grass is important. It is profound to have the words of particle, knot in the thousand character text.	When there are four letters of Eon Jae Ho Ya, Four words old poem of Baekdumun(words of white hair-head) is the words of particle, (In addition, there are other particle such as I, Ya, Yeo, Ui, Hye,)

소위所謂	단어單語	협조協助	독자讀者	어언於焉	쾌재快哉	의호宜乎	혹야或也
so-called	word	help/aid	reader	unawares/short time	delight/joy	of-course	in case

謂위: 생각 함께 consider think together	焉언: 언감생심焉敢生心 I dare not wish
語어: 알리다 tell inform	哉재: 비로소 only-then
助조: 이롭다 beneficial helpful profitable	乎호: 감탄 wow amazed exclaim
者자: 소비자消費者 consumer buyer shopper	也야: 급기야及其也 at the end

한글 영어 표기법

(여기에 없는 한글은 아래 표기를 응용하면 읽을 수 있다.)

ㄱ 가 ga	각 gak	간 gan	갈 gal	감 gam
갑 gap	갓 gat	강 gang	개 gae	객 gaek
거 geo	건 geon	걸 geol	검 geom	겁 geop
게 ge	겨 gyeo	격 gyeok	견 gyeon	결 gyeol
겸 gyeom	겹 gyeop	경 gyeong	계 gye	고 go
곡 gok	곤 gon	골 gol	곳 got	공 gong
곶 got	과 gwa	곽 gwak	관 gwan	괄 gwal
광 gwang	괘 gwae	괴 goe	굉 goeng	교 gyo
구 gu	국 guk	군 gun	굴 gul	굿 gut
궁 gung	권 gwon	궐 gwol	귀 gwi	규 gyu
균 gyun	귤 gyul	그 geu	극 geuk	근 geun
글 geul	금 geum	급 geup	긍 geung	기 gi
긴 gin	길 gil	김 gim	까 kka	깨 kkae
꼬 kko	꼭 kkok	꽃 kkot	꾀 kkoe	꾸 kku
꿈 kkum	끝 kkeut	끼 kki		
ㄴ 나 na	낙 nak			
난 nan	날 nal	남 nam	납 nap	낭 nang
내 nae	냉 naeng	너 neo	널 neol	네 ne
녀 nyeo	녁 nyeok	년 nyeon	념 nyeom	녕 nyeong
노 no	녹 nok	논 non	놀 nol	농 nong
뇌 noe	누 nu	눈 nun	눌 nul	느 neu
늑 neuk	늠 neum	능 neung	늬 nui	니 ni
닉 nik	닌 nin	닐 nil	님 nim	
ㄷ 다 da				
단 dan	달 dal	담 dam	답 dap	당 dang
대 dae	댁 daek	더 deo	덕 deok	도 do
독 dok	돈 don	돌 dol	동 dong	돼 dwae
되 doe	된 doen	두 du	둑 duk	둔 dun
뒤 dwi	드 deu	득 deuk	들 deul	등 deung
디 di	따 tta	땅 ttang	때 ttae	또 tto

뚜 ttu	뚝 ttuk	뜨 tteu	띠 tti	
ㄹ 라 ra				
락 rak	란 ran	람 ram	랑 rang	래 rae
랭 raeng	량 ryang	렁 reong	레 re	려 ryeo
력 ryeok	런 ryeon	렬 ryeol	렴 ryeom	렵 ryeop
령 ryeong	례 rye	로 ro	록 rok	론 ron
롱 rong	뢰 roe	료 ryo	룡 ryong	루 ru
류 ryu	륙 ryuk	륜 ryun	률 ryul	륭 ryung
르 reu	륵 reuk	른 reun	름 reum	릉 reung
리 ri	린 rin	림 rim	립 rip	
ㅁ 마 ma				
막 mak	만 man	말 mal	망 mang	매 mae
맥 maek	맨 maen	맹 maeng	머 meo	먹 meok
메 me	며 myeo	멱 myeok	면 myeon	멸 myeol
명 myeong	모 mo	목 mok	몰 mol	못 mot
몽 mong	뫼 moe	묘 myo	무 mu	묵 muk
문 mun	물 mul	므 meu	미 mi	민 min
밀 mil				
ㅂ 바 ba	박 bak	반 ban	발 bal	
밥 bap	방 bang	배 bae	백 baek	뱀 baem
버 beo	번 beon	벌 beol	범 beom	법 beop
벼 byeo	벽 byeok	변 byeon	별 byeol	병 byeong
보 bo	복 bok	본 bon	봉 bong	부 bu
북 buk	분 bun	불 bul	붕 bung	비 bi
빈 bin	빌 bil	빔 bim	빙 bing	빠 ppa
빼 ppae	뻐 ppeo	뽀 ppo	뿌 ppu	쁘 ppeu
삐 ppi				
ㅅ 사 sa	삭 sak	산 san	살 sal	
삼 sam	삽 sap	상 sang	샅 sat	새 sae
색 saek	생 saeng	서 seo	석 seok	선 seon
설 seol	섬 seom	섭 seop	성 seong	세 se
셔 syeo	소 so	속 sok	손 son	솔 sol
솟 sot	송 song	쇄 swae	쇠 soe	수 su

271

숙 suk	순 sun	술 sul	숨 sum	숭 sung
쉬 swi	스 seu	슬 seul	슴 seum	습 seup
승 seung	시 si	식 sik	신 sin	실 sil
심 sim	십 sip	싱 sing	싸 ssa	쌍 ssang
쌔 ssae	쏘 sso	쑥 ssuk	씨 ssi	
ㅇ 아 a				
악 ak	안 an	알 al	암 am	압 ap
앙 ang	앞 ap	애 ae	액 aek	앵 aeng
야 ya	약 yak	얀 yan	양 yang	어 eo
억 eok	언 eon	얼 eol	엄 eom	업 eop
에 e	여 yeo	역 yeok	연 yeon	열 yeol
염 yeom	엽 yeop	영 yeong	예 ye	오 o
옥 ok	온 on	올 ol	옴 om	옹 ong
와 wa	완 wan	왈 wal	왕 wang	왜 wae
외 oe	왼 oen	요 yo	욕 yok	용 yong
우 u	욱 uk	운 un	울 ul	움 um
웅 ung	워 wo	원 won	월 wol	위 wi
유 yu	육 yuk	윤 yun	율 yul	융 yung
윷 yut	으 eu	은 eun	을 eul	음 eum
읍 eup	응 eung	의 ui	이 i	익 ik
인 in	일 il	임 im	입 ip	잉 ing
ㅈ 자 ja	작 jak	잔 jan	잠 jam	잡 jap
장 jang	재 jae	쟁 jaeng	저 jeo	적 jeok
전 jeon	절 jeol	점 jeom	접 jeop	정 jeong
제 je	조 jo	족 jok	존 jon	졸 jol
종 jong	좌 jwa	죄 joe	주 ju	죽 juk
준 jun	줄 jul	중 jung	쥐 jwi	즈 jeu
즉 jeuk	즐 jeul	즘 jeum	즙 jeup	증 jeung
지 ji	직 jik	진 jin	질 jil	짐 jim
집 jip	징 jing	짜 jja	째 jjae	쪼 jjo
찌 jji				
ㅊ 차 cha	착 chak	찬 chan	찰 chal	
참 cham	창 chang	채 chae	책 chaek	처 cheo

척 cheok	천 cheon	철 cheol	첨 cheom	첩 cheop
청 cheong	체 che	초 cho	촉 chok	촌 chon
총 chong	최 choe	추 chu	축 chuk	춘 chun
출 chul	춤 chum	충 chung	측 cheuk	층 cheung
치 chi	칙 chik	친 chin	칠 chil	침 chim
칩 chip	칭 ching			
칩 chip	칭 ching			
ㅋ 코 ko	쾌 kwae	크 keu	큰 keun	키 ki
ㅌ 타 ta	탁 tak	탄 tan		
탈 tal	탐 tam	탑 tap	탕 tang	태 tae
택 taek	탱 taeng	터 teo	테 te	토 to
톤 ton	톨 tol	통 tong	퇴 toe	투 tu
퉁 tung	튀 twi	트 teu	특 teuk	틈 teum
티 ti				
ㅍ 파 pa	판 pan	팔 pal	패 pae	
팽 paeng	퍼 peo	페 pe	펴 pyeo	편 pyeon
폄 pyeom	평 pyeong	폐 pye	포 po	폭 pok
표 pyo	푸 pu	품 pum	풍 pung	프 peu
피 pi	픽 pik	필 pil	핍 pip	
ㅎ 하 ha				
학 hak	한 han	할 hal	함 ham	합 hap
항 hang	해 hae	핵 haek	행 haeng	향 hyang
허 heo	헌 heon	험 heom	헤 he	혀 hyeo
혁 hyeok	현 hyeon	혈 hyeol	혐 hyeom	협 hyeop
형 hyeong	혜 hye	호 ho	혹 hok	혼 hon
홀 hol	흡 hop	홍 hong	화 hwa	확 hwak
환 hwan	활 hwal	황 hwang	홰 hwae	횃 hwaet
회 hoe	획 hoek	횡 hoeng	효 hyo	후 hu
훈 hun	훤 hwon	훼 hwe	휘 hwi	휴 hyu
휼 hyul	흉 hyung	흐 heu	흑 heuk	흔 heun
흘 heul	흠 heum	흡 heup	흥 heung	희 hui
흰 huin	히 hi	힘 him		

출처: blog.daum.net/pd003/15894497 (노을비 블로그)

273

참고 문헌

- 대동천자문, 김균 저, 이광호 역, 조수현 글씨. 서예문인화 2008년
- 마법천자문, 김영곤 저, ㈜북이십일 아울북, 2004년, 2022년 10쇄
- 윤택진 천자문, 윤택진 벽보시리즈, 출판사 도서출판 새샘
- 김성동 천자문, 김성동 지음, ㈜도서출판 청년사, 2004년
- 천자문, 이동진 편저, 해누리, 2014년
- 다산 천자문, 김대현 편저, 도서출판 다섯수레, 2010년
- 천자문 그 뿌리와 동양학적 사유, 강상규 저, 도서출판 어문학사, 2005년
- 다음(Daum) 영어 번역 프로그램
- 한글 영어 표기법, 노을비 블로그

글로벌 시대를 위한

영어 천자문 에세이

ⓒ 조광호, 2023

초판 1쇄 발행 2023년 3월 31일

지은이   조광호
펴낸이   이기봉
편집   좋은땅 편집팀
펴낸곳   도서출판 좋은땅
주소   서울특별시 마포구 양화로12길 26 지월드빌딩 (서교동 395-7)
전화   02)374-8616~7
팩스   02)374-8614
이메일   gworldbook@naver.com
홈페이지 www.g-world.co.kr

ISBN   979-11-388-1765-3 (03740)